THE FORGOTTEN GERMAN GENOCIDE

THE FORGOTTEN GERMAN GENOCIDE

Revenge Cleansing in Eastern Europe, 1945–50

Peter C. Brown

First published in Great Britain in 2021 by
PEN AND SWORD HISTORY
An imprint of
Pen & Sword Books Ltd
Yorkshire – Philadelphia

Copyright © Peter C. Brown, 2021

ISBN 978 1 52677 374 6

The right of Peter C. Brown to be identified as Author of
this work has been asserted by him in accordance with the Copyright,
Designs and Patents Act 1988.

A CIP catalogue record for this book is available from the British Library.

All rights reserved. No part of this book may be reproduced or transmitted in
any form or by any means, electronic or mechanical including photocopying,
recording or by any information storage and retrieval system, without permission
from the Publisher in writing.

Typeset in Times New Roman 11.5/14 by
SJmagic DESIGN SERVICES, India.
Printed and bound by CPI Group (UK) Ltd, Croydon, CR0 4YY

Pen & Sword Books Limited incorporates the imprints of Atlas, Archaeology,
Aviation, Discovery, Family History, Fiction, History, Maritime, Military, Military
Classics, Politics, Select, Transport, True Crime, Air World, Frontline Publishing,
Leo Cooper, Remember When, Seaforth Publishing, The Praetorian Press,
Wharncliffe Local History, Wharncliffe Transport, Wharncliffe True Crime and
White Owl.

For a complete list of Pen & Sword titles please contact
PEN & SWORD BOOKS LIMITED
47 Church Street, Barnsley, South Yorkshire, S70 2AS, England
E-mail: enquiries@pen-and-sword.co.uk
Website: www.pen-and-sword.co.uk

Or
PEN AND SWORD BOOKS
1950 Lawrence Rd, Havertown, PA 19083, USA
E-mail: Uspen-and-sword@casematepublishers.com
Website: www.penandswordbooks.com

Contents

Introduction		vii
Chapter One	Hitler's Final Solution	1
	The Euthanasia Programme	2
	Bottled Gas	4
	Gas Vans	5
	Observation Stations	6
Chapter Two	The Nazi Camps	9
	Coded Language of Gassing	10
Chapter Three	The Death Marches	21
Chapter Four	Czechoslovakia	24
	The Prague Uprising	34
	Czechoslovak Radio	35
	The Internment Camps	43
	Forced Expulsions	49
	Reprisals	52
	The Death Marches	59
Chapter Five	Hungary	69
	The Phases of Expulsion	83

Chapter Six	Poland	95
	The Katyn Massacre	97
	Kidnapped Children	99
	Deportations	103
	The Warsaw Ghetto Uprising	118
	Flight and Expulsions	128
Chapter Seven	The Removal of Germans from Eastern Europe	134
Chapter Eight	Germany	137
	The Berlin Airlift	145
	The Holocaust Trains	146
	The Yalta Conference	150
	The Nuremberg Trials	151
	The Red Cross	154

Notes	156
Glossary	165
Bibliography	170
Endnotes	177
Index	182

Introduction

The Allied victory that ended the Second World War with the surrender of the Axis powers meant dislocation and revenge against the defeated German army. During the ensuing five years of violence and chaos, the forced expulsion of more than 12 million ethnic Germans from their homes and ancestral lands in Poland, the Czech Republic, Hungary and other Eastern European countries, mostly lands that had formerly been part of Germany and were ceded through the Treaty of Versailles following the First World War, was one of the most significant examples of the mass violation of human rights in recent history. Although they occurred within living memory in time of peace, and in the middle of the world's most densely populated continent, it has been mostly depicted in European-history textbooks as justified retribution for Nazi Germany's wartime atrocities.

In direct contravention of the 1919 Treaty of Versailles, which forced Germany and its allies to accept sole responsibility for causing the First World War and committed it to making territorial concessions, disarming and paying reparations, Adolf Hitler, who came to power in 1933, had steadily and aggressively expanded Germany's borders into the Rhineland from 1936, taking over neighbouring regions and countries with German-speaking populations in order to create a huge economy that would finance and sustain a long-term war in Europe.

The Sudetenland, the German-speaking borders of Czechoslovakia, were ceded to Germany in the Munich Agreement following fears harboured by British and French politicians of a European war. British Prime Minister Neville Chamberlain's endeavours to avoid war meant appeasing Hitler's self-determined right to expand German territories, despite this expansion of Czechoslovakia covering the industrial powerhouses of the Czech state, the factories and mines, and vital fortifications for the defence of the country along the northern, western, and southern borders.

The 'Obersalzberg Speech'[1] was given by Adolf Hitler to Wehrmacht commanders at his home in Bavaria, on 22 August 1939, a week before the German invasion of Poland:

> Our strength consists in our speed and in our brutality. Genghis Khan led millions of women and children to slaughter with premeditation and a happy heart. History sees in him solely the founder of a state. It's a matter of indifference to me what a weak western European civilisation will say about me.
>
> My decision to attack Poland was arrived at last spring. Originally, I feared that the political constellation would compel me to strike simultaneously at England, Russia, France, and Poland. Even this risk would have had to be taken. Ever since the autumn of 1938, and because I realised that Japan would not join us unconditionally and that Mussolini is threatened by that nit-wit of a king and the treasonable scoundrel of a crown prince, I decided to go with Stalin.
>
> I have issued the command, and I'll have anybody who utters but one word of criticism executed by a firing squad – that our war aim does not consist in reaching certain lines, but in the physical destruction of the enemy. Accordingly, I have placed my death-head formations in readiness – for the present only in the East – with orders to them to send to death mercilessly and without compassion, men, women, and children of Polish derivation and language. Only thus shall we gain the living space (Lebensraum) which we need. Who, after all, speaks today of the annihilation of the Armenians?

The grand scheme to divide Central and Eastern Europe was formalised on 23 August 1939 by the Soviet Union and Germany in secret Nazi-Soviet protocols that accompanied the Molotov-Ribbentrop non-aggression pact between the two totalitarian powers. The pact with Stalin gave Hitler a free hand to wage war against Poland, and in return, Germany recognised that the Soviet Union's sphere of interest included Finland, eastern Poland, Moldova, and the Baltic States. The expulsion

Introduction

and eradication of millions of non-Germans and Jews carried out by the Nazis during the Second World War set the precedent for the expulsion of entire German communities after 1944.

The American, British and Free French armies were no less culpable than Stalin's Red Army for the brutal treatment of captured Wehrmacht soldiers. At the Tehran Conference, a strategy meeting of Joseph Stalin, Franklin D. Roosevelt, and Winston Churchill which ran from 28 November to 1 December 1943, they agreed in principle to the partitioning of Germany. They also agreed to the annexation of Königsberg by the Soviet Union and the displacement of Poland (whose government-in-exile in London was neither informed, nor consulted) to the West. This allowed the USSR to keep the Polish territories obtained by the German-Soviet pact, for which the territories acted as (partial) compensation. The future Poland would receive the eastern territories of Germany. The new frontiers of Poland were not specified because the British wanted to avoid the protests of the Polish government in London. Roosevelt too wanted to avoid protests from Americans of Polish origin.

After the Conference, when leaks revealed what was considered to be a plot by the British and Americans against Stalin's ambitions to the detriment of the Poles, both Anthony Eden (in the House of Commons on 15 December 1943) and Roosevelt (in front of the Congress on January 11 1944) gave false denials. It was envisaged that the eastern boundary could be defined by a line called 'Curzon Line A'; not the true Curzon line of 1919 which left Lviv to Poland (named 'B' by the Soviets). The German-Soviet route of 1939 that gave this city to the USSR. As for the western border, it could follow the course of two rivers, the Oder and the Neisse (Oder-Neisse line).

It was not specified, however, whether it was the Western Neisse (which had its source in Bohemia and flowed into the Oder near Nysa) or the Eastern Neisse (which had its source in Silesia and flowed in the Oder near Gubin), which was later to be discussed. Stalin also made his claims in Asia: South Sakhalin and the Kuril Islands, Japan's Northern Territories. Concerning the operations in the occupied Balkans, Churchill announced to Stalin his intention to support communist partisans in Yugoslavia led by Tito rather than the Chetniks' legitimist group obedient to the Yugoslav government-in-exile in London. The former was led by Draža Mihailović.

Churchill made this decision based on reports that the Partisans inflicted much more damage on the Germans than the Chetniks. He did not suspect that these reports largely exaggerated the number of dissident groups and minimised Mihailović's forces. This was due to the influence of the 'Five of Cambridge', a group of agents of the British Secret Intelligence Service who were, in fact, working for the NKVD (People's Commissariat for Internal Affairs). At the conclusion of the conference, the three leaders agreed that the troops of the three powers would remain in close contact for all matters concerning operations in Europe. In particular, it was agreed that a cover plan to mystify and disorient the enemy on operations would be agreed between the relevant personnel.

A savage mentality started at dinner on the second day of the meeting, when Stalin suggested a toast to eliminating 50,000 men from the German staff. Churchill was aghast at this. Roosevelt, in a humorous tone, suggested killing 49,000 men. His son Elliott chipped in by saying that when the Red Army, American and British rolled into Germany, they would not only wipe out top German soldiers but also thousands of Nazis. The most humane of all, Churchill walked out of the room in anger. Such vengeful acts were against the Geneva Conventions of 1929, and if the leaders harboured such feelings towards the Germans, it was bound to percolate all the way down to the foot soldiers of the Allied armies.

In his speech to the House of Commons on 15 December 1944, Churchill vigorously advocated the 'Orderly and humane' expulsions of the German populations (what is nowadays referred to as 'ethnic cleansing') that remained beyond the new eastern borders of Germany from Poland, Czechoslovakia, and Hungary (but not Yugoslavia), asserting that as far as he could judge, it seemed to be the most satisfactory and efficient solution. Commentators recalled that only eighteen months earlier, on 10 March 1943, Viscount Simon declared in the House of Lords that it would be the policy of the British government to destroy the Nazi regime and to deal 'suitably and severely'[2] with the men who had inspired outrages in occupied territory. 'But let it be quite clearly understood and proclaimed all over the world,'[3] he added, 'that we British will never seek to take vengeance by wholesale mass reprisals against the general body of the German people. Our methods will be the methods of justice.'[4]

By April, with progressive victories by American, British, and Soviet troops taking over occupied towns, and liberating prisoners,

Introduction

the Third Reich was facing its inescapable demise. In the face of that prospect, thousands of Germans chose suicide over occupation. As well as this being the preferred method among high-ranking officials like Heinrich Himmler, Paul Goebbels and Adolph Hitler, it was also the avenue taken by many civilians. Numerous German cities experienced mass suicides at the end of the war, but it was the small Pomeranian town of Demmin (now in Mecklenburg-Vorpommern) that witnessed the starkest example of this when, between 30 April and 2 May 1945, the Second Belarussian Front had advanced through Western Pomerania in a merciless rampage, and laid waste to 70 per cent of the town Demmin, with soldiers looting homes, committing rape, and executing people at random. Although death toll estimates vary, more than 900 civilians had killed themselves during the ensuing mass panic – acknowledged to be the largest mass suicide ever recorded in Germany.

Nearly 11 million German soldiers had been captured by the end of the Second World War, but despite the majority of the German army fighting on the Eastern front, the Russians took only around 3.1 million prisoners; a surprisingly low number when compared to the Americans, who took 3.8 million, the British who took 3.7 million, and even the French, who had captured 250,000 Germans.

At the Potsdam Conference, which was held at the Cecilienhof (Cecilia Court) Palace in Potsdam, Germany, from 17 July – 2 August 1945, Winston Churchill sought to mitigate the terms of the expulsions when he met with the Soviet leader Joseph Stalin and United States President Harry Truman, and confirmed the agreements decided at their previous meeting at the Yalta Conference of February 1945, where they negotiated terms for the complete disarmament, denazification, and demilitarisation of Germany. They also agreed in principle that the border of Poland's territory would be moved west, and that the remaining ethnic German population would be subject to expulsion. The leaders of the émigré governments of Poland and Czechoslovakia were assured of their support on this issue.

After 1945, almost all Germans presented themselves as the true victims of the Nazi regime. Despite the vast majority of the Volksdeutsche (German speakers) in Eastern Europe having greeted Hitler's conquests as a form of national 'liberation', and benefited materially from the plunder of their Jewish, Czech and Polish neighbours, the post-war peace was perhaps the most brutal time for the more than 12 million Volksdeutsche living outside the borders of the former Reich.

Hitler's Speech to the Commanders in Chief on 22 August 1939:

> It was clear to me that a conflict with Poland had to come sooner or later. I had already made this decision in spring, but I thought I would turn on the west for a few years, and only afterwards to the east. I wanted to establish an acceptable relationship with Poland in order to first fight against the west, but this plan, which was agreeable to me, could not be executed. It became clear to me that Poland would attack us in case of a conflict with the west. Poland wants access to the sea. The further development became obvious after the occupation of the Memel region, and it became clear to me that under circumstances, a conflict with Poland could arise at an inopportune moment.[5]

Hitler enumerated his personal factors as reasons for the reflections:

> … no one will ever have the confidence of the whole German people as I do. There will probably never again be a man in the future with more authority than I have. My existence is therefore a factor of great value … A personal factor is the Duce. His existence is also decisive. Italy's loyalty to the alliance will no longer be certain. The basic attitude of the Italian court is against the Duce. Above all, the court sees the expansion of the empire a burden. The Duce is the man with the strongest nerves in Italy. The third factor favourable to us is Franco. We can ask only benevolent neutrality from Spain. But this depends on Franco's personality. He guarantees a certain uniformity and steadiness of the present system in Spain. We must take into account that Spain does not as yet have a fascist party of our internal unity. On the other side a negative picture as far as decisive personalities are concerned. There is no outstanding personality in England or France.
>
> For us it is an easy to make decision. We have nothing to lose; we can only gain. Our economic situation is such, because of our restrictions, that we cannot hold out more than a few years. Göering can confirm this. We have no

Introduction

other choice, we must act. Our opponents risk much and can gain only little. England's stake in the war is unimaginably great. Our enemies have men who are below average. No personalities. No masters. No men of action. Besides the personal factor, the political situation is favourable for us; in the Mediterranean rivalry among Italy, France and England, in the Orient tension, which leads to the alarming of the Mohammedan world.

The English empire did emerge from the last war strengthened. From a maritime point of view, nothing was achieved. Conflict between England and Ireland. The South African Union became more independent. Concessions had to be made to India. England is in great danger. Unhealthy industries. A British statesmen can look into the future only with concern. France's position has also deteriorated particularly in the Mediterranean.

Further favourable factors are these: Since Albania there is an equilibrium of power in the Balkans. Yugoslavia carries the germ of collapse because of her internal situation. Romania did not grow stronger. She is liable to attack and vulnerable. She is threatened by Hungary and Bulgaria. Since Kamal's death, Turkey has been ruled by small minds, unsteady, weak men. All these fortunate circumstances will no longer prevail in two to three years. No one knows how long I shall live. Therefore conflict better now.

The creation of Greater Germany was a great achievement politically, but militarily it was questionable, since it was achieved through a bluff of the political leaders. It is necessary to test the military. If at all possibly, not by general settlement, but by solving individual tasks. The relation to Poland has become unbearable. My Polish policy hitherto was in contrast to the ideas of the people. My propositions to Poland (Danzig corridor) were disturbed by England's intervention. Poland changed her tone towards us. The initiative cannot be allowed to pass to the others. This moment is more favourable than in two to three years. An attempt on my life or Mussolini's could change the situation to our disadvantage. One cannot eternally stand opposite one another with cocked rifles. A suggested compromise would have demanded that we change our convictions and make agreeable gestures. They talked to us again in the language of Versailles. There was danger of losing prestige. Now the probability is still great that the West will not interfere. We must accept the risk with reckless resolution. A politician must accept a risk as much as a military leader. We are facing the alternative to strike or be destroyed with certainty sooner or later.

The following reasons strengthen my idea. England and France are obligated; neither is in a position for it. There is no actual rearmament in England, just propaganda. It has done much damage that many reluctant Germans said and wrote to Englishmen after the solution of the Czech question; the Führer carried his point because you lost your nerve, because you capitulated too soon. This explains the present propaganda war. The English speak of a war of nerves. It is one element of this war of nerves for present the increase an armament. The construction programme of the Navy for 1938 has not yet been filled. Only mobilisation of the reserve fleet. Purchase of fishing steamers. Considerable strengthening of the navy, not before 1941 or 1942.

Little has been done on land. England will be able to send a maximum of three divisions to the Continent. A little has been done for the air force, but it is only a beginning. Anti-aircraft defence is in its beginning stages. At the moment, England has only 150 Anti-aircraft guns. The new gun has been ordered, but it will take a long time until enough have been produced. Fire directors are lacking. England is still vulnerable from the air. This can change in two to three years. At the moment the English air force has only 130,000 men, France 72,000 men, and Poland 15,000 men. England does not want the conflict to break out for two or three years.

The following is characteristic of England. Poland wanted a loan from England for rearmament. England, however, only gave credit in order to make sure that Poland buys in England, although England cannot deliver. This means that England does not really want to support Poland.

Introduction

She does not risk 8 million pounds in Poland, although she put half a billion into China. England's position in the world is very precarious. She will not accept any risks.

France lacks men (decline in the birth rate). Little has been done for rearmament. The artillery is antiquated. France did not want to enter on this adventure. The West has only two possibilities to fight against us:

1 Blockade. It will not be effective because of our anarchy and because we have sources of aid in the East.
2 Attack from the West from the Maginot Line. I consider this impossible.
3 Another possibility is the violation of Dutch, Belgian, and Swiss neutrality. I have no doubt that all these states as well as Scandinavia will defend their neutrality by all available means. England and France will not violate the neutrality of these countries. Actually England cannot help Poland. There remains an attack on Italy. A military attack is out of the question. No one is counting on a long war. If Mr Von Brandutch had told me I need four years to conquer Poland, I would have replied: then it cannot be done. It is nonsense to say that England wants to wage a long war.

We will hold our position in the West until we have conquered Poland. We must be conscious of our great production. It is much bigger than in 1914 – 1918.

The enemy had another hope, that Russia would become our enemy after the conquest of Poland. The enemy did not count on my great power of resolution. Our enemies are little worms. I saw them in Munich. I was convinced that Stalin would never accept the England offer. Russia has no interest in maintaining Poland and Stalin knows that it is the end of his regime no matter whether his soldiers come out of a war victorious or beaten. Litvinow's replacement was decisive. I brought about the change to Russia gradually. In connection with the commercial treaty we got into political conversation. Proposal of a non-aggression pact. Then came a general proposal from Russia. Four days ago I took a special step, which brought it about that Russia answered yesterday that she is ready to sign. The personal contract with Stalin is established. The day after tomorrow, von Ribbentrop will conclude the treaty. Now Poland is in the position in which I wanted her.

We need not be afraid of a blockade. The East will supply us with grain, cattle, coal, lead and zinc. It is a big arm, which demands great efforts. I am only afraid that at the last some Schweinehund will make a proposal for mediation. The political arm is set further. A beginning has been made for the destruction of England's hegemony. The way is open for the soldier, after I have made the political preparations.

Today's publication of the non-aggression pact with Russia hit like a shell. The consequences cannot be overlooked. Stalin also said that this course will be of benefit to both countries. The effect on Poland will be tremendous. Göering answers with thanks to the Führer and the assurance that the armed forces will do their duty.[6]

Chapter One

Hitler's Final Solution

As their impending defeat became increasingly clear in 1944 and into 1945, the Nazi regime began a desperate undertaking to destroy all documentary evidence of their various crimes against humanity, including internal reports, personal correspondence, and various propaganda materials.

The earliest piece of verbal evidence from Hitler pointing to his personal premeditation of the Final Solution is a statement he made to journalist Josef Hell during an interview in 1922:

> Once I really am in power, my first and foremost task will be the annihilation of the Jews. As soon as I have the power to do so, I will have gallows built in rows … Then the Jews will be hanged indiscriminately … until all of Germany has been completely cleansed of Jews.[1]

This shows that Hitler had begun premeditating, at least in its most basic form, a campaign of genocide against the Jews prior to him taking power. However, in another statement made to the Czech foreign minister František Chvalkovský during a meeting on 21 January, 1939, he said, 'We are going to destroy the Jews … The day of reckoning has come.'[2] Yet despite the abundance of transcripts of Hitler's public statements and speeches regarding the 'Jewish Question', no definitive written orders are known to exist.

His direct responsibility for planning and implementing the Holocaust can be firmly established by diary entries by high-ranking Nazi bureaucrats which point to his personal ordering of it. An example of this can be seen in a diary entry by Minister of Propaganda Joseph Goebbels dated 12 December 1941:

> With respect of the Jewish Question, the Führer has decided to make a clean sweep. He prophesied to the Jews that if

they again brought about a world war, they would live to see their annihilation in it. That wasn't just a catch-word. The world war is here and the annihilation of the Jews must be the necessary consequence.[3]

Goebbels had made further reference in his diary to Hitler's ordering of the Final Solution a year later, on 14 February 1942: 'The Führer once again expressed his determination to clean up the Jews in Europe pitilessly ... Their destruction will go hand in hand with the destruction of our enemies ... The Führer expressed this idea vigorously and repeated it afterwards to a group of officers.'[4] Another private Nazi record that points to Hitler's having ordered the Final Solution is a handwritten note by Reichsführer-SS Heinrich Himmler from a meeting with Hitler at the Wolfsschanze on 18 December 1941, which simply read: 'Jewish Question/to be exterminated like the partisans.'

The Euthanasia Programme

Following a petition by the parents of a severely disabled infant to have him put to sleep, Hitler sent one of his personal physicians, Karl Brandt, to go to the village of Pomssen, in the south-east of Leipzig, to investigate the case. Following his own examination of the child, Brandt consulted with paediatrician Dr Werner Catel and Dr Helmut Kohl, and they concluded that the child was beyond help. Brandt had been given the authority by Hitler to have the child killed, and if any legal action were to be taken, it would be thrown out of court, and subsequently, the mercy killing (Gnadentod) of five-month-old Gerhard Herbert Kretschmar who, until 2007, had been known only as 'Child K', took place on 25 July 1939, and marked the beginning of one of the most hideous programmes of the Second World War – the 'Euthanasia programme', which ultimately resulted in the deliberate killing of about 200,000 people with mental and/or physical disabilities.

Three weeks after Gerhard Kretschmar's death, the Nazis set up the Reich Committee for the Scientific Registering of Hereditary and Congenital Illnesses. The committee registered the births of all babies born with defects identified by physicians. While Hitler moved against Jews, Sinti, and Roma, he also included those whom he personally viewed as 'marginal humans'; the Aryans whom he considered unworthy of life – people with birth defects, senility, epilepsy, hearing loss, mental illnesses, personality disorders, Down's Syndrome, chronic alcoholism, as well as those who had vision loss, or delays in their development, or who suffered from certain orthopaedic problems.

Experiments with poisonous gas aimed at killing handicapped people, whose life had been deemed unworthy by the regime, were carried out during the so-called 'T4 Action' in National-Socialist Germany from October 1939, and proved satisfactory. It killed quickly, and was easier and cheaper than firing squads that required many soldiers and bullets. It was also much less traumatising for the executioners because they didn't have to see the faces of the victims – which is exactly what happened to the *Einsatzgruppen* units of the SS and the German Police on the Eastern Front as they had to follow the front, and secure territories at the rear of the Wehrmacht and Waffen-SS, by executing communists and male Jews (and later, in the course of the summer of 1941 all Jews, including women, elderly people and children).

Hitler, who maintained a fixed policy of not issuing written instructions relating to anything that could later be classified as crimes against humanity, made an exception in the case of the 'T4 Euthanasia Programme', to overcome opposition to it within the German state bureaucracy. He signed the involuntary euthanasia order, antedated to 1 September 1939, which authorised his physician Karl Brandt and the National Leader Philipp Bouhler, to implement the programme to execute the mentally and physically disabled on the basis that it would help German people get rid of existences that would be a burden in the international struggle for life.

The Reich's Interior Ministry and the regional and authorities of the Länder (states) responsible for the asylums sent out the first registration forms to all mental hospitals and psychiatric clinics in Germany. The one-page forms were designed to select those inmates that were to be killed. The completed forms were registered in the office of the KdF in Tiergartenstraße 4 in Berlin (from which 'T4' was derived), copied and sent to three medical experts, who decided upon the death or life of the patients based solely on the information provided by the registration form. A red cross meant murder, a blue dash meant survival. The final decision was made by the senior referees, among them Herbert Linden of the Reich's Interior Ministry, and Werner Heyde, Head of the T4 medical department. Patients were generally rendered somnolent by being given morphine and scopolamine injections, or narcotic tablets, to create a 'Twilight Sleep' before being taken, in groups of ten, to the gas chamber. Families were advised of the patient's death by form letters which stated that the patient had succumbed to 'heart failure' or 'pneumonia'. The central T4 clearing office received care allowances for the period of time that elapsed between the killing and the attestation of death – usually two weeks – and by the time the programme was terminated on 24 August 1941, it had generated several million Reichsmarks in revenue.

However, the programme had already been initiated, and was being covertly used in the Nazi concentration camps, and would further be applied in occupied Poland, where the murder of the handicapped was a precursor to the Holocaust. Heinrich Himmler, who had witnessed one of the gassings liked what he saw, and gassing would later become the extermination method of choice during the Final Solution. The killing centres to which the handicapped were transported were the antecedents of the Nazi death camps, and many of the physicians who became specialists in the technology of cold-blooded murder in the late 1930s, later staffed those camps, having long since lost all their moral, professional, and ethical inhibitions.

Carbon monoxide exhausted by truck engines was the first method used to kill the victims, who would be placed in a sealed hermetic truck and the exhaust gas would kill them. The problem was the high pressure (that led at least one truck to explode) and the time needed to asphyxiate the prisoners. In Auschwitz Rudolph Hess, an aide of the camp commander, had the idea of using the pesticide Zyklon B. Impregnated in small crystal substrates, the hydrogen cyanide (prussic acid) was vaporised when it came in contact with air. Poured into the gas chambers, Zyklon B would kill in six to twenty-five minutes, depending on the season, because it needed an ideal temperature of 27°C. In other camps, like Belzec or Treblinka, the carbon monoxide remained in use: the engine of an army tank provided the poison.

Bottled Gas

From November 1939, mentally ill people were systematically killed with carbon monoxide gas in Fort VII in Poznan. Under the command of Lange, the inmates of the asylums near Poznan were driven to the camp, locked in casemates and suffocated with carbon monoxide from pressurized steel bottles. The corpses were buried in mass graves in a forest near Oborniki, 30km (18.6 miles) north of Poznan. The handling of the corpses was done by Polish prisoners of Fort VII assigned to SS-Sturmbannführer Herbert Lange. The method of carbon monoxide bottle gassings was subsequently implemented at the Euthanasia killing site Brandenburg in the Reich. In January 1940, Lange moved on from the stationary gas chambers in Fort VII to a motorised mobile homicidal gas chamber.

Gas Vans

Alois Brunner, the right-hand-man to Adolf Eichmann, the supreme logistician of the Holocaust who plotted the transports across Europe to the extermination camps in occupied Poland, was responsible for the creation of gas vans, which initially operated outside ghettos and concentration camps in Eastern Europe. Nazi SS Colonel Walter Rauff was instrumental in the modification of scores of trucks into mobile 'gas chambers'. Under his command, Division II D3a of the Reich Security Main Office ordered six 3,175kg (3.5 t) four-wheel drive Opel Blitz trucks to be adapted, along with the first five of thirty of the larger 6,350kg (7 t) Saurerwagens ordered for the end of 1941. The box structures with tight-closing double doors at the rear were purchased from Gaubschat delivered / Berlin-Neukölln. The conversion to the gas wagon was carried out in the workshop of Unit II D 3 a. A witness, Harry Wentritt, described it in 1961 before the Court in Hannover, as follows:

> There was an exhaust gas hose attached, which was conducted from the outside to the floor of the car. In this car, we drilled a hole in the diameter of about fifty-eight to sixty millimetres, in the thickness of the exhaust pipe. A metal pipe (exhaust pipe) was welded to the inside of the car, above this hole, which could be connected to the exhaust hose connected to the outside. At the start of the engine and after connections, the exhaust gases of the engine went through the exhaust into the exhaust hose and from there

to the exhaust pipe, which was installed inside the vehicle, where the gas then spread.

The box structure was clad in the inside with sheet metal. An initially attached small viewing window was omitted in later versions. Rauff delegated the task of keeping the gas vans, which carry between twenty-five and sixty people at a time, which operated in the Soviet Union and other Nazi-occupied areas to the SS chemist, August Becker, who kept Rauff fully informed on the gas van killing operations.

On the pretext that they needed to shower to become clean, and that their clothes had to be disinfected, up to fifty people with mental and physical disabilities, and later Jews and other prisoners, were escorted to the undressing room, where they gave up their valuables and clothes. Having then been led up steps to the 'washrooms', they found themselves in a sealed compartment. The doors were closed and locked, and the van was driven away towards pre-cleared spaces in nearby woods or forest. During the short journey, the carbon-monoxide exhaust fumes were piped directly into the compartment, asphyxiating the passengers. The dead were subsequently buried in mass graves. In September 1944, the Nazis destroyed the camp and tried to erase the evidence of the mass murders by digging up and cremating all of the bodies from the mass graves. Around 7,000 Jews, Roma, communists, Jehovah's Witnesses and the disabled died in gas vans.

Observation Stations

Between October 1939 and August 1941, more than 70,000 German handicapped people were killed by gas, after a selection made by SS physicians. Regional governors were eager to clear out their institutions to make way for wounded soldiers, and having seen what was going on in Poland, they jumped at the chance to implement similar programmes on the home front, and what had begun as a regional solution to 'hospital overcrowding' soon spread across Germany. The administrators established gas chambers at six killing centres, referred to as 'Observation Centres', in Germany and Austria: Hartheim, Sonnenstein, Grafeneck, Bernburg, Hadamar, and Brandenburg.

Herbert Lange was transferred directly from duties in the T4 euthanasia programme, murdering psychiatric patients in Posen, to

Chelmno, which had been selected as the site of the first experiments by gas chambers for the mass killings of Jews as part of the 'Final Solution'. In November 1941, they took over the grounds of an empty manor house called 'The Castle' in Chelmno, and converted it into a base camp with barracks and a reception area for deportees. For security reasons, the main gate to the site was constructed as a sluice: when the guards opened one gate, the other one was closed. Several other buildings of the former estate were located within a 2.5–3 m (8 ft) high wooden fence and densely planted trees.

Each afternoon, Jews were brought under guard by train from Łódź via Kolo junction (where they transferred to open rail cars running on a narrow-gauge track), or from nearer locations by lorry, to the castle or Schloss. Upon arrival, they were told that some of them would go to work to Austria or further eastward, others would work at his estate; they would be fairly treated and receive good food. They were told that for sanitary reasons they had to take a shower first. They were then gathered in the castle courtyard, subdivided into groups of fifty, and told to undress. They were forced to hand over all valuables. They were then told they were about to be transferred to a work camp, but first they had be disinfected and showered. They were taken down into the castle cellar to a 'washroom' which led via a ramp into a waiting van. Vicious beatings ensured that none hesitated or declined to go inside. After fifty to seventy persons were jammed into the van's freight compartment, the exhaust pipe was connected to an opening in the compartment and the engine switched on. After about ten minutes those inside were dead. The driver, usually a member of the 'Schutzpolizei', then drove the van 4km (2.5 miles) to a camp in the nearby Rzuchowski Forest. Here, the SS had prepared long deep trenches, dug out by Jewish slave labour (after spring 1942, the bodies were cremated on site). Ten minutes were allowed for the exhaust fumes to evaporate, and then a team of forty to fifty Jews, wearing leg-irons to prevent their escape, hauled the corpses out of the van and dumped them in the graves. The bodies were searched for jewellery and gold teeth, which were extracted, and then another team of Jews sorted the clothes and objects of those killed so that they could be made available to Germans in the Reich. No less than 370 wagon loads of clothing were supplied by these means.

The Gas chambers at Auschwitz were hidden in the basement of the crematoria, and so were not visible from the outside. Victims selected on the arrival ramp of the camp train terminus were led straight to the chambers. Numerous bath and shower signs written in different languages were aimed to assure the victims, as were many shower heads in the chambers. In other extermination camps, there were no false shower heads. The chambers were the heart of the national-socialist death industry, and their location under the crematoria ensured maximum efficiency and rapidity. Not limited to extermination camps, gas chambers were installed in some concentration camps. Mauthausen, Sachsenhausen, Ravensbrück, Stutthof, Neuengamme, Natzweiler, and Dachau, were equipped with gas chambers and crematoria, although the camps were not designed for mass killings.

As the Third Reich embarked upon its plan of conquest and genocide, a way of identifying and cataloguing Jews had to be found straight away, so they were targeted for efficient asset confiscation, ghettoization, deportation, enslaved labour, and, ultimately, annihilation. It was a cross-tabulation and organisational challenge so monumental, it called for a specialised system. International Business Machine (IBM) founder Thomas Watson cooperated with the Nazis, despite international calls for an economic boycott, and leased IBM's Herman Hollerith punch-card technology for very high fees, to automate Hitler's persecution of the Jews. The data generated employing counting and alphabetisation equipment supplied by IBM through its German subsidiary Dehomag, and other national subsidiaries, was instrumental in the efforts of the German government to concentrate and ultimately destroy ethnic Jewish populations across Europe.

It was first used in Germany, and then rolled out across Nazi Europe, recording the identification of the Jews in the 1933 censuses, registrations, and ancestral tracing programmes, to the running of railroads, and the organisation of concentration camp slave labour. IBM and Dehomag custom-designed complex solutions, one by one, as required by the needs of Reich, with continuous upkeep and service. The machines became the sole source of the billions of punch cards Hitler needed. IBM and its subsidiaries helped create enabling technologies, step-by-step, from the identification and cataloguing programmes of the 1930s to the selections of the 1940s.

Chapter Two

The Nazi Camps

During the earliest years of the Third Reich, a variety of detention facilities were established under National Socialism by German authorities to confine those whom they defined as political, ideological, or racial opponents of the regime, including German Communists, Socialists, trade unionists, and others from left and liberal political circles. Based on an extra-legal jurisdiction authorised by Hitler, the concentration camps literally stood outside the laws of the German state.

The concentration camp at Dachau, in Upper Bavaria, was established in 1933 and served as a model for an expanding and centralised concentration camp system under the management of the Schutzstaffel (SS). Most prisoners consisted of German communists, Socialists, Sinti and Roma (Gypsies), Jehovah's Witnesses, homosexuals, and persons accused of 'asocial' or socially 'deviant' behaviour by the Germans, who were undesired to sustain the German war effort. In 1934, the IKL – Inspektion der Konzentrationslager (Concentration Camps Inspectorate) was created by the SS-Oberführer Theodore Eicke, the second commandant at Dachau, as the central SS administrative and managerial authority for the concentration camps of the Third Reich. Working for the 'Reich Leader SS' Heinrich Himmler, the IKL would administer thirty-two main camps and with more than 1,000 satellite camps.

Further Nazi German camps and subcamps were set up before and during the war, with six major and most renowned camps – Chelmno, Beł`ec, Sobibór, Treblinka, Auschwitz-Birkenau and Majdanek, being established in Nazi-occupied Poland between 1941 and 1945. These were Concentration Camps, Extermination Camps, Labour Camps, and Prisoner of War Camps.

Coded Language of Gassing

A coded language was designed to record the death of the inmates of concentration camps, and from its inception: '14 f 1' signified natural death, '14 f 2' – suicide or accidental death, '14 f 3' – shot while trying to escape, '14 f I' – execution. SS physicians based at each of the camps pre-selected a pool of potential victims, the selection process involving a two-tier approach. Officially, SS camp physicians were directed by the Inspectorate to create a pool of potential victims who were suffering from incurable physical diseases, or who through physical ailments, were permanently unable to undertake physical labour; unofficially, the Inspectorate also applied other criteria, which were not transmitted in writing, covering racial and eugenic criteria for selection. The covering code for this 'Special Treatment' was '14 f 13' – the 'euthanasia' of sick or infirm prisoners. Questionnaires had been transmitted to all the camps before the physicians' arrival, but the SS had already filled in the obligatory information: name, date and place of birth, last residence, family status, citizenship, religion, race, and date of arrest.

Himmler had provided support services for T4 killing operations, which were organised by Viktor Brack, an active member of the SS who had a close relationship with Himmler, but once Himmler and Bouhler had reached an agreement on the killing of concentration camp prisoners, Brack simply coordinated the killing operation and the T4 medical personnel selected the actual victims from this pool. At least twelve physicians were assigned to visit the concentration camps. One of the first, Dr Friedrich Mennecke, head of the Eichberg hospital and its children's ward near Wiesbaden, visited the Sachsenhausen Nazi concentration camp in Oranienburg, Germany, early April 1941. The preliminary work of selection had been carried out before his arrival. Mennecke thus only needed to check the completed information, enter the diagnosis, and make the final decision. However, for the Jews interned at Sachsenhausen, as well as all the other camps, the physicians did not even bother to enact the pretence of a physical examination.

Unlike T4, the deaths were recorded by the registry office responsible for each concentration camp. The camp was noted as the place of death and a fictitious cause of death created, although from early 1942 death notices were no longer sent to the next-of-kin of the deceased. The camp at Natzweiler-Struthof, located in the Vosges Mountains, had been established too late to be included and were all selected for 14 f 13. Mennecke, having been personally responsible for selecting over 2,500 'euthanasia' victims, was awarded specialty certification for his 'work', and like many other perpetrators, he enjoyed the privileges and the money that T4 distributed.

The 14 f 13 policy changed as a shortage of manpower became critical, and on 28 March 1942, the office of the Inspectorate of the Concentration Camps wrote to all camp commandants:

> A camp commandant's report has made it known that of fifty-one prisoners selected for special treatment 14 f 13, forty-two had 'again become fit for work' after a certain time, so that it was no longer necessary to apply special treatment to them. This case clearly shows that the regulations were not observed at the time of the prisoner's selection. Only those categories of prisoner referred to in the regulations should be brought before the medical commission, particularly those who are no longer fit for work.[1]

An order from Himmler in April 1943 further reduced the application of 14 f 13: 'Only mentally ill prisoners should be selected by the competent medical commissions for operation 14 f 13. All other prisoners who are unfit for work are to be excluded from this operation. Bedridden patients should be given suitable work that can be performed in bed.'[2] This order did not, however, prevent camp physicians using their own initiative to continue to kill prisoners unfit for work. Prisoners were now either killed at the camp itself or sent to a camp equipped with gas chambers.

The T4 killing centres were closed down as a result of this further change of policy, but under a new order on 11 April 1944, the selection of prisoners for 'euthanasia' was made by the camp physicians. The total number of victims of 14 f 13 is uncertain, but is thought to exceed 20,000. The programme was relatively small in scope in comparison to the killings in the death camps, but the transferred practices of the 'euthanasia' programme to the concentration camps, helped to create the dual purpose labour and extermination camps.

Chełmno (December 1941 – January 1945) was the first of the extermination camps; the site chosen due to the village's position in the Warthegau region of western Poland, west of the Łódź ghetto, where many of the victims came from. The first phase of executions, from 7 December 1941 until March 1943, were of victims who were deported from nearby places: Babiak, Dąbie, Deby Szlacheckie, Grodziec, Izbica Kujawska, Kłodawa, Koło, Kowale Pańskie, Nowiny Brdowskie and Sompolno. In mid-January, the SS also started to exterminate the Jews from the Łódź ghetto. Between 16 and 29 January 1942, 10,003 Jews were killed, from 22 February – 2 April 34,073, from 4–15 May 11,680, and from 5–12 September 1942, 15,859. By early 1943, all the other Jews of Warthegau had been killed. Also among the victims were 15,000 Jews from Germany, Austria, Czechoslovakia and Luxemburg, 5,000 Romany, several hundred Poles and an unknown number of Soviet POWs, as well as eighty-eight Czech children from Lidice.

On 7 April 1943, the SS blew up the manor house and the two furnaces, but following that, a last unexpected transport arrived, carrying Jews who were suffering from typhus. The Germans, afraid of being infected, ordered them to go to the first storey of the castle building. Dynamite was placed in the basement and the building was blown up, together with the Jews.

Bełżec was situated between the cities of Zamość and Lwów, around 0.5km (0.31 miles) south of the railroad station of Bełżec in the Lublin district of South-East Poland. Its site on the border between the Lublin District and the German District of Galicia (formed after 'Operation Barbarossa') was chosen because the Jews of both regions could be processed, and for ease of transportation by the railroad junction at nearby Rawa-Ruska and the highway between Lublin-Stadt and Lemberg. The camp, overseen by Obersturmführer Richard Thomalla, civil engineer and the camp construction expert in the SS, was built for the sole purpose of implementing the secretive Operation Reinhard, which operated from 17 March 1942 to the end of June 1943. Local builders were employed, who were overseen throughout the construction process by a squad of Trawniki guards. The work included building barracks with showering facilities for the prisoners and digging deep anti-tank trenches across the northern perimeter of the camp. The work was completed in February 1942 with the fitting of a tank engine and the exhaust piping systems for gassing.

Bełżec was originally a slave labour camp, managed initially by Christian Wirth, an SS officer who had been a killing expert since his participation in the first Aktion T-4 gassing of handicapped people at the Brandenburg Euthanasia Centre, and one of the leading architects of the programme to exterminate the Jewish people of Poland, and thirty SS and around 100 selected Soviet prisoners and Ukrainian Guards. The site was completely camouflaged to prevent the local population seeing the activities within the camp each time the twenty or so cattle/freight cars, carrying eighty to one hundred victims crammed into each, arrived after being detached from the Holocaust train at the railway station. During its short existence, an administration area and three gas chambers were added. Of the 430,000 sent to the first death camp at Bełżec between March and December 1942, there were only two survivors.

Groups of prisoners who had been selected to remain alive as Sonderkommandos (forced labourers) at Bełżec worked in the killing area to remove bodies from the gas chambers, and to bury the victims in mass graves. 600,000 people, mainly Jews and a few hundred Roma, were murdered, 80,000 of them within the first few weeks of operation. The bodies were exhumed again in late spring 1943 by the Sonderkommandos, who cremated them and dismantled the camp. The site was ploughed by the Germans, a manor house was constructed, and trees and crops were planted to disguise the area as a farm. The region was overrun by Soviet forces in July 1944.

Sachsenhausen Concentration camp in Oranienburg, 35km (22 miles) north of Berlin, had been used primarily for political prisoners since 1936, but with changes in the composition of the prison population, had over 11,300 prisoners in its confines by 1939. The camp was used as a training centre for Schutzstaffel (SS) officers, where trials were carried out to perfect the most efficient and effective methods of execution for use in the death camps. To this end, 'Station Z', which was designed specifically for the extermination of prisoners, was built by prisoners on the orders of the SS. On 29 May 1942, with high-ranking Nazi officials in attendance, it was put into operation, and ninety-six Jews were shot there on that day. In March 1943, a gas chamber was added and was in use until the end of the war.

Sachsenhausen was also the site of 'Operation Bernhard', one of the largest currency counterfeiting operations ever recorded. The Germans forced inmate artisans to produce forged American and British currency, as part of a plan to undermine the British and American economies. The unit ceased production in early 1945 with the advance of the Allied armies. The equipment and supplies were packed and transported, with the prisoners, to the Mauthausen-Gusen concentration camp in Austria, arriving on 12 March. However, Operation Bernhard was officially closed down at the start of May, and the prisoners were transported to the nearby Ebensee concentration camp, where an order had been issued that the prisoners were to be killed.

In April 1945, orders were given for the evacuation of the 33,000 remaining prisoners, who set out on a death march northwards towards the sea in groups of 400. The Nazis' aim was to put them on to a ship and then sink it. Over 6,000 prisoners died on the death march before it was liberated near Schwerin by the Soviet and US armies. Around 3,000 prisoners, almost half of them women, remained in the camp until it was liberated by Soviet soldiers on 22 April 1945. As in other camps, many former prisoners continued to die for a short time after liberation as a result of their imprisonment, despite the medical care that they received.

When Buchenwald concentration camp, situated on the northern slope of Ettersberg, a mountain five miles north of Weimar, in Thuringen, Germany, was established in July 1937, it was one of the first and the largest of the camp type within Germany's 1937 borders. Many actual or suspected communists from all over Europe and the Soviet Union were among the first internees, soon to be joined by Jews, Poles and other Slavs, the mentally ill and physically disabled, political prisoners, Romani people, Freemasons, prisoners of war, as well as ordinary criminals and sexual deviants.

All prisoners worked primarily as forced labour in local armaments factories, but the insufficient food and poor conditions, as well as deliberate executions, led to 56,545 deaths at Buchenwald of the 280,000 prisoners who passed through the camp and its 139 sub-camps. It was liberated by the Americans on 11 April 1945, they found 21,000 survivors, including 4,000 Jews and 1,000 children. As the American forces were closing in from 6 April, the Germans began already begun to evacuate the camp, with between 15,000–25,000 inmates dying in the process. From August 1945 to March 1950, the camp was used by the Soviet occupation authorities as an internment camp, NKVD special camp No. 2, where 28,455 prisoners were held, of whom 7,113 died.

Sobibór (May–July 1942 and October 1942 – October 1943) was established in the Lublin district of South-East Poland and was the site of the murder of around 500,000 Jews. SS-Obersturmführer Franz Stangl was the first camp commandant who had around thirty SS soldiers (many of these had previously worked on the T4 Euthanasia Programme in Germany) and a further 90–120 Ukrainians as camp guards. Around a thousand Sonderkommandos were selected from the strongest of those who arrived at the camp to work on the processing of new arrivals and their belongings.

Upon arrival, the Jews were taken directly to the reception area where they were informed that they had reached a transit camp en route to a labour camp and were given the opportunities to write to their loved ones to let them know they were safe. They were then told that they had to take a shower and have their clothes disinfected before they continued on their journey the next day. After the men and women were separated, the children going with the women, they were ordered to remove their clothing and hand over their valuables. They were then marched to the gas chambers – around 450–550 at a time. The whole process, from arrival to burial, took just two or three hours. At the end of 1942, the Germans ordered the digging up and cremation of the bodies to hide the evidence of the killings. The camp was closed down at the end of 1943 after a prisoners' uprising in October. After the uprising, the Nazis destroyed Sobibór, and the whole area was ploughed, planted with crops and given to a Ukrainian guard.

Treblinka was a forced labour camp managed by German SS and Trawniki Guards (Central and Eastern European collaborators recruited from Soviet Prisoners of War). Located in a forest north-east of Warsaw, it operated between 23 July 1942 and 19 October 1943 as one of the camps used in the final phase of Operation Reinhard. More than 700,000 Jews, along with 2,000 Romani people (Indo-Aryans), were killed at Treblinka in just five months. Treblinka was split into two separate units. Treblinka I was a forced labour camp where the prisoners worked in the forest, where the wood was cut and gathered to fuel the cremation pits, or in the gravel pit or irrigation area. The commandant was Sturmbannführer Theodor van Eupen, who ran the camp with several SS men and almost 100 Hiwi guards (voluntary assistants).

More than half of its 20,000 prisoners died from summary executions, hunger, disease, or brutal mistreatment. Treblinka II was an extermination camp where a small number of Jewish men who were selected upon arrival became its Sonderkommandos, and were forced to bury victims' bodies in mass graves. When the last of the Jews were gassed, the 1,000 Sonderkommandos who would be left in the camp were aware that they would also be killed, and so organised a revolt. On 2 August, armed with shovels, picks and a few weapons stolen from the arms warehouse, they set fire to part of the camp and broke through its barbed-wire fence. Around 300 of them escaped, and around a third of them survived recapture by the Germans. The gassing ended in October 1943, and from December, the inmates were no longer carrying any specific sentences, and the camp continued to operate officially until 23 July 1944, when the imminent arrival of Soviet forces led to its abandonment. The ground, like other camps, was ploughed over to disguise the genocide.

Auschwitz was the infamous concentration camp situated in Oświęcim, Poland, less than forty miles south of Krakow, and was made up of three camps, Auschwitz (the main camp), Birkenau (the largest extermination camp), and Monowitz-Buna, with three labour subcamps. The original camp was established in 1940 to house political prisoners, but by the autumn of 1941, a new camp (Birkenau) was constructed on the site of the village of Brzezinka, situated two miles away. After the population of the village were evicted from their homes by the Nazis, their properties were demolished and used as building materials for the Auschwitz-Birkenau camp, which began operating as a death camp between March 1942 and January 1945. Experiments with mass killing methods had been going on at Auschwitz since June 1941, and in August, 500 Soviet prisoners of war were gassed to death with Zyklon-B, a cyanide-based pesticide. The SS soon placed a huge order for the gas with a German pest-control firm, an ominous indicator of the coming Holocaust.

The trains arrived carrying Jews from almost every country in Europe, with some of the journeys lasting for days. Each train carried more than one thousand people crammed into cattle wagons with standing room only, and many died during the journey as a result of suffocation, illness, or hunger. Until the spring of 1944, the victims were unloaded on a ramp alongside the main railway lines at Oświęcim, in front of the awaiting SS officers and guards, Kapos (prisoners who had the authority to supervise other Jews) and Sonderkommandos and, following a selection process of which Jews would be sent straight to their deaths in the gas chambers and which Jews would remain alive temporarily, were then forced to walk the short distance to the camp. Over 80 per cent of Jews, invariably the elderly, women and children, were sent straight to their deaths in the gas chambers upon arrival at the camp. When it was known that 440,000 Hungarian Jews were to be sent to the camp, railway tracks were laid right into the camp, through the now infamous gatehouse building.

The Jews selected for work were sent to a separate building for registration, where they were tattooed on the left arm with a registration number (Soviet prisoners of war were tattooed on their left breast), shaved of all body hair, disinfected and showered before being given the infamous striped pyjamas, hat and a pair of wooden clogs before being marched to the blocks to begin their life within the camp. Categories of prisoners were distinguishable by triangular pieces of cloth sewn onto on their jackets below their prisoner number. Jews wore a yellow badge, the shape of the Star of David, Political prisoners, mostly Poles, had a red triangle, while criminals were mostly German and wore green. Asocial prisoners, which included vagrants, prostitutes and the Roma, wore black. Purple was for Jehovah's Witnesses and pink for gay men, who were mostly German.

The prisoners were housed in brick or wooden barracks. The brick barracks were constructed in the autumn of 1941 and designed to accommodate forty people, but depending on the number of transports arriving at the camp, very often more than 700 would be placed in each of them. Prisoners were packed into sixty spaces, with three bunks in each space, and slept on straw spread over the wooden bunks.

In each block of the wooden barracks, which had once been stables, were wooden three-tiered bunks, and the prisoners slept under thin blankets or rags on straw mattresses. Despite each barrack having two stoves with a brick heating flue running between them, no fuel for them was provided, and as a result, many prisoners died during the extreme cold of the Polish winters. The prisoners also had no access to water for washing during the first two years of the camps' existence.

A Zigeunerlager (Gypsy camp) at Birkenau was built by Soviet Prisoners of War from formerly Polish lands in Lithuania, Byelorussia, and Ukraine, who carried out the earth-moving and drainage labour in the marshy terrain two miles from the main camp at Auschwitz, built the access roads, and laid the foundations under the barracks. It was initially used for the imprisonment of Sinti and Roma (Gypsies) arriving primarily from Germany, Austria, the Protectorate of Bavaria and Moravia, and Poland, with smaller groups arriving from France, the Netherlands, Yugoslavia/Croatia, Belgium, the USSR, Lithuania, and Hungary. Around 23,000 men, women, and children (including the more than 370 children reckoned to have been born there) are estimated to have been imprisoned in the camp. Treated as asocial prisoners, they were marked with black triangles. A series of camp numbers, prefaced with the letter Z, were given to them and tattooed on their left forearms. Insufficient food and the severe overcrowding in the Zigeunerlager led to a dramatic deterioration in hygienic and sanitary conditions, which led in turn to frequent epidemics, especially of typhus and starvation diarrhoea. These epidemics resulted in a high mortality rate among the prisoners. When typhus was detected among a group of approximately 1,700 Polish Sinti and Roma men, women, and children who arrived on 23 March 1943 from Białystok, north-east Poland, they were sent directly to the gas chamber in fear of an outbreak, and their bodies cremated. It would not be the only occasion.

The head physician between the end of May 1943 and August 1944 at Birkenau was SS-Hauptsturmführer Dr Josef Mengele, who, along with Dr Horst Schumann or Dr Carl Clauberg, and other prominent doctors pertaining to the Nazi apparatus, ignored all ethical concerns and took advantage of carrying out pseudo-medical experiments such as euthanasia, live organ removal, and genetic manipulation with thousands of prisoners. Mengele, who had a predilection for twins, would personally select victims on the train platform upon their arrival at the camp. The few survivors were mutilated or otherwise incapacitated for life. In the seventeen months that the Zigeunerlager was in operation, 21,000 people or were murdered in the gas chambers.

The 60th Army of the First Ukrainian Front, a unit of the Soviet Army, opened the gates and entered the Auschwitz camp complex on 27 January 1945. They discovered around 7,000 surviving prisoners across the three main camps of Auschwitz I, Auschwitz-Birkenau and Buna Monowitz (which housed the predominantly Jewish prisoners who had to do forced labour on the grounds of the affiliated group of German Chemical and Arms manufacturers 'I G Farben'). Among the survivors were 180 children; fifty-two of them under the age of 8.

Majdanek (September 1941 – July 1944) was a German concentration and extermination camp built on the outskirts of the city of Lublin, Poland, but unlike other main Nazi camps, it was located in an area of rolling terrain that was entirely open to view from all sides. Used initially to imprison captured Soviet soldiers, it soon became a detention centre for Jews as part operations for the Final Solution, with mass transports of Jews arriving from the beginning of April 1942. The first 10,000 to arrive at Majdanek were young men from Slovakia, followed by transports from the area that is now the Czech Republic. Jews from Austria, Germany, France and Holland. From mid-1942 until mid-1943, most of the Jews were from the Lublin region itself, and the ghettos of Warsaw and Bialystok. By the time the camp was liberated by the Soviet Army in July 1944, approximately 360,000 victims had been murdered or had died at Majdanek, and 120,000 of them were Jews.

In July 1942, Himmler had ordered that all Jews held in key areas of Poland, except for those needed for essential labour, were to be killed by the end of the year. By the end of that year, more Jews had been murdered than in any other year of the Holocaust, the majority in the newly created extermination camps.

The Allies had been warned by the German industrialist Eduard Schulte via Polish and French intelligence contacts, about the systematic exterminations of Jews in Nazi Germany occupied Europe. Schulte, who had frequent contact with High German government and military officials, learned about 'Operation Reinhard' – the Final Solution concept, and in July 1942 he told Gerhart M. Riegner, the Swiss representative of World Jewish Congress, who in turn notified the Allies, but the information was largely ignored.

Germany was losing the war by 1943, sparking uprisings in some of the extermination camps as the remaining Jews kept alive to dispose of bodies and sort out the possessions realised that the number of transportees was reducing, and that they would be next. Civilian uprisings also took place across Poland, as mostly young Jews, whose families had already been murdered in the Nazi death camps, began to resist Nazi oppression. This made the press in Britain and brought to light the reports of rebellion and mass murder that could no longer be ignored.

Vital funds were still being ploughed into exterminating the Jews in the camps as late as March 1944, while the Allies were driving the German army back, but, now aware that the world had been alerted to the horrors of the camps, the Nazis sought to destroy evidence. In June, Soviet forces liberated Majdanek. The Nazis had already burned down the crematorium chimney but had failed to destroy the gas chambers and barracks. Only a few hundred inmates were still alive.

Wöbbelin was one of over eighty-five sub-camps of the Neuengamme concentration camp in the Bergedorf district of Hamburg, and was constructed on the road between Wöbbelin and the castle town of Ludwigslust under extremely harsh conditions by prisoners from Neuengamme and Bergen-Belsen concentration camps. It was originally intended as a reception camp for various evacuation transports, primarily to house American and British prisoners of war, but it existed for just ten weeks, from 12 February to 2 May 1945. In that time, nearly 5,000 inmates from at least twenty-five nations had been interned there, more than 1,000 of whom died of exhaustion, maltreatment and starvation.

On 2 May, units of the 82nd US Airborne Division and 8th Infantry reached the region, and the Soviet Army stood before Grabow. The guards left the camp around noon, and not long afterwards, American soldiers discovered the camp, which was not marked on any map. They would never forget what they saw there. On the orders of the American military authorities, the victims of Wöbbelin concentration camp were transported by the Americans on 7–8 May, and buried in individual graves in Ludwigslust, Hagenow, Wöbbelin and Schwerin.

Chapter Three

The Death Marches

In the summer and early autumn months of 1944, most of the evacuations from the Nazi concentration camps were carried out by train or, in the case of German positions cut off in the Baltic States, by ship. Towards the end of the war, with Germany's military forces crumbling, the whole Nazi concentration camp system was collapsing. The Germans were unable to cope with housing or feeding the ever-growing numbers of prisoners within the camps, which had rapidly led to widespread starvation and disease. Central SS authorities attempted to persuade the camp commandants to focus on keeping the prisoners alive to be used as forced labourers to serve the German war effort, and those who agreed began frantically evacuating the camps near the front lines. Few of the commandants took these instructions seriously, and according to SS reports, there were more than 700,000 prisoners left in the camps in January 1945. None were concerned about changing the murderous culture of the camps. By this time, most of German East Prussia was under Soviet occupation, and Soviet forces had besieged Warsaw, Poland, and Budapest, Hungary, as they prepared to push German forces back toward the interior of the Reich.

As winter approached, however, with the Allies having reached the German borders and had assumed full control of German skies, SS authorities evacuated concentration camp prisoners, from both east and west, on foot. The prisoners in the East were subjected to the enforced marches to camps in Germany and Austria which led to terrible overcrowding and resulted in many thousands of deaths. The Germans were unable to cope with the numbers within the camps, and could not house or feed the prisoners, which soon led to widespread starvation and disease. The prisoners were first taken by train and then by foot on 'death marches', as they became known, on which the prisoners were forced to march long distances in the bitter cold, with little or no food, water, or rest. Those who could not keep up were shot.

Shortly after the Soviet offensive in eastern Belarus annihilated German Army Group Centre, Soviet forces then overran the first of the major Nazi concentration camps at Majdanek, on the outskirts of the city of Lublin. While this provoked SS Chief Himmler into ordering that prisoners in all concentration camps and sub-camps be forcibly evacuated toward the interior of the Reich, it was too late to complete the emptying of the Majdanek camp. This had allowed Soviet and Western media to widely publicised SS atrocities at the camp, using both footage of the camp at liberation and interviews with some of the surviving prisoners.

The evacuation of Auschwitz and its satellite camps began on 18 January 1945, with nearly 60,000 prisoners being forced on death marches. Thousands of whom were considered too weak or too sick to march were killed in the days before the death march, and the tens of thousands of prisoners, mostly Jews, were forced to march to the city of Wodzisław Śląski, in the western part of Upper Silesia. More than 15,000 died during the marches; shot because they fell behind or could not continue. At Wodzisław Śląski, the prisoners were put on unheated freight trains and deported to concentration camps in Germany, particularly to Flossenbürg, Sachsenhausen, Gross-Rosen, Buchenwald, Dachau, and Mauthausen. The Soviet Army reached Auschwitz on 27 January and liberated the few remaining prisoners.

On 25 January 1945, the evacuation of around 25,000 prisoners, the overwhelming majority of them Jews, began from Stutthof concentration camp, near Sztutowo, in northern Poland. It had been filled to capacity since 1942 after prisoners were transferred from the concentration camps at Mauthausen and Flossenbürg. Following the main evacuation, around 12,000 prisoners were left behind, victims of a typhus epidemic that had struck the camp in 1944, and reached its peak in December. When soldiers of the 48th Red Army, under the command of Colonel S.C. Cyplenkow, liberated the camp on 9 May 1945, they found only 140 surviving prisoners. A further 5,000 inmates from the sub-camps were marched to the shore of the Baltic Sea, where they were forced to walk into the freezing water to be machine-gunned. Other prisoners were sent on a death march to Lauenburg in Eastern Germany, but they were cut off by advancing Soviet forces and forced back to Stutthof. Marching in severe winter conditions and being treated brutally by SS guards caused thousands to die during the march.

The Death Marches

With Stutthof completely encircled by Soviet forces by late April, the remaining prisoners were evacuated by sea on 25–27 April. Again, hundreds of prisoners were forced into the sea and shot. Over 4,000 were sent by small boat to Germany, some to the Neuengamme concentration camp near Hamburg, and some to Flensburg and Lübeck along the Baltic coast. Many drowned along the way, and their naked bodies were thrown in the sea. On approaching Lübeck, the local German authorities forbade their landing on the shore. Nearly all were killed. Shortly before the German surrender, some prisoners were transferred to Malmö, Sweden, and released to the care of that neutral country. It has been estimated that over 25,000 prisoners, around half, died during the evacuation from Stutthof and its sub-camps. One hundred prisoners were liberated from Stutthof on 9 May 1945.

Ahead of the advancing Red Army, many of the ninety-five sub-camps of Buchenwald, near Weimar, Germany, were closed, and the prisoners were sent to the main camp. On 7 April 1945, 28,000 prisoners were forced on a 300km march from Buchenwald through Jena, Eisenberg, Bad Köstritz, and Gera, towards the intended destination of Dachau, Flossenbürg, and Theresienstadt. The remaining 21,000 prisoners in Buchenwald were liberated four days later by the US Third Army.

As late as 19 April 1945, prisoners were still being sent to Dachau Concentration camp, around 16km (10 miles) northwest of Munich. Eduard Weiter, who had succeeded Martin Gottfried Weiss as the commandant of Dachau, suggested to Himmler that the camp be turned over to the Allies. Himmler, in signed correspondence, prohibited such a move, adding that, 'No prisoners shall be allowed to fall into the hands of the enemy alive.'[1] On 24 April, just days before the US troops arrived at the camp, the commandant and a strong guard forced around 7,000 prisoners on a six-day death march southwards to Tegernsee, in Bavaria. Dachau was liberated by the Americans on 29 April, who found approximately 67,000 prisoners, around a third of whom were Jews. After liberation, around 250 a day died from the effects of their prolonged internment. In early May, American troops liberated the surviving prisoners from the march to Tegernsee.

Chapter Four

Czechoslovakia

The world economic depression hit Czechoslovakia at the beginning of the 1930s, its highly industrialised German-speaking districts were hit more severely than the rest of the country, and the economic crisis soon turned into a political one. The consensus that the Prague government disproportionately favoured the Czech areas of the country with unemployment relief contributed to a sharp rise in the popularity of the rightist populist movements German National-Socialist Party and German National Party, whose leaders sought support from the new emerging force in the Weimar Republic Party – the NSDAP (National Socialist German Workers' Party, commonly referred to as the Nazi Party), especially following Adolf Hitler's rise to power in Germany.

Konrad Henlein, the leader of the Sudeten German Party (SdP), which had been formed from the Sudetendeutsche Heimatfront (SHF) some months after the First Czechoslovak Republic had outlawed the German National Socialist Workers' Party, won growing support among the German speakers living in the borderland. From the spring of 1934, Henlein's party was politically and financially supported by the NSDAP, which helped the SdP to increase its political influence among the Sudeten Germans. Its dominant position was confirmed within the German community in Czechoslovakia with more than 65 per cent of the vote in the parliamentary election in May 1935. Henlein's party won forty-four seats in the Czechoslovak Parliament, becoming the second-largest political force – with only one seat less than the Czechoslovak Agrarian Party.

Hitler embarked on a programme of eastward expansion, and on 5 November 1937 he informed his military chiefs of his intention to move against Austria and Czechoslovakia 'at the next opportunity'. Henlein's response, in the fear that Czechoslovakia would be defeated militarily within a few months, was to offer Hitler the SdP as an instrument with which to break up the country from the inside.

During the last free democratic elections before the German occupation of Czechoslovakia – the May 1938 communal elections, the SdP party gained 88 per cent of ethnic-German votes, taking over control of most municipal authorities in the Czech borderland. Despite repeated efforts made by the Czechoslovak President Edvard Beneš, together with the moderate German parties, to limit the SdP's popularity, the party had over 1.3 million members by June, making it one of the largest fascist parties in Europe at the time.

In his address to the foreign organisation branch of the NSDAP at the Nuremberg Rally on 12 September 1938, Hitler reviewed the history of the Nazi Party since 1923, and then declared that their enemies of today were the same as they were then. Attacking the Jews, he said,

> Because we are socialists we cannot tolerate an alien race dominating us. We are fighting the Jews so fanatically because National-Socialism wants to create a true unity of the nation. In this state, even the poorest child must be able to ascend to the highest peak. The formation of the unity of the people demanded an organisation which trained them; its nucleus was the Nazi party. Today that organisation reached into every house, every workshop, and even to Germans living abroad, combining them in one unity.
>
> […]
>
> The leadership [is] quite absolute; it could even adopt unpopular measures, if necessary. 'We are confronted by a united front from the Bolsheviks down to the Democrats. Today we see how international world democrats work hand in hand with Moscow. This insincerity is simply disgusting.
>
> […]
>
> I am asking neither that Germany be allowed to oppress three and a half million Frenchmen, nor am I asking that three and a half million Englishmen be placed at our mercy. Rather I am simply demanding that the oppression of three and a half million Germans in Czechoslovakia cease and that the inalienable right to self-determination takes its place.[1]

Henlein had played a clever political game in influential foreign circles, especially in London, convincing them that he was not Hitler's stooge but a free agent merely demanding self-determination for Czechoslovakia's oppressed Germans. By September 1938, the crisis had elevated and, following British Prime Minister Neville Chamberlain's meeting with Hitler at his private mountain retreat Berchtesgaden, Bavaria, assuring him that the German objectives could be achieved without fighting, the French consented to Chamberlain's policy, thus abandoning their former commitments, and the Soviet Union was under treaty obligation to assist Czechoslovakia only if the French would honour their pledges first. However, Hitler rejected the British plan, despite having been made aware through diplomatic channels that the UK could act against him, and Europe stood on the verge of war for several days before Chamberlain visited him for the second time, at Bad Godesberg. In the meantime, Czechoslovakia had announced general mobilisation, followed in France and Britain with partial call-ups. With the appeasers winning the day, Hitler agreed to receive Mussolini, Chamberlain, and the French premier in Munich.

With the support of Konrad Henlein, the leader of the SdP, Adolf Hitler met with Benito Mussolini, Édouard Daladier, and Neville Chamberlain, at the Munich Conference on 30 September 1938, to demand that the Czechoslovak government cede the Sudetenland to be joined with the Third Reich. Henlein, at Hitler's instigation, agitated for autonomy with the Karlsbad Programme, a list of demands that included self-government for German-speakers and all other minorities of the Sudetenland, substantial changes in Czechoslovak foreign policy including the abandonment of all Czechoslovak defence treaties and Czech cooperation with Germany, and reparations for damages suffered by Sudeten Germans since 1918, when the region was incorporated into the newly formed state of Czechoslovakia.

The Czechoslovaks had no representative at the meeting. Having been informed by Britain and France that it could either resist Nazi Germany alone or submit to the prescribed annexations, the government reluctantly capitulated and agreed to abide by the decision made at the conference. The agreement was readily accepted by most of Europe because it prevented the war threatened by Hitler, who had announced that it was his last territorial claim in Europe, and the choice seemed to be between war and appeasement. It also thwarted Hitler's proposed 'Fall Grün' ('Case Green'), the codename given to his plan for an aggressive open war against Czechoslovakia. But while Chamberlain returned to

England and delivered his 'Peace for our time' speech to crowds in London, over 3 million nationalistic Sudeten and Carpathian Germans found themselves a part of Germany.

The Prague government subsequently relinquished to Germany all frontier districts with populations that were 50 per cent or more German by 10 October. Edvard Beneš resigned the presidency on 5 October, and went into political exile in Chicago, in the United States of America. The agreement set up the new borders for the Czechoslovak state, fulfilling Hitler's and Henlein's demands concerning the incorporation of the Sudetenland into the Third Reich. Berlin had required the Sudeten lands and the ethnic Germans within them as the prelude to the total occupation of Czechoslovakia, and the agreement allowed no possibility of appeal. Wehrmacht troops entered Prague on 15 March 1939, and a new administration was installed.

In physical terms, the Third Reich obtained 40 per cent (11,185 square miles) of the territory of Bohemia and Moravia, which had 3.5 million inhabitants – 2.8 million Germans and 700,000 Czechs. The establishment of the German Protectorate in the remaining Czech lands finally dismembered the Czechoslovak state in 1939; placing it under the control of a newly established Slovak puppet regime which operated under the influence of Germany.

The Slovak Republic, a client state of Nazi Germany from 1939 to 1945, was governed by the Slovak politician and Roman Catholic priest Jozef Tiso. He and his aides had negotiated with Hitler as he prepared for the final takeover of Slovakia. After his return to Bratislava on 14 March 1939 following talks with Hitler in Berlin, during which Tiso signed a 'Protection Treaty' and was promised support for Independence if he separated Slovakia from Czecho-Slovakia (otherwise, the Slovak lands would be divided between Hungary, Poland and the rest of Czecho-Slovakia), all Slovak parliamentarians voted for independence, with Tiso as president.

The Slovak government issued a series of anti-Jewish decrees that forced Jews out of the civil service and the army, and placed them in specially created labour units. The Catholic-National Conservative Group, led by President Jozef Tiso, the radical Catholic and fascist-leaning group, represented by Prime Minister Vojtěch Tuka, and the radical and brutal paramilitary Hlinka Guard, all promoted anti-Jewish policies. While Tiso's group promoted a step-by-step diminishment of Jewish influence, Tuka demanded the complete exclusion of Jews from society, and ultimately their deportation. Germany reneged on the Protection Treaty with Tiso when a border war was fought between Slovakia and Hungary from 23 March to 31 March, resulting in the Hungarian occupation of a narrow strip along the border which had previously been Slovak.

The chief of Czechoslovak Military Intelligence, František Moravec, received a phone call on 14 March 1939 from Colonel Antonín Hron, the country's military attaché in Berlin, during which Hron confirmed the message that Moravec had received a few days earlier via one of his agents that Germany would invade Czechoslovakia the next day. Unlike the Czechoslovak foreign minister, František Chvalkovský, who refused to believe the information, Moravec knew that now was the time to act. He quickly assembled his closest staff along with as many intelligence documents as he could and boarded a plane at Prague Ruzyně Airport to fly to Britain, where he would continue the fight in exile.

The Czechoslovak President Emil Hácha (the successor to Edvard Beneš), together with the Czech Foreign Minister František Chvalkovský, was summoned to attend a meeting with Adolph Hitler in Berlin in the late evening of 14 March 1939, to discuss the future relations between the Reich and the independent Czech lands. Hácha, who was unable to fly due to his heart condition, arrived by train in Berlin at 10.40 pm on Tuesday evening, where he was met by Foreign Minister Ribbentrop and taken to the Adlon Hotel to await Hitler's call. Nearly three hours later, at 1.15 am, Hácha was finally summoned to the Reich Chancellery to see the Führer, who had Hermann Göring and Joachim von Ribbentrop in attendance.

Without any intimate dialogue between the two men, Hácha was offered an ultimatum: accept incorporation into the German Protectorate of Bohemia-Moravia or face destruction. Hácha refused to concede to the demand, but when Göring stepped in, threatening an aerial bombardment of Prague by the Luftwaffe, Hácha suffered a heart attack on the floor of the Reich's Chancellery. After doctors attended to Hácha and had managed to revive him, he eventually recovered enough health to speak to the government back in Prague. Following the call, he reluctantly agreed to give up his country's independence, and signed the surrender document. Within two hours, German tanks and motorised units under the command of General Johannes Blaskowitz had crossed the frontier, and occupied strategic points to prepare the way for the general advance. It was the beginning of six long years of occupation and Nazi tyranny. Adolph Hitler, travelling in an open-top car as part of a motorcade, was enthusiastically welcomed upon his arrival by huge crowds of Germans, held back by double rows of Schutzstaffel (SS) in the main streets of Brno when he entered the city on 17 March 1939. Unlike most Czecho-Slovaks, the spectators viewed the take-over of the country not as an occupation, but as a liberation.

The Nazis were not the only ones to assert anti-Jewish orders. The Czech authorities, despite claims that its autonomous government was forced by the German Reichsprotector to implement anti-Jewish policies, attempted to push through their share of anti-Jewish measures, with the exclusion of Jews from society and the transfer of their property and economic positions into Czech hands being perceived as a means of resisting Germanisation. However, the Germans were given reserved decisive powers through the decree by the Reichsprotector in 1939, mainly focused in the Aryan areas. They would later organise the deportations of Jews. From 1 September 1941, all Jews aged 6 and over had to wear a yellow badge or armband.

Around 26,000 Jews had successfully emigrated from Germany and Austria to Poland or Slovakia by the time of the Nazi occupation on 1 September 1939. In July, the Zentralstelle für Jüdische Auswanderung (Central Office for Jewish Emigration), which was modelled after its forerunners in Vienna, Prague and Amsterdam, had been established to accelerate the process of the emigration of Jews from the protectorate, making 'illegal' emigration much more difficult. The office, which operated under the complete control of the German authorities, oversaw the confiscation of property of would-be emigrants.

Jewish communities of various ideologies joined together and were centralised under the leadership of the Prague Jewish Community, chaired by František Weidmann representing the Czech Jews, and his deputy, Jakob Edelstein, a leading Zionist, and were subordinated to the Central Office for Jewish Emigration. All members had to be registered as well as people of other confessions (or those who were non-confessional) considered by the Germans to be Jews according to the Nuremberg Laws.

The Germans' policy on the Czech territories was initially softer than in neighbouring Poland or the Baltic states, but this changed when Hitler, who was disappointed in von Neurath's ability to sufficiently control political and economic unrest, replaced him with Reinhard Heydrich as Chief of the Central Security Office of the Third Reich, on 27 September 1941. Heydrich's reputation for machine-like efficiency and unflinching cruelty preceded him. He had put together one of the most brutal policing organisations in modern history, the Gestapo. After the Reichstag passed the Gestapo Law on 10 February 1936, which declared, 'Neither the instructions nor the affairs of the Gestapo will be open to review by the administrative courts.'[2] This meant the Gestapo was now above the law and there could be no legal appeal regarding anything it did. Heydrich's control had become almost absolute. He implemented drastic new policies and declared a state of emergency on the majority of the Protectorate territories. Four to five thousand arrests were made, along with the executions of another 400, quickly earning him the nickname 'The Butcher of Prague'. He also masterminded several of the Nazis most insidious acts of aggression, including laying out the blueprint for the Final Solution.

In November 1941, Heydrich ordered the creation of the Theresienstadt Ghetto, to the north of Prague. Jews from all over Czechoslovakia began to be deported to, and concentrated in, this ghetto. The ghetto was also used as a transit camp, with the first transport of people who were deemed least useful: the sick, old and weak, and the very young, departing from Theresienstadt to the Easton 9 January 1942. Some 33,000 people died from the unsanitary conditions and starvation in Theresienstadt alone.

It is estimated that 118,310 Jews were living in the Protectorate of Bohemia and Moravia upon its establishment following the German invasion in 1939. Of these, 103,960 had declared themselves to be of the Jewish faith with the rest being of other faiths or none at all. They became subject to strict limits to their rights and freedoms with more than 400 decrees and regulations restricting all aspects of their public and private lives. Their properties were transferred into Czech hands, special labels were issued to indicate Aryan shops, and synagogues were damaged or, as in Jihlava, burnt down as part of the systematic anti-Jewish policy by fascists.

26,000 Jews paid high fees and left all their property to the Reich so that they could emigrate legally on the path to freedom in the West. The emigration was initially supported by Nazi authorities, encouraging as much of the Jewish population as possible to flee abroad, but over the next two years, the number of states prepared to take in the waves of Jewish emigrants rapidly and continually decreased, until 1941, when the situation led to 'the Final Solution'. 80,000 Jews were deported, initially to Theresienstadt with the help of local Czech Nazi collaborators, and later to Auschwitz and Treblinka, and 10,000 survived the concentration camps.

The assassination of Reinhard Heydrich in an ambush and anti-tank mine attack by Czechoslovak Special Operations Executive agents Jozef Gabčík and Jan Kubiš on a mission codenamed 'Operation Anthropoid', in Prague on 27 May 1942, from which he slipped into a coma and died in Bulovka Hospital on 4 June 1942, was followed by a campaign of terror, coordinated by the Gestapo. 5,000 anti-fascists were arrested and all but 400 were imprisoned; they were summarily executed without a trial to spread fear throughout the country, and to suppress the growing anti-fascist resistance movement. The culmination of the German terror was Hitler's order for the extermination of the whole population of two Czech villages, Lidice and Ležáky.

On 9 June, two companies of police in battledress and a squad of Security Police joined Gestapo agents from Prague in the agricultural village of Lidice, in the Kladno district, where they systematically stormed properties and rifled through belongings. All 173 males in the village aged 15 and over were herded out of their homes and confined in a barn belonging to the Horák family, before being lined up in rows of ten at a time, and shot. A further eleven men who were not in the village at the time were later arrested and executed soon afterwards. The 198 women and 98 children from the village were driven to Kladno, where they were locked up in the gymnasium of the secondary school. They were left there for three days, without food or adequate sanitation, until they were deported to Ravensbrück concentration camp, where a few of the children, who were considered racially suitable and thus eligible for Germanisation, were handed over to SS families. The older women were separated from the rest and were sent onto the Auschwitz death camp. The village of Lidice was set on fire and the remains of the buildings destroyed. The reason given was that the Gestapo in Kladno had intercepted a letter belonging to a local family by the name of 'Horák', who had a son in the Czech army in Britain. The letter was labelled as 'suspicious' and led to the ensuing action: the Nazis selected thirty Jewish prisoners from the Terezin concentration camp and transported them to the village, where it took them thirty-six hours to dig a hole for all 173 bodies to conceal the evidence.

The small hamlet of Ležáky was targeted after evidence was found that residents had aided the agents of the Special Operations Executive who were directly involved in the assassination of Reinhard Heydrich, by providing a hiding place for their radio transmitter. The German police and the SS surrounded the village on 24 June and shot all thirty-three adults, both men and women. The village was razed to the ground. Thirteen children were spared, two of whom were deemed racially valuable, and were selected for Germanisation, but the remaining eleven children were sent to the Chełmno extermination camp, where they were gassed in summer 1942, together with one girl from Lidice. Unlike Lidice, Ležáky was not rebuilt after the war, and only memorials remain today.

Beneš and his advisors discussed the 'good' Germans being allowed to stay in Czechoslovakia, but the reverberations of Lidice and Theresienstadt and the rising wave of anti-German Czech nationalism were too strong, and Beneš' advisors recommended that he pursue the expulsions to the end. The idea of a nation-state without the minorities started to take shape between 1942 and 1943 through the diplomatic efforts undertaken by President Beneš, but his plan to expel the German minority from Czechoslovakia initially failed to win the support of the Western powers. However, when Stalin recognised the Czechoslovak government-in-exile, and expressed himself in favour of the transfer of Germans, both the United States and Great Britain changed their positions and accepted Beneš' plans for the transfer.

The Czech Press began conducting a mass propaganda attack against the Germans, recalling the crimes committed during the occupation. The presence of the Red Army also strengthened Anti-German sentiments. The actions of the Soviet soldiers against German civilians were legitimated by denazification which was identified with de-Germanisation.

The Czechoslovak government introduced numerous measures discriminating against their German minority. Germans could go out only at certain times of the day. They were forbidden from using public transportation or walking on the pavement; they could not send letters or go to the cinema, theatre, or pub; and they could not own jewellery, gold, silver, precious stones and other items. They were issued with ration cards, but were not allowed meat, eggs, milk, cheese or fruit, and had restricted times for buying food. The Germans were also sometimes forced to work as slaves on farms, in industry, or the mines.

Beneš, who took every opportunity to preach hatred towards the Germans, stated in a radio broadcast on 27 October 1943 that:

> The end of the war will be written with blood. What the Germans have done in our lands since 1938 will be revenged on them multifold and mercilessly. The whole nation will participate in this endeavor, and no Czechoslovak will refuse to exercise just revenge for our nation's suffering.[3]

The already-crazed population had already been incited via radio by President Beneš after his return to Prague from exile in London to, 'Take everything from the Germans. Leave them only a handkerchief to weep into.'[4] Czechoslovak vigilante groups had been formed, and the situation had become lethal for German civilians with gruesome and horrifying attacks.

In a radio broadcast from the Czechoslovak government-in-exile in London on 3 November 1944, the wartime Minister of National Defence Sergěj Ingr, urged his compatriots:

> When our day comes, all of our people will resound the battle-cry of the Hussites; Beat them kill them, let nobody survive. Everybody should now begin to arm himself, as best as possible, to be able to attack the Germans. He who cannot find firearms should resort to other weapons and hide them, weapons that pole, pierce or cut the Germans.[5]

The Germans had ceased to be recognised as human beings, and become more of a single-entity monster to be dealt with.

The Protectorate order was breaking down. German signposts and signage were being repainted with Czech place names, and the Czech flag could be seen hanging from many a window. Czech tram conductors were refusing payment in marks. A police unit which refused to take part in an anti-partisan action around Můstek was cheered by crowds, and false news of American troops already in the vicinity of Ruzyně and making their way towards Prague echoed through the capital, as well as the real news that Emanuel Moravec, the most notorious Nazi collaborator, attempted to drive to a radio station under German control in the hope of broadcasting an appeal for calm, when the vehicle he was travelling in ran out of fuel. Moravec shot himself in the head with a pistol, presumably to avoid capture by the partisans.

During this time, the former Czechoslovak legionary František Slunečko, known under the codename 'Alex', activated his network of confederates within the police, administration and news services. The city was important to the Germans because it was the nerve centre of Bohemia. Its bridges and communication lines could be used to go west and escape the advancing Red Army, yet despite this the Germans still posed a formidable threat in the city, possessing much better equipment that the resistance; at 11.00 am, he issued the order for police units loyal to the resistance to ready themselves and subsequently occupy strategic points across the city. They had all the reason to fight desperately and dedicate their efforts to regaining control in order to reach the American lines, and the long-standing resentments finally erupted in spontaneous and brutal violence when the population of Prague rose up against the Nazis.

The Prague Uprising

During the last week of the war, an infectious panic swept through the city. German soldiers were captured, beaten, doused in petrol and burned to death, and dozens were hung from the city's lamp posts with swastikas carved into their flesh. Thousands of German civilians were taken from their homes and interned in cinemas, schools, and barracks as makeshift detention centres, where they were brutally interrogated in the attempt to discover their political affiliations. Those who had sought sanctuary in cellars, or in the homes of their Czech friends and acquaintances, to avoid the mob were subjected to brutal beatings, raped, and on many occasions, slaughtered.

Unexpected assistance came in the form of the 1st Division of the Russian Liberation Army, a German armed forces unit made up of Soviet POWs who, after some persuasion by the resistance leaders, defected and was marching towards Prague on 5 May 1945. They arrived in the city from the south, and engaged German troops in Petřín and several other locations in the city. The main engine of violence was the voluntary

1st Czechoslovak Independent Brigade, commanded by General Ludvik Svoboda, aided by the Russian Liberation Army, led by Lieutenant-General Andrey Vlasov.

The uprising proved to be a great obstacle to the trapped German units, who wanted desperately to be captured by the Americans, to avoid being captured by the Soviets. The general capitulation had been signed in Reims in the late afternoon of 8 May and was going to take effect from 9.00 pm that evening, with the resulting ceasefire allowing the German forces to withdraw from the city. The Germans launched a final general offensive on Prague in retaliation for the uprising, but their progress was severely hampered by the thousands of barricades that had been erected by Czech civilians, who had become targets of their aggression.

Despite the ceasefire, not all Waffen-SS units obeyed, and fighting continued until 9 May, when the Red Army entered the almost-liberated city. The uprising was brutal, with both sides committing war crimes. More than 1,600 insurgents, 300 RLA soldiers, 1,000 German and 692 Soviet soldiers died. General Dwight Eisenhower ordered George Patton's US Third Army not to go to the aid of the Czech insurgents because it would undermine the credibility of the Western powers in post-war Czechoslovakia. The uprising was seen as a symbol of Czech resistance to Nazi rule, and the liberation by the Red Army was used by the Czechoslovak Communist Party to increase popular support for communism. The number of victims had been cited as 250,000, but files from the SBZ/German Democratic Republic, which were not accessible until 1990, showed that this figure was actually much higher and must now be set at no less than 460,000.

Czechoslovak Radio

During its six-year occupation, the Nazi regime decreed that all broadcasts be made in German, and used the radio to distribute propaganda. Fourteen members of the pre-war staff of Czech Radio had been removed and either imprisoned or executed by the Nazis, some for political reasons and others because they were Jewish. With all radios being licensed, the Nazis were able to demand that licensees took their radios in for inspection. Around 1.1 million sets had their shortwave capacity removed, and a red sticker applied that read in Czech and German: 'Attention! Listening to short wave radio is punishable by death!'[6]

This didn't affect the estimated 100,000 radios that were being used without a licence, or the owners of the sets that had been restricted by the authorities from using a small removable device known as a 'Churchilka', which was widely available on the black market, and allowed shortwave foreign broadcasts to be received. The Germans, being aware that control of the airwaves might prove decisive in the event of an uprising, increased security at the Post Office owned building of Czech Radio at 12 Fochova Třída (now known as Vinohradská Street) in the centre of Prague. Around ninety SS guards were posted inside the building, and a barbed-wire fence was erected outside the entrance, with two machine guns controlling entry and exit.

The radio staff, who had started planning for the takeover of the radio station in 1944, removed all signage inside the building so that the SS guards would get lost, and hid inside the radio studio overnight on 4 May. On the morning of 5 May 1945, Czechoslovak Radio broadcaster Zdeněk Mančal, who had just started his shift, announced in a mix of Czech and German: 'It is just six o'clock.' The simple announcement defied Nazi censorship by broadcasting in Czech, but informed the listeners of the collapsing Protectorate of Bohemia and Moravia that the end of the occupation in Europe had come.

The SS guards tried to interrupt the broadcast but were unable to find the newsroom due to the lack of signage, and just after midday, elements of the 1st Battalion of the government army, a lightly armed police force, arrived. The Nazi flag was torn down and American and Czechoslovak flags raised over the building. They then assisted members of the radio station staff to enter the building via the rooftops of the adjacent houses and across the neighbouring courtyard at Římská Street, completely unaware that Waffen-SS were guarding the building. Gunfire could be heard over the live radio, which was still in the control of the Czech employees who had barricaded themselves in the newsroom.

At this time, the lowest three stories of the building were still held by the SS, but the Balbínova Street entrance was held by the resistance. At 12.33 pm, the radio announcer broadcast a call to Czech policemen and ordinary citizens to come to the aid of the beleaguered building, issuing the famous message: 'Calling all Czechs! Come to our help at once. Calling all Czechs.'[7] This message marked the beginning of the

Prague uprising. Fierce fighting inside the building and in the streets nearby continued for the rest of the afternoon. The German forces left in the city surrounded the radio station, and had set up machine-gun nests in front of the National Museum, before surging up Wenceslas Square and forcing the groups of protesting Czechs into the side streets. But it wasn't enough. The Czechs had seized the old Town Hall, from which the city-wide loudspeaker system was operated, as well as the main telephone exchange at Žižkov.

The SS inside the radio building, all heavily armed with machine guns and grenades, moved from room to room, confused and slowed down by the lack of signage in the building, and unaware that Czech policemen had taken control of the upper stories, and encountered resistance on the second floor. The Czech police suffered considerable loss of life due to their inferior weaponry, mostly pistols, but they were eventually able to drive the SS soldiers into the basement and then into the courtyard. The fire brigade flooded the basement, and the SS men were forced to surrender at 5.30 pm.

Around 17,000 fighters had joined the action by the evening of 5 May. The uprising spread all over the city of Prague. At 7.20 pm, a radio broadcast urged Praguers to build barricades to prevent the Germans from moving troops and armour into the city. Over 1,600 had been constructed by the morning of 6 May. The SS sent in armoured cars carrying troops in an attempt to swarm the building, but they were overrun by the Czechs, who seized the vehicles and the weapons. The Germans then called in an airstrike by the Messerschmitt Me 262 jet-powered fighter that had been strafing and bombing the city. The weather was good, and the Czech resistance had no anti-aircraft defences. A Me-262 bombed the building and destroyed, besides other departments, the newsroom in the basement, causing sufficient damage to prevent the Czechs from broadcasting from the building for the rest of the uprising. However, Czech broadcasts resumed eighty minutes later from a transmitter in a secret location in the suburb of Strašnice, before moving again the following day to St Nicholas Church, which was used by Czech partisans as a concealed broadcasting site. The Germans, unaware that the base for the broadcast had been moved, continued to attack the building in Fochova Třída, which went on to be hit by more than forty shells.

A Czechoslovak Radio broadcast raised hopes about liberation from the West when it announced the advance of the General Patton's 3rd Army through Plzeň, 90km west of Prague. But the US high command issued an order to halt the advance. After consultation with the Soviets, they were very wary of moving any further east and breaking the occupation lines agreed upon at the Yalta Conference. Even Churchill's call to Truman urging that US troops should take Prague were dismissed. Despite entreaties, no Allied airstrikes were made, nor any air-drops of vital supplies to the defenders of the city.

Available documentation has it that 123 Waffen-SS, mostly with frontline experience from the Eastern Front, were barricaded in a nearby school at Na Smetance, a major Nazi stronghold at the beginning of the uprising, and had placed two heavy machine-guns on the first floor, which covered both the surroundings of the school and the entirety of Balbínova Street, causing a great number of casualties among the resistance fighters. Sergeant Thomas Vokes and Private William Greig had escaped from Stalag 8b near Lamsdorf, Poland, and were taken in by a Czech family. They were fed and clothed and then taken to the local railway station, to catch a train to Prague. The head of the family, Frau Babca had arranged for them to be met in Prague and given a place to hide in the then Hopfenštokova Street. They arrived in Prague as the uprising was just beginning. They volunteered to aid the resistance movement and were asked to help defend the precious radio station building. They were given a rifle each and spent many hours lying on stairs by a small door, defending the station from German attacks. Behind the door was a tunnel, and it was at the end of the tunnel where the broadcasting equipment was set up.

The Czech resistance was running increasingly short of ammunition when on 7 May, more Wehrmacht and Waffen SS units arrived from the north and started attacking the city. Some of the most intense fighting took place in Strašnice, just east of Žižkov, and the resistance forces were pushed back into the city. At 2.41 am, General Alfred Jodl, representing the German High Command, had signed an unconditional surrender at Allied headquarters in Reims, France, to take effect the following day, ending the European conflict of the Second World War. The surrender was officially ratified, and just after midnight on 8 May, it was signed on behalf of the German High Command by Field Marshal Wilhelm Keitel, Colonel-General Hans-Jürgen Stumpff and General-Admiral Hans Georg von Friedeburg. Soviet Marshal Georgy Zhukov signed the document on behalf of the Supreme High Command of the Red Army and British Air Marshal Arthur W. Tedder as deputy of the Supreme Commander Allied Expeditionary Force.

The effect of the Reims signing was limited to a consolidation of the effective ceasefire between German forces and the Western Allies. Fighting continued unabated in the east, however, especially as German forces now intensified their air and ground assault against the Prague uprising. The situation was becoming desperate, with almost continuous casualties suffered by the resistance. Vokes presented a seemingly foolish idea to Staff Captains Václav Kopecký and Jaroslav Záruba, the insurgent commanders. They would go and talk with the Germans in person, negotiate and discuss with them their terms of surrender in the name of the queen. In one house, the resistance fighters found a compliant woman who willingly cleaned and ironed every crease of the uniforms for the British soldiers. Both lads were now spick-and-span. Courageously, they made their way up to the school, together with both insurgent commanders, and one more fighter who was carrying a white flag.

Bravely and with absolute self-confidence they proceeded to the main entrance. They let themselves be ushered to the guard commander-in-chief. The Germans seemed fairly unsettled at the sight of British soldiers. Vokes and Grieg were playing their parts to perfection. They informed the German commander in a pretty matter-of-fact style that they had come to negotiate on behalf of a British parachute division dropped as a part of the advance guard of allied armies which were currently approaching Prague. Vokes added boldly, 'Unless you accept the unconditional surrender immediately you will be crushed by the allied air forces in a few hours' time.'[8] The commander of the German guard signed the surrender document at 11.40 pm sharp. Moreover, he agreed in writing that the SS soldiers would leave a car full of weapons and ammunition to the resistance fighters.

Czechoslovak Radio announced, 'Prague is calling all listeners! Germany has capitulated unconditionally, the Czechoslovak News Agency in London announced at 3.22 pm today, 8 May.'[9] A truce was sought by the German troops, and agreed by the resistance leaders. The vast majority of the Germans left the city under the ceasefire, desperate to evade capture by the Soviets, and surrendering to the Americans.

Some SS units remained and continued the fight around Pankrác and Dejvice until the next day, when the first Soviet tanks started arriving from Dresden. Around 1,700 Czechoslovaks died during the uprising, and more than 3,000 were injured. The Germans lost around 1,000 men, and the Soviets, who arrived in the closing phase of the uprising, lost around thirty men. The liberating Russian Army troops lost around 300 men, but worse was in store for them. After surrendering to the Western allies, they handed them back to the Soviets, who saw them as traitors.

Czechoslovak politicians aimed to completely remove the German and Hungarian minorities from their territories. They were all Czechoslovak citizens before the Munich Pact in 1938, but were now considered collectively as war criminals, based on the actions such as Konrad Henlein. During the last years of the war, Beneš had been working towards the problem through the transfer or assimilation of these minorities, whom he considered the greatest obstacle in the way of reshaping post-war Czechoslovakia into a nation-state. Beneš revoked the citizenship of Germans and Hungarians by decree #33, and maintained that any peace agreement must include a provision stating that, 'Hungarians whose Czechoslovak citizenship will now be revoked will be recognised by Hungary as Hungarian citizens and will be settled on its territory, and Hungary will bear responsibility for these individuals from the moment they cross Hungary's border and will provide for them.'[10] Although they could again express a choice for Czechoslovakia, the public authorities retained the right of individual decision. The exceptions were those with an active anti-Nazi and anti-fascist past, who fought against Henlein and Hungarian irredentism, who fought for Czechoslovakia, and who after the Munich Pact and after 15 March, were persecuted for their loyalty to Czechoslovakia.

Klement Gottwald, the leader of the Czechoslovakian communists, set up a rival Czechoslovak government in Moscow, and, at a meeting in Kosice in April 1945, Gottwald and Beneš worked together to create a new Czechoslovak government – the National Front, which was a mixture of Soviet-supported communists and non-communists. All the political groups in Czechoslovakia at the time, including the previous government-in-exile, agreed that the country should be formed into a nation-state. The resulting Kosice Government Programme was created under the supervision of the central committee of the all-Soviet Communist Party.

The resettlement of about 700,000 Hungarians envisaged at Kosice was subsequently reaffirmed by the National Front, but its success depended heavily on the acquiesence of the Allied victors of the Second World War. Beneš had previously received the necessary approval of the United States, Great Britain and the Soviet Union to transfer the German and Hungarian population out of Czechoslovakia, but when they saw the specifics of the plan at the end of the war, the American and British leaders did not support it. It did, however, fit in with Joseph Stalin's Central European policy, and on 21 March 1945, the Soviet Foreign Minister Vyacheslav Molotov informed Beneš that the Soviet Union would support him. With the loss of support of the Western powers, who supported negotiations with Hungary, the Czechoslovak government turned to an internal solution, and decided to eliminate the Hungarian minority through Slovakisation and Slovak colonisation.

More than 40,000 Hungarians were resettled to the Czech borderlands by the government, provoking a protest from the United States, and a warning from Hungary about the potential re-annexation of the solidly Hungarian areas. Following that, Czechoslovakia pressed for a bilateral population exchange to remove Hungarians and increase its Slovak population, changing the ethnic makeup of the country. This plan was initially rejected by Hungary, but realising that the Allies were not interested in the fate of the Hungarian minority, and would not halt the deportations, Vladimír Clementis, the Vice-Minister of Foreign Affairs, and János Gyöngyösi, Minister of Foreign Affairs of Hungary, despite considering the agreement to be a major fiasco, finally signed the bilateral agreement with Czechoslovakia in Budapest, on 27 February 1946.

Czechoslovakia was liberated from the East to the west in May 1945 by the Soviet troops and the Romanian Army, supported by Czech and Slovak resistance, with only south-western Bohemia being liberated by US forces under General Patton. Although the American troops were eager to head east and liberate the capital city of Prague, they were told to stay put in Konstantinovy Lázně where its command posts had been established. President Harry Truman and General Dwight Eisenhower were both keen to avoid conflict with Stalin, who saw Eastern Europe as the spoils of war after sacrificing millions of Soviet lives to defeat the Nazis. General George Patton was ordered to halt his advance west of Prague. In the end, most of Czechoslovakia was occupied by the Red Army, sealing its fate as a Soviet satellite state.

With the borderland cities and their environs subject to ethnic cleansing, the authorities started to confiscate the property of the

German speakers. Internment centres and labour camps were opened by the local authorities, which served not only to gather the tens of thousands of Sudeten Germans who were to be expelled, but also to ease some of the tension within the community.

The Potsdam conference had brought an end to the turbulent phase of wild expulsions, effectively postponing the transfers, and in an attempt to minimise the reaction of the Czech population who had struggled against Nazism before Munich, a compulsory work scheme for those with specialised skills was introduced, which in part, ensured that the economic situation was improved after years of Nazi usurpation. Unskilled workers up to the age of 40 were ordered, in the atmosphere of confusion and fear, to clean the streets and fill potholes.

The months immediately after the war were particularly strained as small areas of Nazi resistance remained in the region, and the German civilians found themselves in a reverse situation to that which had applied at the time of the Protectorate, and were forced to leave their homes and leave their property. New regulations were rolled out during the summer of 1945, which limited the civic and personal freedoms of the Germans. Most of these were modelled on the laws implemented by the Third Reich on the Czechoslovak territory during the occupation. All Germans had to wear white armbands, marked with an 'N' ('Nemec' – 'German' in Czech) in clear view, which made them easy targets for any expression of rage and disgust in the streets. Among numerous cases of violence, the worst took place in the city of Přerov, where Czechoslovak soldiers rounded up and shot more than 260 Carpathian Germans, most of them women and children. The Germans were forbidden to use public transport, including trains (except when travelling to work and back), and telephones. Public gatherings were prohibited, as was sitting on park benches or walking on the sidewalks. All letters were censored.

In some regions, the Red Army was the first to arrive after the Wehrmacht retreat and unleashed brutal revenge for the fearsome war through a great deal of damage to property and buildings, and the assaults, rapes, mass rapes, and rape-murder against German women and girls. But in contrast to their treatment by the Czechs, the Russian soldiers occasionally fed hungry German children, while the Czechs had let them starve. Soviet troops would also occasionally give the weary Germans a ride on their vehicles during their long treks out of the country, while the Czechs only ever looked on with contempt and indifference.

The Ministry of Interior issued a circular concerning the beginning of mass transfer on 31 December 1945, for which 107 Transfer Collection Centres had been established, and the Czech authorities also issued guidelines which included food rations and the weight of personal property to be restricted to 30–50kg and 1,000 Reichsmarks per person. Implementing the transfers, the Czechoslovak government used orders, guidelines, and other regulations, which included the pre-Munich legal order, particularly the Act on Aliens No.52/1935sb, and the Austrian Act No.88/1871 on Police Expulsion and Deportation, by the Ministries of Interior and National Defence. The skilled workers were exempt from transfer were relocated to the Federal Republic of Germany by 1950–1, along with the reunification of families. The policy of relocation was stopped in April 1951 by the Ministry of the Interior, and the policy was implemented by national committees.

The Internment Camps

One of the worst camps in post-war Czechoslovakia was the old Nazi concentration camp of Theresienstadt. It became part of the battlefront on 8 May 1945, when scattered German military and SS units continued fighting Soviet forces in the vicinity. On the following day, Soviet troops entered the camp, and assumed responsibility for its prisoners. By the end of August 1945, most of the former prisoners had left the camp, to be replaced by ethnic Germans arrested by the Czech and Soviet authorities.

At least 180,000 ethnic Germans had been interned in Czechoslovakia as of November 1945, and another 170,000 were interned in Yugoslavia. The internees included many German civilian women and children, as well as German-speaking Jews. In many cases, former Nazi concentration camps and detention centres like Theresienstadt were converted overnight into camps for ethnic Germans. Linzervorstadt camp in Budvar was administered by a former Czech internee of Dachau, who had the motto 'Arbeit Macht Frei' ('Work Sets You Free') over the camp gates replaced with 'Auge für Auge, Zahn für Zahn' ('Eye for Eye, Tooth for Tooth'). The conditions at Linzervorstadt, as well as the other camps, were fraught with danger, making it clear that the Czechs savoured the opportunity to pay back the Germans, and the Czech camp commandant made sure that the inmates suffered accordingly. Inmates were stripped naked and shorn of their hair upon arrival at the camp, forced to run a gauntlet while being beaten with rubber truncheons and then, during their stay in the camp, systematically flogged, tortured and made to stand at attention in all-night roll calls.

The largest population in the camps were women and girls, having been separated from the men, which was often the case in ethnic cleansing, and subjected to sexual abuse and exploitation in violent and obscene ways. They were often stripped and beaten just for the entertainment of the guards while they screamed 'Nazi whores' or 'Pigs' at them. All the inmates were constantly abused and beaten, and given minimal rations, but were still expected to work hard twelve-hour shifts. The despair and hopelessness drove many inmates to simply give up and kill themselves. In 1946 alone, 5,558 Germans committed suicide.

According to a German Red Cross report in 1964, 1,215 internment camps were established, along with 836 Forced Labour camps and Disciplinary Centres, and 215 prisons on Czechoslovak territory. Special Courts sentenced 21,469 persons to prison and 713 were executed for crimes committed during the Nazi occupation. A further 6,989 deaths occurred in the internment camps. Under the Czech administration, the people, including children and juveniles, were locked up because they were Germans, and suffered the same atrocious conditions as did the prisoners during wartime, as the Czechs deliberately copied the practice and methods of the concentration camps of the National Socialist regime; the only discernible difference being that the word 'Jews' had been replaced with 'Germans'.

As announced in chapter eight of the Košice Programme, the loyal German and Hungarian citizens, and above all, those who proved their faithfulness to the Republic in the difficult times, would not be affected, but the culprits would be severely and pitilessly punished. The Czechoslovak citizens of German and Hungarian nationality, who were Czechoslovak citizens before the Munich Pact in 1938, would have their citizenship confirmed, and their eventual return to the Republic permitted, only in the following categories: for anti-Nazis and anti-fascists who fought against Henlein and Hungarian irredentism, who fought for Czechoslovakia, and who, after the Munich Pact and after 15 March, were persecuted for their loyalty to Czechoslovakia, and imprisoned in jails and concentration camps, or those who fled abroad, where they participated in the struggle for the restoration of Czechoslovakia.

It was also very difficult for Czechoslovak authorities to distinguish between the German children they sought to deport and the Germanised children they hoped to save for the Czech nation, and four years of Nazi occupation had not made the task easier. The American diplomat George Kennan, had noted of one Bohemian town shortly after the Nazi occupation in 1939: 'It became difficult to tell where the Czech left off and the German began.'[11] Legally, a person's declaration of nationality on the 1930 census was decisive in Czechoslovakia, but there was a multitude of problem cases. Several hundred thousand people, for example, had declared themselves German during the Nazi occupation, only to attempt to reclaim Czechoslovak nationality after the war. Thousands more were entwined with Germans in mixed marriages.

The government also considered that its highest moral duty was to turn over to the courts, and to punish, all war criminals, traitors and active helpers of the German and Hungarian oppressors, without delay. Subsequently, the Czechoslovak citizenship of the other Czechoslovak German and Hungarian citizens was cancelled, although the public authorities retained the right of individual decision. The German and Hungarian transgressors, who were under indictment for crimes against the Republic and the Czech and Slovak nations and who were condemned, would lose their citizenship and would be expelled from the Republic forever – if not under sentence of death.

Czechoslovak politicians had stressed at the end of the war that the notion of collective responsibility for war crimes would be ascribed to the whole German population, and the German speakers who moved to the Czech Protectorate after Munich would be immediately expelled from the country as the consequence of the crimes committed by them during the war. Vladimír Clementis, the Czechoslovak deputy foreign minister and one of the leading figures of the Communist Party, stressed that, 'Until this issue was dealt with, none of the other important social, economic, and institutional problems of the country could be addressed.'[12]

The cooperation of the Soviet authorities and, to a lesser extent, of the American, British and French authorities in their respective zones of occupation was a necessary condition upon which the wild expulsions could be carried out. The British zone was the main destination of the 'Reich' Germans who had been domiciled there before the war, and the British did not want to repatriate the Sudeten Germans from their zone to

Czechoslovakia, whereas the French expressed their will to accept certain categories of Czechoslovak Germans into their zone of occupation.

The resettlement of German minorities in Central Europe was discussed at the Potsdam Conference in July-August 1945, and on 3 July, the Czechoslovak Ministry of Foreign Affairs submitted memoranda to the Allies regarding the transfer of German and Hungarian minorities. The future of the Hungarian population living in Czechoslovakia and other countries neighbouring Hungary was not debated during the Potsdam conference, nor was a final determination of Hungarian-Czechoslovak borders, and the post-war Czechoslovak government proposed not only the transfer of German minority, but also that talks should be held with the Allied Control Commission (ACC) in Budapest to debate the Hungarian issue.

The Czechoslovak authorities made their official position clear to the American, British and Soviet diplomatic representatives on 16 August 1945, together with planned expulsions based on the decree of the Czechoslovak President Beneš (the first from the series of Beneš decrees which would become a symbol of anti-German policies), which was issued on 2 August 1945, depriving the German speakers of their Czechoslovak citizenship. The deportees would be allowed to take their personal property with them, subject to a weight limit of 60Kg, and sufficient foodstuffs for four days had to be ensured for each transferred person. The allied powers approved these decrees.

It was only after the publication of the outcome of the Potsdam Conference on 16 August 1945, that the Czechoslovak Ministry of Foreign Affairs informed the British, American, and Soviet embassies in Prague that he intended to start direct negotiations with the ACC in Budapest regarding conditions for potential exchanges of the population with Hungary. The proposed transfer was to be pursued through the exchange of population since the Czechoslovak estimate suggested that around 345,000 Slovaks living in Hungary wished to return to Czechoslovakia. Under the memoranda, Czechs and Slovaks considered the transfer of both Germans and Hungarians to be the basis for the future safety of the State, and to contribute to the preservation of peace in Central Europe. The Hungarian question was reserved for a solution at a separate peace conference. It was clear that a bilateral agreement on the exchange of population endorsed by the great powers was a more preferred solution.

The Czechoslovak authorities planned that 250,000 Germans should be relocated in December 1945 and a further 125,000 in January 1946 to end the main transfer by August 1946. The Czechoslovak government discussed the transfer scheme on 14 December. However, the food, weather, and transport conditions in Germany delayed the beginning of the organised transfer, which began in January 1946. At least 1.5 million Germans were resettled from the Czechoslovak Republic to the American zone, and 750,000 to the Soviet zone in Germany, and by the autumn of 1946, the mass organised transfer had all but ended. The transfers were renewed for a short time in 1947 to the two zones, after which only around 200,000 Germans remained in Czechoslovakia.

The notion of collective responsibility for the German war crimes was generally accepted by the majority of the Czech population, and the minority voices risked being defined as anti-Czech by the communist and nationalist press if they criticised or protested against the abuses committed against the Germans during the transport, or about the conditions inside the labour camps.

The exiles who had sheltered in Britain from fascism had long-awaited to be repatriated to Czechoslovakia, but when the opportunity arose after the end of the war, the refugees were hesitant. Few were prepared for the complexities of their homecoming, reception, and treatment, which to a large extent were determined even before the war had ended by a potent combination of Great Powers politics, ethnic division, territorial claims, and economics. Many Czechoslovaks consequently emigrated, or from February 1948, fled from the new authoritarian regime, Communism, making Britain their permanent home.

Throughout the republic, men and women worked to repair the damage caused under the sorrowful occupation of the Nazis, while the Czech people looked to Beneš, who had seen many governments come and go, for guidance. Beneš knew, however, that the delicate balance upon which the nation's independence rested, would prove to be the most demanding of his whole career, and that Czech foreign policy would have to be strongly orientated towards Moscow. Post-war Czechoslovakia was all but surrounded by Russia and Soviet-dominated countries, and only through the American zone in Germany could the nation look out upon the West. He made a mutual assistance treaty with Russia, and later ceded to it the province of Bohemia, which was mainly inhabited by Ukrainians.

On his return to Prague in 1945, after more than six years in exile, Beneš was greeted as a hero by his people, who looked to him to lead the country out of its dilemma and into security and peace, and to somehow maintain its working alliance with Russia without severing its traditional friendship with the Western democracies. Beneš publicly announced his programme for the expulsion of the Sudeten Germans, which, as far as the people were concerned, sanctioned the start of the period that was known as the 'wild expulsions', which lasted until the autumn of 1945. But there was nothing 'wild' about this first wave of what Czech officials referred to as Národní Ocista (National Cleansing). These expulsions, which resulted in the removal of up to 2 million Germans from Eastern Europe, were planned and executed by troops, police and militia, under orders from the highest authorities, with the full knowledge and consent of the Allies.

The Germans were given very little time to pack their things and leave, sometimes no more than fifteen minutes, and they were allowed to take only bare essentials with them. They had, almost overnight, lost their livelihoods and jobs, and were now being threatened with violence if they did not vacate their homes. The cumulative distress among the Germans led to mass suicides in towns and villages throughout the former Sudetenland. Whole families would dress in their Sunday finest, surrounded by flowers, crosses and family albums, and then kill themselves by poisoning or hanging.

Beneš had first publicly declared his support for the 'principle of the transfer of populations' in September 1941, after which he successfully lobbied the Allies for their approval of the expulsions throughout the war. His justification for territorial transfers was grounded in the principle of guilt, in particular, the collective guilt of the German minority in the destruction of the Czechoslovak state and that minority's collaboration with Hitler. Based on the premise that the Slovak population was just as responsible for the post-Munich break-up of the state, the Sudeten German Social democrat politician Wenzel Jaksch questioned how the expulsion of solely the Sudeten Germans could be justified based on collective guilt/collective responsibility if the Slovaks were also not expelled, to which Beneš responded that 80 per cent of the Slovaks had not abandoned their loyalty to Czechoslovakia.

Speaking in Lidice on 10 June 1945, the anniversary of the massacre of the inhabitants and the destruction of the village, Beneš held the whole German nation responsible for Nazism, stating that, 'I hold all the German people responsible for Nazism and its crimes. And let us not forget that the principles, the collaborators and executors of these crimes were Germans of Bohemia; this must have political consequences.'[13] The new Czech prime minister, Zdeněk Fierlinger, had received assurance from Stalin that although the Red Army would not help with the deportation of Germans and Magyars (Hungarians), it would not stand in his way. A period of wild expulsions ensued, during which the Czechs showed particular brutality in dealing with Germans, and ignoring all existing regulations protecting the minorities, and causing extreme concerns to the Americans and British that the mass influx of Germans into their respective zones in Germany would destabilise them.

Forced Expulsions

Within two days of the liberation by the Allies, the German soldiers were pushed into the unfamiliar role of victim, and, no longer organised, the beleaguered soldiers were left to their own devices to try to make their way back home. It was at this time, and for a further five years, that the worst peacetime violence in history was carried out in the form of brutal reprisals by partisans and civilians, driven by years of ethnic tensions in the countries of Eastern Europe exploited by Hitler in his drive towards war.

Revenge was taken upon the substantial German-speaking minority of Czechoslovakia, included ethnic Germans, who had engaged in favour of Hitler's Reich, and the German-speaking community which, for many years had been accused of oppressing the Czech nation. The majority of these people were older men, women and children, and many of whose families had lived in Eastern Europe for centuries. Loudspeakers mounted in streets announced that revenge will be carried out on Nazi war criminals and their Czech collaborators. All signage over shops and hotels, in market places and on billboards which were in the German language, was broken up, torn down or painted over. German soldiers who had been captured were tortured and shot in the streets by Slovak Revolutionary guards.

Anti-fascists and communists were supposed to be protected from forced migration by decree of the president of the Czechoslovak Republic, but they were often targeted along with the rest of the German population, even though they 'proved their faithfulness even in times of great difficulty',[14] and had been persecuted by both the Nazis and the Czechs. The wild transfers were carried with significant violence and hostility to the newly captive German populations by mobs, soldiers, the police, and others acting under the colour of authority. A perpetual state of anxiety reigned as no one was any longer sure of his or her life. Any amount of sacrifices they made under the Nazi regime of terror were completely overlooked, and the centuries of coexistence and shared history with the Sudeten Germans was lost forever in a seemingly instantaneous change in attitude after the Czech government and nation unilaterally agreed to the mass transfer of the people they now perceived as a threat to the newly liberated state.

The same rationing system that was originally introduced by Germans after the Invasion of Poland, was put into place by the Police Director, and allocated according to race and ethnicity. During the early evening of 29 May 1945, police and assistance troops began to gather all recipients of food coupons (which were marked with a 'D' (German), which numbered 18,072 according to police reports, and at 10.00 pm on 30 May, the first groups of thousands of Germans began a forced march south towards the Austrian border thirty-four miles away. By midnight, most of the group had reached the town of Rajhrad, around eight miles away from Brno and, after a period of rest, arrived during the next morning at a small, recently abandoned concentration camp close to the town of Pohořelice, nine miles further south. Women and children were given shelter in barns, which were locked, but any thoughts of safety dissipated when Romanian soldiers arrived in trucks, broke in and began robbing the women of any wedding bands or jewellery they might have hidden away, before beating and raping them. Many were killed or died as a result.

Over half a million people consisting of the large ethnic German minority, specifically all the women, boys under the age of 14, and men over the age of 60, were ordered to leave the city immediately upon the issue on 30 May 1945 of the order No. 78/1945 by the Zemský Národní Výbor (Provincial National Committee), and forced to march to the German and Austrian borders. Working men were expelled after their positions were filled. With much of the city in ruins from combat and bombing raids, their soon-to-be-vacated homes were confiscated, as the Germans had done with the apartments of the Jews, and allocated to the homeless, but in particular, to factory workers.

The *London Daily Mail* reported on the same day, 30 May, on the wild expulsion of an estimated 30,000 Germans from Brno in Czechoslovakia in the hope of arousing public support for the expellees:

> Shortly before 9.00 pm, young revolutionaries of the Czech National Guard marched through the streets calling on all Germans citizens to be standing outside their front doors at nine o'clock with one piece of hand luggage each, ready to leave the town forever. Women had ten minutes in which to wake and dress their children, bundle a few possessions into their suitcases, and come out on to the pavement. Once outside they had to surrender all jewellery, watches, furs and money to the guardsmen, retaining only their wedding rings. Then they were marched out of town at gunpoint to the Austrian border. It was pitch dark when they reached the border. The children were wailing, the women stumbling.

Two days later, many of the people were suffering from exhaustion, so the guards selected approximately 10,000 people, just over half the number that set out, and who were still able to walk, and escorted them for fifteen miles to Mikulov, in South Moravia, close to the Austrian border. As they neared it, the Czech border guards pushed them over the frontier towards the Austrian border guards, which was when more trouble started. The Austrians refused to accept them. And the Czechs refused to readmit them. The expellees were pushed into fields for the night, and in the morning a few Romanians were sent to guard them. The field became a makeshift camp, but there were no rations; some people survived only because of the food which the guards gave them from time to time.

Following protests by the Soviet Occupation Authorities in Austria as well as the Austrian representatives in Brno, word got through that day that the Czechoslovak government had been persuaded to stop the expulsion, and subsequently an estimated 10,000 expellees were held in the camp at Pohořelice, even though their number far exceeded the camp's capacity. With no provisions for food, healthcare or adequate accommodation, and with the surrounding villages filled almost to capacity with German minorities, and able to accept only a thousand more, it wasn't long before an epidemic of Shingellosis (Dysentery) broke out. Official records indicate that 455 people died of disease and malnutrition and were buried nearby, but Sudeten German sources suggest that over three times that number had died and that many of the victims had been murdered.

It wasn't until 5 July, however, that a proper camp administration was established and a regular food supply provided, and because the Austrian authorities refused to accept any people before their Austrian origin was proven, meticulous identification of the expellees had to be carried out. As a result, 2,000-2,500 of the camp inmates, most of whom had been confirmed as having Czech origin or had Czech relatives in Brno, were selected and allowed to return to Brno, which sparked a wave of anti-German protests in the city. Families in surrounding villages accommodated around 1,000 expellees, and records show that 1,807 mostly elderly people were relocated to the former correctional Institute for Juveniles in Mušlov, 2½ miles from Mikulov. Individuals with German or Austrian citizenship were allowed to go to Austria. The camp at Pohořelice was officially dissolved on 7 July, despite there being eighty Brno German expellees still interned, the majority of whom were ill in the provisory hospital on the site.

The fate of expellees who ended up in the Western occupied zones of Germany differed greatly from those in the Soviet zone. The processing of these people varied according to where they came from and where they were sent. Around 1.75 million Sudeten Germans, the largest group, ended up in the American zone, while approximately 750,000 had originally been sent to the Soviet zone a number of these people later fled to West Germany. Although ethnically German, they had evolved as a part of Austria, and with their dialect and cultural traditions being so fundamentally different to those of the existing German population, their reception was mixed. Many felt that they had helped to bring about the war in Europe, and so were expected to adapt to a reformulated identity that would provide them with a semblance of belonging. Some of the Sudeten Germans, however, felt that it was their patriotic duty to resist any attempts at integration, as it might be interpreted as giving up on claims to their right to self-determination.

Reprisals

When Czechoslovakia was created in 1918, Sudeten German leaders failed in their attempt to form German-speaking provinces that would join Austria. The minority was not happy in the new state. German-owned export industries took a hard hit in the Great Depression, and in elections held in 1935 and 1938, the Sudeten Germans overwhelmingly voted for Konrad Henlein's far-right Sudetendeutsche Partei that later helped force Czechoslovakia to cede its German-speaking borderlands to Nazi Germany.

Although they were not responsible for the occupation or hardships of the Czech people, the Sudeten Germans' call for independence ultimately led to the Munich Conference and the annexation of the Sudetenland, and it was the political opportunism and expansionism of Hitler's Germany that caused Czechoslovakia's loss of sovereignty. By the time the war was over in 1945, hatred of the Germans was part of society, and the Czechs took an act of ugly revenge; there would be no pardoning of their national oppressors. The intense inter-ethnic hatred that resulted from centuries of cultural antipathy, and the brutality of the Nazi occupation could not restrain violence performed by individuals and soldiers against German civilians, and the Sudeten Germans, who were labelled as inherent perpetrators of war.

The Czechs, no less than the Poles, attacked, subdued, beat and murdered German civilians. Precipitated by news of the arrival of the Red Army, Germans, often whole families, committed suicide by the thousand. Hunger and sickness also took countless lives. The German writer Juergen Thorwald wrote,

> Crowds of Czechs awaited the transports of German prisoners in the streets to pelt them with stones, spit into their faces, and beat them with any object that came to hand. German women, children, and men ran the gauntlet, with arms over their heads, to reach the prison gates under a hail of blows and kicks. Women of every age were dragged from the groups, their heads were shaved, their faces smeared with paint, and swastikas were drawn on their bared backs and breasts. Many were violated, others forced to open their mouth to the spittle of their torturers.[15]

On 9 May, with the fighting ended, the mob turned its attention to the thousands of Germans locked in prisons. Thorwald continues:

> Several trucks loaded with German wounded and medical personnel drove into the [prison] court […] The wounded,

the nurses, the doctors had just climbed from their vehicles when suddenly a band of insurgents appeared from the street and pounced upon them. They tore away their crutches, canes, and bandages, knocked them to the ground, and with clubs, poles, and hammers hit them until the Germans lay still.

So began a day as evil as any known to history … In the street, crowds were waiting for those who were marched out of their prisons … They had come equipped with everything their aroused passions might desire, from hot pitch to garden shears. They grabbed Germans, and not only SS men, drenched them with gasoline, strung them up with their feet upper-most, set them on fire, and watched their agony, prolonged by the fact that in their position the rising heat and smoke did not suffocate them. They tied German men and women together with barbed wire, shot into the bundles, and rolled them down into the Moldau River. They beat every German until he lay still on the ground, forced naked women to remove the barricades, cut the tendons of their heels, and laughed at their writhing. Others they kicked to death.[16]

On 9 June 1945, the Czech Military Authorities summoned 8,000 German men and boys to the sports stadium at Chomutov. Stadiums such as this around the country were used to hold prisoners as well as become places of torture and execution. Stripped to the waist, they were inspected for any tattoos or Waffen-SS markings, and anyone with the small black ink 'Blutgruppentätowierung' (SS blood group) sign, which was applied to the upper arm of all of its members, were pulled aside and beaten to death with wooden clubs and iron bars in front of everyone. The Germans who were not arrested were forced to wear white armbands, and were subject to anti-German decrees, and were then expelled en masse. Almost 3.5 million people had been stripped of their citizenship, their homes and their property with no compensation.

On 18 June 1945, a military transport stood at the station in the village of Horní Moštěnice near Přerov in the Olomouc Region of the Czech Republic, where members of the 17th Infantry Regiment of Petržalka (former members of the 1st Czechoslovak Army Corps) led by Officer (later Lieutenant) Karol Pazúr, were returning to their base from Prague. On the same day at around noon, another transport arrived with rolling stock consisting of six wagons carrying 267 Carpathian Germans and Hungarians (71 men, 120 women and 74 children) from Dobšinej, Kežmarok, Gelnica, Młynice and Janova Lehota near Žiar nad Hronom, who were returning to their homes in central Slovakia. They had been evacuated to the north-western Bohemia by the command of German authorities in December 1944.

Pazúr told his fellow soldiers that the deportees included collaborators of Nazis and also SS members who were to blame for war atrocities. They were removed from the train and escorted outside the city to a hill Švédské šance, where they were made, along with locals from the nearby village of Lověšice, who were under the threat of death if they did not cooperate, to dig a mass grave. Pazúr then named a firing squad to execute them, and all but two were shot in the back of the neck. One ethnic Slovakian woman and her boy, Paul Molnar, were exempt from the killing, Molnar's father was shot.

Brno, located in the south-eastern part of the Czech Republic, at the confluence of the Svitava and Svratka rivers, was liberated by the Soviets on 26 April after the Soviet 53rd Field Army, together with an attachment of the Czechoslovak Special Purpose Company, when it broke through German defences. The ethnic Germans who had not fled the city in fear ahead of the Soviet advance were rounded up and incarcerated in Kounic College, which had been used as a Nazi prison during the war. Following the exhumation of rows of bodies of victims of the Gestapo from the grounds outside the college, prisoners were selected and forced to erect three wooden gallows in the courtyard where, during May and June 1945, at least 300 Germans were executed.

Late in the evening of Wednesday, 30 May 1945, under the direction of the Národní výbor města Brna (National Committee of the City of Brno), around 18,000 ethnic German inhabitants of Brno were forced to leave the city (known in infamy as 'The Brno Death March') for camps across the border 56km (35mi) away in Austria. Only about half of expellees actually crossed the border. Few among them were men since most male adults had been conscripted into the Wehrmacht and were by then prisoners of war. In the early hours of the next morning, the march stopped in Pohořelice, halfway between Brno and the border, and the women and children were accommodated in the abandoned concentration camp nearby.

The next day, 1 June, with many people too exhausted to continue, the guards selected around 10,000 people who were still able to walk, and continued to the Austrian border near Mikulov. In the meantime, the unarranged expulsion of the large numbers of people from Brno had drawn protests from the representatives of Austria in Brno, as well as the Soviet occupation authorities in Austria. They persuaded the Czechoslovak government to stop the expulsion, and around half of the expellees thus remained in the camp of Pohořelice. While some Germans were later allowed to return to Brno, hundreds of others fell victim to diseases and malnutrition in the following weeks. During their encampment, being locked inside large barns, they were brutally treated by the organisers of the march, who were young Czechs, and workers from the Brno arms works in Zbrojovka. When two trucks of Romanian soldiers arrived, they broke through the locked doors of the barns and began raping the women. There was indiscriminate shooting and people were killed or were beaten and robbed of any earrings, rings or trinkets they had on them. At around 4.00 am the next day, they were loading the trucks with corpses. Around 1,700 expellees are believed to have died, mostly on the march itself, while others succumbed to epidemics of Shigellosis (closely related to E. coli) that spread in the Pohořelice camp.

Nothing had been heard about an expulsion until papers were received at the homes of the Germans which gave the instruction to leave their homes and property and had a luggage allowance of only 24kg per person. Upon arrival at the station halls, they were subjected to a strict search of their person and of their luggage. Any clothing and shoes deemed new or fairly new were confiscated, which often meant having to change there and then into clothes from their luggage or taken from other persons. All documents, money, rings, jewellery, and anything else that could be utilised was also seized, and anyone who refused to cooperate was subjected to verbal and physical abuse.

The feelings of hostility towards the Germans seemed completely justified to the Czechs as they vented their anger on the expellees, who left the halls both destitute and traumatised by the abandonment of their homes, and the humiliation and abuse they had suffered at the hands of the Czechs. The rough treatment of people who resisted or objected to the treatment echoed the observed and rumoured actions of Nazis during the occupation to keep the expellees under control, and the guards often used violence and fear to enforce obedience.

While the troops and police were on the ground dealing directly with the Germans, and deciding how brutally to treat them, the government's commitment to diplomacy and democracy was put into doubt. The Czech leaders seemed oblivious to the international repercussions and consequences that might manifest themselves in the years to follow. While their primary concern was eliminating the German threat to the Republic, they turned a blind eye to the violation of human rights and the outright violence being carried out against their former citizens. The perpetrators of the wild expulsions were even given amnesty, which further undermined Czechoslovakia's credibility as a democratic nation.

Throughout the summer of 1945, trains of German expellees continued to pour into Berlin and other German and Austrian cities. The Western journalists who had travelled to Berlin to cover the Potsdam Conference were aghast at the scenes they encountered at the railroad stations, with the dead and dying littering the platforms. Charles Bray, Germany correspondent of the *London Daily Herald*, described finding four dead Germans on a visit to Stettin Station, with 'another five or six … lying alongside them, given up as hopeless by the doctor, and just being allowed to die.'[17] Bray discovered the suffering of the German expellees 'gave me no satisfaction, although for years I have hoped that the Germans would reap the seeds they had sown.'[18]

The powers occupying Germany were anxious to stop the wild expulsions which, by the end of 1945, had chased some 750,000 Germans from the country, partly out of concern for the human rights violations and on humanitarian grounds, but mainly because of the huge demands placed on their resources by the tens of thousands of refugees crossing the border every day. This led to the organised transfers, which were primarily supervised by the government of Czechoslovakia, the United States and the Soviet Union, who regulated the number of expellees and monitored the conditions in which they lived during the transfers. These were less traumatic for those involved, and more uniformly enforced. Luggage limits were more lenient, allowing up to 50kg per person to try to ensure that the emigrants should have the basics for their needs for their life in Germany. This still provoked strong feelings with the Germans and Czechs involved; the Great Powers had been betrayed by the pre-war Munich agreement which had allowed the occupation to happen in the first place.

On 25 February 1946, all German expellees were examined by a medical doctor and given a week's ration of food before boarding the first train, which included a Red Cross compartment staffed by German nurses. The Czech commandant overseeing the proceedings confirmed that none of the expellees' possessions had been confiscated and that they were provided with adequate clothing if it was something they lacked. Foreign diplomats and representatives from the media were invited to witness the staged conditions of the initial organised 'voluntary transfers', as the expulsions were guised under, which made for a suitably reassuring spectacle for the observers to report back upon.

Away from the media spotlight, the conditions of the organised expulsions were not nearly as favourable. A very large number of German expellees were transported while suffering from infectious diseases contracted while they were interned in the camps, and the Red Cross was repeatedly reporting that the trains from Czechoslovakia were consistently dispatched with insufficient food rations for the journey. Two trains per day left for the American Zone; the carriages of the trains consisted of largely obsolete stock, with no room for the expellee's baggage if there was any; a systematic pillaging had been carried out by both military and civilian personnel. Many able-bodied and skilled were held back during this time in direct violation of the requirement that families were not to be separated.

From 1 April 1946, several trains every week were leaving the Karlovy Vary in western Bohemia as the transfers of ethnic Germans and German speakers got under way. The trains were mostly comprised of sets of cattle and coal wagons while there were no regulations on the necessity of heat, food, or protection from the elements during the wild period of expulsions. Exposure to the elements for people travelling in the wagons was the major cause of deaths during the transfers, but even that was slightly paled by those who were forced to march on foot to the border, with many of the old, sick and injured dying along the way. Being perceived as a threat to their newly formed state, the Czechs were not concerned about comfort or well-being as they worked as quickly as they could to remove that threat.

In the elections held in May 1946, the communists, although winning only 38 per cent of the popular vote, became the largest single political party. The communists were able to put their leaders in key positions, and Moscow-trained Czechoslovak Communist Party (CPCz) leader Klement Gottwald was installed as Czechoslovakia's prime minister. Gottwald was a firm supporter of the expulsion of ethnic Germans from Czechoslovakia, gaining mainstream credibility with many Czechs through the use of nationalist rhetoric, exhorting the population to 'prepare for the final retribution for 'White Mountain', for the return of the Czech lands to the Czech people. We will expel for good all descendants of the alien German nobility.'[19]

The end of the post-Potsdam organised expulsions was celebrated on 26 October 1946 at Karlovy Vary (Carlsbad) railway station, along with a ceremony in the local theatre with the participation of leading members of the Czechoslovak cabinet. The transports had been stopped because the Americans asked for a break, being afraid of the diminishing capacity of the area under US control to receive the Germans. Nevertheless, the Czechoslovak authority still counted on some additional transports being sent to the American zone; 2,165,135 Germans had been expelled: 1,415,135 to the American zone and 750,000 to the Soviet zone. Around 300,000 German speakers still remained in Czechoslovakia, but by 1948, most of them had left for Germany fearing further persecution following the rise to power of the communists.

The Death Marches

Facing the prospect of an unknown future was more terrifying than death itself in the face of limited provisions, sexual violence, and verbal and physical abuse, and many Germans took the only way out they could: by taking their own lives to stay in their homeland and avoid the suffering experienced by their friends, families, and neighbours. Many of the so-called 'death marches' took days and even weeks to complete as the expellees were herded in long columns towards Germany, Austria, or Poland, carrying all the possessions they still had, and unceasingly urged forward by the constant threat of violence and death that hung over them on their journey.

The few crumbs of bread given out by the Czech and Soviet guards was not nearly enough to sustain them on the journey, and parents had no way to improve the situation for their children as they walked extremely long distances in the summer heat. Taunted by their captors with the hope of returning home after the expulsions had been carried out only exacerbated their suffering. They soon became vulnerable to sickness, and exhaustion, the absence of food and water and disease caused the deaths of many Germans along the way, especially among the elderly and the young children, who rapidly became emaciated. The columns of people were encouraged to keep moving by gunshots and the cracking of whips. If anyone was unable to continue marching, they were harassed, beaten, and sometimes killed. Added violence continued at the whim of the guards. Even when they were faced with exhaustion, the expellees had no choice but to continue, since any slowing or stopping would be met with violence at the hands of the Czechs and Soviets. They would be beaten until they started moving again at gunpoint, or if they didn't move quickly enough, were shot. The same treatment was applied to the sick, who were expected to keep up with the march, regardless of their health.

Their arrival in Germany, Austria, or Poland was not the end of the ordeal for the Germans. With many of the expellees including children and the elderly, it was difficult to find a suitable place to settle, and the huge numbers of expellees pouring into the border regions only made things worse, forcing large numbers of them to continue walking on, racked by fever and contaminated with lice, trying to find a way to survive as they looked for food, shelter, and work. Chances were remote for them as they were entering war-torn countries with few belongings and even fewer prospects of a stable life. For many, who could bear no more after their recent experiences of hostility and physical abuse, the uncertainty of the future, and the fact that that they were no longer welcome in their homeland, it resulted in suicide. While some of the Germans were able to find work and relatively secure homes in their strange new countries and surroundings, many others were reduced to begging on the streets and living off scraps.

During the afternoon of 31 July 1945, an ammunition dump exploded in Krásné Březno, in the largely ethnic German city of Ústí nad Labem (previously known as Aussig). During the incident, the confirmed body count was forty-three, with seven of them identified as Czechs, and dozens more having been injured. Rumours very quickly spread that German partisans were responsible, and almost immediately after the explosion, a massacre of ethnic Germans, who had to wear white armbands after the war and so were easy to identify, began in four places in the city.

German men, women and children were mercilessly beaten, bayonetted, hanged, shot, or drowned in a fire pond. Others, including a woman with a baby and pram, were thrown into the River Elbe and were then shot at while they tried to swim to safety. The perpetrators of what would become known as 'The Ústí Massacre', were Revolutionary Guards (comprised of various vigilante groups), along with Czech and Soviet soldiers, and around 300 Czech civilians who had just arrived from Prague by train. Local Czechs, including the mayor, Josef Vondra, tried to help the victims, as did many local Czechs. But the death toll continued to rise. Finally, a state of emergency was declared and a curfew imposed. By 6.25 pm, the streets had been cleared by the army. Controversy still surrounds the event, which had been shrouded in secrecy for many years, and while only indirect evidence is known to survive, it is still hypothesis whether or not the explosion of the ammunition store, which was located next to a factory that produced engines for the German Messerschmitt aircraft, had been planned in advance by communists within the Czechoslovak secret services, or through the British and American Allies.

Postelberg (now Postoloprty), in the province of Saaz (now Žatec) in Bohemia, was where one of the largest planned murders of German civilians was carried out. When the Soviet army pulled out of this newly liberated area, soldiers of a special unit of the 1st Czechoslovakian Corps, under the command of Captain Vojtěch Černý, moved in from the end of May to 7 June 1945, to clean 'hostile elements' from the city and its surroundings. With help from a troop of Revolutionary Guards, led by former municipal police officer Bohuslav Marek, and civilian Czechs anxious for their anticipated real estate, they mounted attacks on the region's trapped ethnic Germans.

An investigation carried out by a Czechoslovak parliamentary commission in September 1947, unearthed the bodies of 763 ethnic Germans in many mass graves (including 225 buried by the school) and sand pits, and several corpses were found inside houses. All of them had been shot or beaten to death. Czech prosecutors have blamed policeman Bohuslav Marek and Vojtech Cerny, an army captain, but they were long since dead. Any official documents about the events in Postelberg disappeared into the Interior Ministry archives.

In the spring of 1946, the campaign to elect the first post-war parliament was under way. Czechoslovakia was one of the most progressive democracies of the post-war world, and every citizen over the age of 18 was required by law to vote. Over 7 million went to the polls, the communist party was in the lead with 114 of the 300 seats from the new constituent assembly, where all delegates confirmed their allegiance to the state by shaking hands with Zdeněk Fierlinger, the prime minister of the outgoing provisional government. As the new prime minister, communist Klement Gottwald prepared to head the coalition government, called the National Front. From the official residence, President Beneš issued a hopeful declaration of the political aims of reborn Czechoslovakia, and its role as 'a Central European peace factor in the new family of nations which has emerged out of the hard trials of this war … the United Nations Organisation'

The United States Ambassador Laurence Steinhardt brought support and friendship from America. His success as a New York lawyer and diplomat with three years of service as ambassador to Russia had made him well aware of the influence which Russia could bring to bear upon its small neighbour to the west, and his close friendship with the Czech foreign minister Jan Masaryk involved meetings that deepened his concerns for Czechoslovakia's future.

Prompt economic reconstruction was vital and began with the rebuilding of the badly damaged transportation system and the hundreds of bridges and thousands of kilometres of railway track that were destroyed in the fighting that swept the country. The United States shipped over 200 million dollars' worth of supplies to start them on the road to recovery, and to compensate for the shortage in manpower, every able-bodied Czech donated some of his time to the effort. The work of rehousing the thousands who lost their homes during the war was very quickly under way, and Czechoslovakia extended its system of low-cost housing which, before the war, was one of the most progressive in Europe. High priority on the task of economic reconstruction was given to the work of restoring mills and factories, which employed the labour of prisoners of war and careful salvage, to regain its pre-war position as the industrial leader of central Europe. Farming and agricultural machinery provided by UNRAA (the United Nations Relief and Rehabilitation Administration), the farmers were able to produce good harvests, enabling the nation escaped the famines that overtook many of its neighbouring countries.

The post-war life also brought other great changes. Under one of the first post-war decrees, nearly all key industries were ordered to be nationalised. 'State Property' was marked on all large factories, and workers' councils worked under state-appointed managers. Despite being handicapped by lack of business experience and labour shortages, the managers were able to keep production at a high level. The biggest of all the nationalised industries, the Škoda Works, sent a substantial share of its output to Russia, which already had a decisive voice in the country's economic affairs. Despite the peacetime needs, Škoda was still equipped to produce arms and heavy tools of war.

Hardliners in Slovakia became the main target for the Communist Party's attacks as they tried to convince citizens that the Slovak Democratic Party and the Hlinka Guards, who in 1942 headed the deportations of Slovak Jews to the Nazi concentration camp of Auschwitz, were connected. The communists claimed that during the Nazi regime, supporters of independent Slovakia had conspired against the nation. Citing high treason, 380 Slovaks, mostly those enrolled in the Democratic Party, were arrested, and the Ministry of the Interior Václav Nosek put non-communist politicians under close surveillance. He also fired eight non-communist commanders in the police and replaced them with communists, who then claimed they had discovered an espionage scheme carried out by American military attachés in Prague.

The open abuse of the police and security forces tried the democratic ministers, who demanded that the non-communist commanders be reinstated and that the Party cease its political attacks. Both Nosek and Gottwald refused to give in to the demands, and with the Trade Unions showing their support for the Communist Party, the communists set up armed 'action committees' in industrial plants, farms and villages. Violent communist-led demonstrations erupted, and armed trade unionists rioted in the streets of Prague, attacking the offices of the political opposition. The army was the only force that could oppose the communists, and it was run by communist General Ludvík Svoboda.

In Prague, the Czechoslovaks discussed whether or not to join the Marshall Plan. On 7 July 1947, the democratically elected government, despite a third of the ministers being communist, unanimously agreed to attend the conference in Paris that was scheduled to begin on 12 July. Premier Joseph Stalin immediately summoned the Czech prime minister, Klement Gottwald, to Moscow. Foreign Minister Jan Masaryk went with him; they arrived during the afternoon of 9 July, and waited. At around 11.00 pm, they were summoned to the Kremlin, where they were told by Stalin that the delegation from Czechoslovakia should not go to Paris to attend the conference on the Marshall Plan. They were then warned that, 'If by 4.00 am on 11 July, you have not refused to attend, then be prepared. This will have serious consequences on our relations with you.'[20] Subsequently, the same government that had previously unanimously accepted the plan, rejected it. There was no more discussion as far as the Marshall Plan was concerned. When the Czech delegation left Moscow, Gottwald read a prepared statement in which he couldn't hide his discomfort. 'Long live the eternal friendship and the alliance of the Soviet Union and Czechoslovakia. Long live the heroic Soviet people and their great leader, Generalissimo Stalin.' Masaryk was shattered by the experience. He had gone to Moscow as a minister of a free state, but returned as Stalin's slave.

In September 1947, Stalin resurrected policies from the pre-1939 Communist International (Comintern) platform, through which he planned to control the countries of the Eastern Bloc. He also instructed communist parties in the West to take the initiative in seizing power. Despite American propaganda reporting that the common form was a sinister shadowy conspiracy of evil, the Soviet Union's economic associate, Comecon, the Council for Mutual Economic Assistance, offered Russian aid to Eastern Bloc countries. It sent grain to Czechoslovakia after a bad harvest. Both Comecon and Cominform (the Information Bureau of the Communist and Workers' Parties) were a direct response to the Marshall Plan. Cominform followed the political-ideological line that the Soviet Union wanted to adopt in the socialist countries, and the aim of Comecon was to provide economic assistance to prevent those countries from being torn from its sphere of influence.

Communist Premier Gottwald launched an aggressive campaign to turn the country into a communist state, and through a series of carefully-plotted moves throughout the republic, he marshalled his political strength to force the resignation of anti-communists from the government. With characteristic party discipline, his orders were followed in detail by revolutionary communist action committees, and to demonstrate his strength and purposes, his henchmen threatened a nationwide general strike, and also presented Beneš with a list of so-called reactionaries who would be punished if he did not sign the communist government's set of proposals. No opposition to the Communist Party was allowed. President Beneš found himself in a difficult situation. Although he was committed to socialism and had wanted the USSR to be a significant role-player in Eastern Europe because he did not want Germany to gain power again, he was repelled by the Stalinist model.

In February 1948, Czechoslovakia's economic reconstruction was interrupted by a political coup. With Russia's interest in Czechoslovakia having steadily increased since the end of the war, following a pattern all too familiar to the people of Eastern Europe. The Marshall aid received from the United States had already put a strain on the relationship with the Soviet Union after it claimed that the acceptance of such help would breach the existing friendship treaty, but with the fast pace of post-war industrialisation, the citizens began to see the Communist Party in a different light. Responding strongly to criticism, several non-communist ministers were targeted with parcel bombs in November of 1947, most likely courtesy of the communists.

On 21 February 1948, tens of thousands of workers and students poured into Prague's Old Town Square, and by the evening, the People's Militia, which was formed from armed units from the Communist Party members and supporters, and comprised of 7,000 members, together with revolutionary action committees, was hastily equipped and set on alert during the communist takeover of power. They occupied offices across the country and took over the police and the labour unions. Two days later, around 2.5 million workers went on strike. Wenceslas Square was filled with demonstrators on 25 February, and threatened to march on Prague Castle, the seat of government, if the president refused to give in. The unions sent a delegation to President Beneš demanding that he respect the people's will and appoint a new, thoroughly socialist government. Disillusioned, and afraid that a civil war would start, President Beneš capitulated that same day, and finally, the bloodless communist coup was completely successful. Communist leader Klement Gottwald returned to Wenceslas Square to announce victory to the cheering crowd. In just five days, the communists had taken over Czechoslovakia's government. Stalin's rule was imposed upon the Czechs, and the red flag flew in the centre of Prague. On that day, Czechoslovakia, until then the last democracy in Eastern Europe, fell to the Communist Party of Czechoslovakia (KSČ), triggering more than forty long years of totalitarian rule.

The communist takeover in Prague shocked Washington, where the case for Marshall Aid was still being argued before a partially isolationist congress. President Harry S. Truman emphasised to Congress that a draft to keep their occupying forces in Germany until peace was secured was of vital importance; that they must be prepared to pay the price for peace, or assuredly, they would pay the price for war. The Czech coup was the final straw. Even the isolationists could see that the Russians were advancing westward with the takeover of Czechoslovakia, and passed the legislation.

Truman announced to a joint session of Congress on 17 March 1948 that,

> The Soviet Union and its agents have destroyed the independence and democratic character of a whole series of nations in eastern and Central Europe. It is this ruthless course of action, and their clear design to extend it to the remaining free nations of Europe that has brought about the critical situation in Europe today.[21]

He also asserted that,

> The door has never been closed, nor will it ever be closed, to the Soviet Union or any other nation which will genuinely cooperate in preserving the peace.[22]

Jan Masaryk died a mysterious death on 10 March 1948. Early reports from the free radio of Europe gave the cause as suicide, but it could just as easily have been murder. He either fell or was pushed off the balcony of his office on the third floor of Czernin Palace, and was found dead on the pavement below. A frail and sick Beneš resigned on 6 June 1948, and Gottwald became president while the Chairman of the Constituent National Assembly, Antonín Zápotocký, took up the post of prime minister. When Beneš passed away on 3 September 1948, so did the democratic hopes, dreams and tradition of Czechoslovakia, only to be miraculously resuscitated during November of 1989.

By the end of the expulsion process in early 1949, only around 8 per cent of the pre-war population of Germans remained in Czechoslovakia; those who had not been expelled were expected to assimilate into the host society, and special efforts and measures were put into place to forestall a refugee group form of an entity from developing and possibly becoming prey for the remnants of National Socialists. The measures reversed bans on the former expellees forming organisations, a limited German-language press was allowed to circulate, and ethnic Germans were granted a small number of opportunities in which they could practice their culture. It had become easier since 1948 for Germans and Hungarians to reacquire their Czechoslovak citizenships, and by 1953, it was compulsorily restored.

Toward the end of the 1960s, West Germany was seeking to re-establish relations with Czechoslovakia, and with the signing of the Prague Treaty in 1973, the Sudeten Germans commenced a vigorous programme of lobbying for their perceived rights, and the recognition and upholding of the rights of ethnic Germans remaining in Czechoslovakia.

The Beneš decrees acted as an anchor point in allowing the Sudeten Germans, the majority of whom supported Hitler's destruction of Czechoslovakia in 1938, to portray themselves as victims of injustice. De Zayas believes that the expulsions and transfers were unjust on the grounds that although the Nazis had committed appalling atrocities upon the Czechs, they were, for the most part, committed by members of the SS, the majority of whom were not Sudeten Germans. The simple German farmer living in the Sudetenland had little contact with the Czechs and could not have been held responsible for any abuses committed by the NSDAP in the Protectorate. Yet, he was left to pay the bill for the crimes of the Nazi regime.

The decrees have also been a bone of contention at the governmental level between the two countries since the end of the war. An attempt was made by the then prime minister, Václav Havel, in a speech of 15 March 1990 to the visiting German President, Richard von Weizsäcker, about reconciliation with the Sudeten Germans, and gave a personal apology for injustices committed against them after the war:

> A certain madman in boots crushed our first attempt at a democratic state when on 15 March 1939, he burst into this castle to announce to the world that violence had triumphed over freedom and human dignity … Fifty-one years ago, an enemy broke in uninvited. Today, a friend is here at our invitation. That former visit brought the death of our pre-war democracy. Today's visit heralds our new democracy. That former visit marked the beginning of all our recent

misfortunes. Today's visit coincides with their end ... The time is ripe for us to shake hands at last with a friendly smile, certain that we no longer have reason to fear each other, because we are connected by mutual respect for human life, human rights, civil liberties, and general peace, a respect we have paid for dearly.[23]

In 2002, Czech courts reaffirmed the validity of a 1946 law that retroactively legalised 'just reprisals for actions of the (German) occupation forces and their accomplices ... even when such acts may otherwise be punishable by law.' This statute continues to prevent the investigation or prosecution of any murder, rape or torture of Germans that took place in Czechoslovakia before 28 October 1945, when the first postwar Czechoslovak parliament was reconvened.

Chapter Five

Hungary

Following Adolf Hitler's rise to power in 1933, the Hungarian Government, which maintained similar authoritarian ideologies, became interested in forming an alliance with Nazi Germany inorder to get assistance in retrieving land it had lost after the First World War. Over the next five years, Hungary moved closer to Germany. As it strengthened its ties with Nazi Germany, the persecution of Jews increased significantly. Soon after the Anschluss – the annexation of Austria into Nazi Germany on 12 March 1938, Hungary began issuing anti-Jewish legislation and on 29 May, Prime Minister Béla Imredy, whose foreign policy became increasingly pro-German and pro-Italian, passed the 'First Jewish Law' which limited the role of Jews in the Hungarian economy and liberal professions to 20 per cent. He drafted a harsher Second Anti-Jewish Law, which reduced the role of Jews in Hungarian economic life even more, setting the limit to 6 per cent, before his resignation in February 1939. Under Prime Minister Pál Teleki, who succeeded Imredy, the Second Anti-Jewish Law was adopted on 4 May 1939 and became law the following day. The Hungarian Government further limited the Jews in the economic realm by distinguishing them as a racial rather than a religious group.

The Munich Agreement, which was signed by Germany, Italy, France, and Britain, on 29 September 1938, stipulated that Czechoslovakia must cede Sudeten territory that had formerly belonged to Hungary, to Germany. Germany then handed it back to Hungary to cement the relationship between the two countries. In March 1939 Hungary created a Munkaszolgálat – a Draft Labour Service not unlike the one established at the end of 1919 for civilians who were either unwilling or unable to serve in the regular army, but this 'new' Labour Service was not directed only at Jews, but at 'politically unreliable' people belonging to minorities, sectarians, leftists and Roma as well. The draft forced Jews aged between 20 and 48 years of age into Labour Service Battalions, which were run by Hungarian Army officers – the vast majority of whom were extremely anti-Semitic; the Jews were treated with gratuitous hatred-fuelled cruelty and brutality while they worked in heavy construction, mining, and building military fortifications. Men who worked in mine quarries would frequently be pushed to their deaths off the man-made cliffs and embankments.

The Jews were not issued with any uniforms and had to wear their own civilian clothing. A decree implemented by August 1941 further stipulated that Jewish labourers had to wear yellow armbands, and Christian labourers, who were considered to be Jews by racial definition, had to wear white armbands. The work units were stationed all over Hungary, with 130,000 men sent to work at the Eastern Front in occupied Ukraine under the direction of gendarmes and army men. These were mostly members of the anti-Sematic fascist Arrow Cross Party, and subjected the slave labour to atrocities such being forced to clear minefields by marching across them (the men would reveal mines by stepping on them, with the obvious consequences to life and limb) so that the regular troops could advance, burying the dead on the forward lines without any kind of protection while bullets from both sides of the lines flew past the forced labourers, and building tank traps and trenches, and fixing roads under the same conditions. The Munkaszolgálat began to grow following the German invasion of the Soviet Union in June 1941, and by 1942, over 100,000 Jewish men had served in these units and great numbers of Munkaszolgálatos, as they were referred to, were lost within the framework of the forced labour they performed pursuant to the draft; being killed, dying through malnutrition (the guards deprived them of most of their rations), or succumbing to disease in the unsanitary conditions they were kept in.

Hungary joined Germany, Italy, and Japan in the Axis Alliance after it was given possession of Northern Transylvania in August 1940. It received more land in March 1941, which had been given to the Kingdom of Serbs, Croats and Slovenes (from 1929 Yugoslavia) by the Allies after the First World War when, despite its alliance with the Yugoslav Government, it answered Hitler's request for military cooperation to support his invasion of Yugoslavia. By that time, with all its new territories, the Jewish population in Greater Hungary had reached over 725,000, not taking into account around 100,000 Jews who had converted to Christianity, but were still racially considered to be 'Jews' under the racial laws then in effect.

Yugoslavia was partitioned by the Axis powers, who exploited ethnic tensions to reinforce their new territorial boundaries. Germany annexed northern and eastern Slovenia, occupied the Serb Banat, which had a significant ethnic German minority, and established a military occupation administration in Serbia proper, based in Belgrade. Italy annexed southern and eastern Slovenia, occupied the Yugoslav coastline along the Adriatic Sea (including Montenegro) and attached Kosovo-Metohija to Albania, which Italy had annexed in April 1939, and Hungary annexed the Bačka and Baranja regions in north-eastern Yugoslavia, while Bulgaria occupied Macedonia and the tiny Serb province of Pirot. Conflicts in the policies between Germany and its Axis partners had a severe impact on the fate of the Jews living in Yugoslavia.

Most Jews and Roma were interned by the German military and police authorities in detention camps during the summer of 1941, and their situation was further jeopardised following an uprising initiated by the communist-led partisan movement and by the Serb Nationalist Chetnik Movement of Draza Mihailovic, which inflicted serious casualties upon the German military and police personnel. The response by Hitler was that, for every German death (including those of ethnic Germans in Serbia and the Banat), German authorities were to shoot 100 hostages.

German military and police units used this order as a pretext to shoot virtually all-male Serb Jews, approximately 8,000 people – around 2,000 actual and perceived communists, Serb nationalists and democratic politicians of the interwar era, and approximately 1,000 male Roma. Jewish women and children were rounded up and incarcerated in the Sajmište (Semlin) Nazi Concentration and Extermination Camp located at the former Belgrade fairground site close to the town of Zemun, Croatia. The Reich Central Office for Security sent a gas van – a truck with a hermetically sealed compartment that served as a gas chamber – to Belgrade in early 1942, and between March and May, 6,280 people – virtually all Jews – mostly women and children from Sajmište camp, were killed.

Shortly after Hungary had joined Germany in its war against the Soviet Union on 27 June 1941, officials of the agency responsible for the foreign nationals living in Hungary decided to deport foreign Jews (Polish and Russian Jews among them), and Hungarian Jews who could not produce documentation of their citizenship were also deported. Many Jewish communities, especially in the Governorate of Subcarpathia (a region in the easternmost part of Czechoslovakia that was then a part of Hungary), were deported in their entirety. The Hungarians loaded the Jews into freight cars and took them to Kőrösmező (now Yasinia, Ukraine), near the pre-war Hungarian-Polish border, where they were transferred across the former Soviet border and handed over to the Germans. By 10 August, around 14,000 Jews had been deported from Hungary to German-controlled territory. Once in German hands, the Jews, often still in family units, were forced to march the 104 miles (168km) from Kolomyia to Kamianets-Podilskyi.

Despite the anti-Jewish laws causing many hardships, most of the Jews of Hungary lived in relative safety until July, when the Hungarian Government transferred responsibility the Jews who were randomly designated as 'Jewish Foreign Nationals' from Carpato-Ruthenian Hungary to the German Armed Forces. Ostensibly, these Jews, who did not have Hungarian citizenship despite some of them having lived there for many generations, were sent to a location (where burial pits had been dug in advance) near the city of Kamianets-Podilskyi, in western Ukraine. There, during the opening stages of 'Operation Barbarossa' (the code name for the Axis invasion of the Soviet Union), one of the first large-scale mass-murder of Jews was carried out on 27 and 28 August, when 23,600 men, women, and children were massacred in this action (including 16,000 who had earlier been expelled from Hungary) by Einsatzgruppen – mobile Nazi death squads under the command of the Higher SS and Police Leader for the southern region, SS General Friedrich Jeckeln.

The executions were preceded by similar killing sprees between 9 July and 19 September 1941, in the cities of Zhytomyr, which was made Judenfrei ('free of Jews') after three mass-murder operations conducted by German Police Battalion 320, the Einsatzgruppen, Hungarian soldiers, and the Ukrainian Auxiliary Police, in which 10,000 Jews perished, followed by the killing of 28,000 Jews by the Einsatzgruppe 'D' in Vinnytsia on 22 September 1941, and the massacre on 29 September of 33,771 Jews at Babi Yars.

Hungarian Prime Minister László Bárdossy passed the 'Third Anti-Jewish Law' in August 1941, which was closer to Nazi Nuremberg Laws in its tone and racial definition, and prohibited the marriage and sexual intercourse of Hungarians with Jews (and became commonly known as the Race Protection Law). Bárdossy, who had been appointed Foreign Minister in January 1941, had succeeded Pál Teleki as prime minister after his suicide on 3 April (Teleki had signed a non-aggression and 'Treaty of Eternal Friendship' with Yugoslavia on 12 December 1940, opting to remain out of the German-Yugoslav conflict, but also proposed and enacted far-reaching anti-Jewish laws). Three days after Teleki's death, the German Luftwaffe bombed the city of Belgrade without warning. The Yugoslavian armed resistance was quickly crushed by the invading German Army, and the Hungarian Government, on the orders of the Regent Admiral Miklós Horthy, dispatched the Hungarian Third Army to occupy the province of Vojvodina, which comprised Banat, Bačka, Baranja and Syrmia, in northern Serbia. Eventually, 250,000 soldiers would be sent there, along with 45,000 Jewish forced labourers, and thousands of non-Jewish labourers. Finally, in December 1941, Hungary joined the Axis Powers in declaring war against the United States, completely cutting itself off from any relationship with the West.

In early January 1942, the Hungarian occupational authorities began raiding towns and villages in the southern Bačka region of Yugoslavia, starting with Čurug, and then moving on to Gospođinci, Titel, Temerin, Đurđevo and Žabalj, to suppress partisan resistance, and detain at random any 'suspicious' individuals. The region lost 19,573 people; resistance members and civilians killed outright in the raids or losing their lives after being sent to Nazi Concentration and Forced Labour Camps. On 20 January, Hungarian troops shot around 3,000 Serbian and Jewish hostages in the occupied north-eastern city of Novi Sad.

Following the Russian military breakthrough at Voronezh in January 1943, and the destruction of the Second Hungarian Army, several thousand servicemen perished in the inhuman conditions while taken prisoner by the Soviets on the snowfields of Ukraine. Many froze to death, starved, or died as a result of disease. Some among the retreating German and Hungarian armies took their revenge on the servicemen who were exhausted to breaking point. On 30 April, 800 labour servicemen were murdered near the Ukranian village of Doroshich, when Hungarian soldiers padlocked and set fire to the hospital's infirmary barracks, which housed 800 servicemen suffering from typhoid fever. Those who managed to leap from the burning inferno were gunned down.

The Soviet army was able to force back the Hungarian and other Axis invaders and, following the German defeat at Stalingrad on 2 February 1943, which made it clear that the Nazis would not emerge from the war victorious, Miklós Kállay, the Hungarian prime minister, sought an armistice with the Allies, and attempted to pull out of the alliance with Germany. In response, Hitler launched 'Operation Margarethe' in March 1944, and ordered Nazi troops to occupy Hungary. Horthy was forced to remove Prime Minister Miklós Kállay from office. Kállay, like Horthy, knew that Germany was losing the war, and had put out numerous feelers to the West. Although the Jews endured economic and political repression under Kállay's government, they protected them from the 'Final Solution'. The government had expropriated Jewish property; banned the purchase of real estate by Jews; barred Jews from working as publishers, theatre directors, and editors of journals; proscribed sexual relations between Jews and non-Jews; and outlawed conversion to Judaism.

On 19 March 1944, Adolf Eichmann and a group of SS officers arrived in Budapest to take charge of Jewish matters, and ten days later, anti-Jewish legislation was enacted which set in motion the machinery the most concentrated and brutalised ghettoization and deportation process of the Nazis' Final Solution programme. Hitler had set up a new government that he thought would be faithful, with Döme Sztójay, the former Hungarian Minister in Berlin, as prime minister. The Jewish leaders were shocked to find that they were completely isolated. Most of their top-ranked patrons collapsed with the traditional political elite and were arrested by the Gestapo in one fell swoop, while others were hidden or simply replaced. In mid-April, the Hungarian government decided to put an end to this unclear legal situation and legalised the Jewish Council, with the body being incorporated into Hungarian Competence under the name 'Temporary Steering Committee of the Jewish Association of Hungary'. Although the Hungarian government was publicly shaking hands with its Jewish citizens, the Jewish leaders pretended that nothing had changed with the occupation, and behaved according to their traditions. They made huge efforts to arrange supplies to the Jews, while continuing with their efforts to persuade the German and Hungarian authorities to prevent and stop the deportations.

Under Sztójay's reign, which was governed with the aid of the German politician and SS-Brigadeführer Edmund Veesenmayer, the

Hungarian authorities issued anti-Jewish legislation that called for the isolation of the Jews of Hungary, and gendarmerie units concentrated the approximately 16,000 Jews of the Bačka and Baranja in May 1944 in transit facilities at Bačka Topola, Baja, and Bácsalmás, and then in early June, deported the Jews to the border of the Generalgouvernement (General Governorate for the occupied Polish Region) and released them into the custody of German police, who transported them to Auschwitz-Birkenau. Accompanying the German occupation forces was a Sonderkommando unit headed by the German-Austrian SS-Obersturmbannführer Adolf Eichmann (who was one of the major organisers of the Holocaust), whose job it was to begin implementing the 'Final Solution' within Hungary. By 18 July, over 430,000 Hungarian Jews had been deported to Auschwitz-Birkenau in forty-eight trains. Most were gassed.

More Jews would have perished had not it been for the efforts of Swedish diplomat and humanitarian Raoul Wallenberg, who arrived in Hungary on 9 July 1944 with the mission of saving as many Jews as possible. By various means, including issuing special Swedish passports and bribing guards and officials, as well as setting up a programme for feeding the Jews of Budapest, his actions saved many tens of thousands from extermination. In September 1944, he was forced to go into hiding to avoid the Gestapo. He was later reported to have died on 17 July 1947 while imprisoned by the KGB secret police in the KGB headquarters and affiliated prison in Lubyanka, in the Meshchansky District of Moscow.

Judenräte (Jewish Councils) were established throughout Hungary under German Command, following additional anti-Jewish decrees that had been passed in great haste. The central Judenräte called the Zsidó Tanács was established in Budapest under the Leader of the Jewish Council, Samu Stern. Movement of Jews was restricted and their telephones and radios confiscated to isolate them from the outside world. Their communities were forced to wear badges in the form of a Yellow Star. Jewish property and businesses were seized, and from mid- to late April, the Jews of Hungary were forced into ghettos. The Ghettoization began on 15 April in Transcarpathia in the east, and the process moved westward across the country until early June, when deportations from the countryside were complete. In small communities and villages, Jews were herded together and transported to the nearest town, or a ghetto erected on its outskirts, and from there to holding camps, most of which were brick factories, and whole Urban Jewish communities were generally forced to live in cramped conditions within an existing Jewish district, or in ruined parts of the town.

The ghettos were short-lived, however, as within two to six weeks, the Jews of each ghetto were put on trains and deported. Between 15 May and 9 July 1944, around 430,000 Hungarian Jews were deported, mainly to Auschwitz, where the majority were gassed on arrival. Ironically, the Draft Labour Service that had been introduced in March 1939 became something of a haven for thousands of Jews who otherwise would have been deported to extermination camps, although they lived an uneasy existence. Negotiations were entered throughout the spring of 1944 between the Hungarian-Jewish journalist and lawyer Rezső Kasztner (Rudolf Israel Kastner), Joel Brand, and other members of the underground Zionist Group 'Aid and Rescue Committee', and the SS to try to save lives.

An offer of 'Blood for Goods' was made by Adolf Eichmann, in which a certain number of Jews would be spared in exchange for large amounts of goods, including trucks. Kasztner negotiated directly with Eichmann, and later with the mid-ranking SS commander, Kurt Becher, and in late June 1944, a list of 1,700 people to be released was drawn up, which included leading wealthy Jews, Zionists, rabbis, Jews from different religious communities, and Kasztner's own family. They were transported out of Budapest on 30 June on what came to be known as the 'Kasztner Train', which consisted of thirty-five cattle trucks. After a period of detention at the 'exchange camp' at Bergen-Belsen, near Celle in Lower Saxony, Germany, they eventually reached safety in Switzerland. As many as 8,000 Jews had already fled from Hungary, mostly to Romania, through the assistance of Zionist Youth Movement members, who forged identity documents and provided them with food.

Horthy replaced Sztójay with the anti-fascist General Géza Lakatos on 29 August 1944, but he could not fulfil his duties due to health problems, so under the brief Lakatos regime, acting Interior Minister Béla Horváth ordered the Hungarian Gendarmerie to prevent any Hungarian citizens from being deported. Subsequently, the Jews of Budapest continued to live in relative safety until 15 October, when Horthy publicly announced that Hungary had declared an armistice with the Allies, and withdrawn from the Axis.

The Hungarian army ignored the armistice, fighting desperately to keep the Soviets out, in an attempt to keep Hungary tied to their alliance, topped the government with 'Operation Panzerfaust' and, by kidnapping his son Miklós Horthy Jr., forced Horthy to abrogate the armistice, and depose the Lakatos government. Ferenc Szálasi, the leader of the fascist, violently anti-Semitic Arrow Cross Party was given power, and Horthy himself was taken to Germany as a prisoner (He ultimately survived the war and spent his last years exiled in Portugal, dying in 1957).

Horthy was forced to resign in October 1944 and was placed under arrest by the Germans and taken to Bavaria. At the end of the war, he came under the custody of American troops. Horthy had been under pressure from two sides since June 1944: the Nazis and the majority of the Hungarian government wanted the remaining Jews deported, while prominent individuals close to Horthy and international representatives, including Pope Pius XII, King Gustav of Sweden, and President Franklin D. Roosevelt of the United States, tried to persuade him to stop the deportations. The military situation at the time undoubtedly favoured the Allies and, with the publication of the Auschwitz Protocols, more and more information had come to light regarding the workings of the death camps. Horthy's decision to suspend the deportations was influenced not so much by the Protocols, since he had been aware for some time of the realities of the 'Final Solution', but rather by the international outcry they generated. On 6 July, Horthy issued a directive to suspend the deportations. At this point, only the deportation of the Budapest Jews remained.

A reign of terror ensued in Budapest under Szálasi as he attempted to resume deportations of Jews, but Germany's rapidly-disintegrating communications largely prevented this from happening, and almost 80,000 Jews were killed in the city itself, shot on the banks of the Danube River by firing squads, and then thrown into the river, which would carry their bodies away. Thousands of others were subjected to torture, rape, and murder, and forced on death marches to the Austrian border. During the Soviet siege of the city in December, 70,000 Jews were forced into a ghetto, where thousands died of cold, disease, and starvation.

After putting an end to the death marches on 21 November 1944, the Arrow Cross government crammed the Jews of Budapest into two ghettos. The 'small' or 'international' ghetto in Újlipótváros, Budapest's 13th District, contained those who held protection papers issued by a neutral state, which were also forged in great number. The international ghetto area around Szent István Park and Pozsonyi Road was, by December, soon overcrowded with almost 40,000 people living there, often with up to sixty people sharing one room.

Soviet forces crossed the Hungarian border in September 1944, and as they pushed westward, Sztojay's government proceeded to muster new armies. The Hungarian troops again suffered terrible losses, but now had a motive to protect their homeland from Soviet occupation. Soon Hungary itself became a battlefield, and its armies were slowly being destroyed. The Hungarian First Army participated defensively alongside the German 1st Panzer Army in October as the Red Army advanced towards Budapest.

The Germans and pro-German Hungarians loyal to Szálasi fought on regardless after 28 December 1944, when a provisional government was formed in Hungary under the acting prime minister, Béla Miklós. The following day, Budapest was completely encircled by Soviets and Romanians, and the battle turned into the Siege of Budapest. By 16 January 1945, most of the Hungarian First Army had been destroyed, and four days later, Miklós' Provisional National Government accepted and signed the terms of an armistice presented by the governments of the Soviet Union, the United Kingdom, and the United States of America, on 20 January in Moscow. From within Hungary, 32,000 ethnic Germans were arrested and transported to the Soviet Union as forced labourers. In some villages, the entire adult population was taken to labour camps in the Donets Basin. Hungary was finally liberated by the Soviet army by April 1945, and the Germans, with the Arrow Cross in tow, had completely vacated Hungarian soil.

With the invasion of Yugoslavia in 1941, the Germans had acquired the large copper mines in the area of Bor, in Eastern Serbia, and with the majority of Yugoslav Jews having been annihilated, and Serbs being seen as potential partisans, Germany turned to Hungary for a labour force. Despite objections raised by Vilmos Nagybaczoni Nagy, the Minister of Defence, the government agreed, and the first companies left for Bor in the summer of 1943. By the summer of 1944, around 6,000 Hungarian servicemen were sent to the copper mines.

The labour force was housed in eight camps around the mines, and while these were under the control of the Hungarian army, the work in the mines was supervised by armed members of the German paramilitary work organisation. The Engineering organisation 'Todt', which was responsible for the Reichsautobahnen (Autobahn) project and, having been 'incorporated' into Ministry of Armaments and War production in February 1942, following the death of its founder, Fritz Todt, and working under Albert Speer, the construction projects included air-raid shelters, underground refineries and armaments factories, and administered construction of the Nazi concentration camps in the late phase of Nazi Germany. The conditions and treatment of servicemen varied slightly between the camps, but at the end of 1943, when Lieutenant Colonel Ede Marányi took over as commander of the camps, the already strict discipline was replaced with a cruel and anti-Semitic system of beatings, truss-ups and executions. Thousands of labourers died from abuse, malnourishment, cold, and disease.

Adolf Eichmann was deployed to Hungary on the 19 March 1944 to carry out the extermination of its Jewish population, and aimed to deport more than 800,000 people to the camps in the East. Despite the likelihood of defeat in the war by this stage, genocide was still a priority for the Nazis. Arriving with just a few German staff, Eichmann was reliant on the collaboration of the Hungarian authorities to achieve this aim. The Hungarian authorities cooperated enthusiastically with Eichmann's plans. In just over two months, over 200 camps and ghettos had been established and filled with the Jewish population. 437,402 Hungarian Jews were deported in between May and July 1944, primarily to Auschwitz, where almost all of them were murdered.

In the meantime, the neutral states planned rescue actions for the Jews of Budapest. Raoul Wallenberg was sent as secretary of the Swedish Foreign Ministry in July 1944, with instructions to save as many Jews as possible. He issued thousands of Swedish identity documents to Jews to protect them from Nazi deportation, and is credited with ultimately saving as many as 20,000, which allowed them to ask for the protection of the neutral Swedish government. During the autumn of 1944, Wallenberg repeatedly intervened to secure the release of bearers of certificates of protection and those with forged papers. His aide, the Swiss diplomat Carl Lutz, served as vice-consul, and is credited with saving over 62,000 Jews, the largest rescue operation of Jews of the Second World War.

Two transports of Jewish inmates from Budapest prisons, and the internment camps of Kistarcsa, Budapest, and Bácstopolya, in the north Bačka District of Vojvodina, Serbia, were sent by the German authorities at the end of April 1944. The mass transport of Hungarian Jews to

Birkenau took place between 16 May and 11 June, and by October, 437,402 Hungarian Jews had been deported, with all but 15,000 of them going to the Auschwitz complex, where 90 per cent of them were immediately killed.

Following a coup d'état led by King Michael I of Romania on 23 August 1944, which removed the government of Ion Antonescu, the Hungarian Ministry of Defence called the Hungarian servicemen and labour force back from Bor. The evacuation took place in two waves. The first contingent of around 3,600 people suffered brutal treatment and significant losses from their escorting Hungarian-speaking Swabian (ethnic Germans) and Bosnian SS troops by the time they reached the Szentkirályszabadja camp near Lake Balton. On the night of 7–8 October, between 700 and 1,000 men were machine-gunned into mass graves at Cservenka, in the West Bačka district of Serbia. After this, stragglers in the column of survivors were shot at random by Hungarian soldiers.

Once back on Hungarian soil, the remaining Labourers of Bor were driven first north, and then towards the western border. With Marányi taking over command again, the executions resumed with twenty-two being shot in the outskirts the village of Abda, near Győr, 196 were killed at Kiskunhalas, sixty-three were murdered at the Debrecen-Apafa shooting-range, and on 26 October, an entire labour service company of 216 men were exterminated at Pusztavám. The survivors of the first contingent were marched on to the Nazi Concentration camps of Dachau, Buchenwald, Oranienburg-Sachsenhausen and Flossenbürg.

The second contingent of around 2,000 servicemen left Bor on 29 September 1944, but was liberated by Tito's partisans in the Serbian mountains the same day. The most brutal of the Hungarian officers and soldiers were shot on the spot, and while many of the freed servicemen joined the partisans, most of them sought sanctuary in Romania.

Whereas Czechoslovakia independently expelled over 3 million Sudeten German civilians, the expulsion programme to remove the Danube Swabians in Hungary was carried out under the direct observation and cooperation of the Americans, the Soviets, and a sometimes reticent Hungarian communist government. The Soviet Red Army had obliterated the Third Reich and its allies of Hungary and Romania by the summer of 1945, and along with the United States and Great Britain, agreed that the transfer to Germany of German

The public execution of Polish civilians by Germans in the city of Bydgoszcz, following the invasion of Poland in September 1939. (*Włodzimierz Jastrzębski: 'Terror i zbrodnia'. Interpress, Warszawa 1974*)

Suppression of the Warsaw ghetto uprising. Nowolipie Street looking East, close to the intersection with Smocza Street in the Jewish Quarter of Warsaw. Captured Jews are led by German Waffen-SS soldiers to the assembly point for deportation (Umschlagplatz). Photo taken between 19 April and 16 May 1943. The woman on right has been identified as Hasia Szylgold-Szpiro.

Suppression of the Warsaw ghetto uprising. Captured Jews, with the Neyer family at the front of the column, are led by German Waffen-SS soldiers towards an assembly point for deportation (Umschlagplatz). Their homes burning in the background.

17-year-old Lepa Svetozara Radic´ was publicly executed on 8 February 1943 for her role in the resistance movement against the Axis powers. Lepa was a Bosnian Serb member of the Yugoslav Partisans, and was hanged for shooting at German troops. With the noose around her neck, her captors offered her a way out of the gallows by revealing her comrades' and leaders' identities. She told them that she was not a traitor and that, 'You will know them when they come to avenge me.' (*Danilo Gagovic´*)

Child survivors of Auschwitz, wearing adult-size prisoner jackets, stand behind a barbed wire fence. In 1940, after Hungary assumed control of the previously Romanian region, antisemitism increased, and Jews could no longer travel freely. By 1942, Jews were forbidden to hire Aryan labourers, and Alexandru had to fire all his farm hands. In 1943 Jews were required to wear the yellow star. (*United States Holocaust Memorial Museum, courtesy of Yad Vashem and Raymund Flandez*)

Jews from Subcarpathian Ruthenia who have been selected for death at Auschwitz-Birkenau, wait in a clearing near a grove of trees before being led to the gas chambers. This photo from a negative, and other negatives found by the Czech researchers were used in the pre-trial investigations for the Frankfurt Auschwitz trials of 1963-1965. (*United States Holocaust Memorial Museum, courtesy of Yad Vashem and Raymund Flandez*)

Ministers of the Arrow Cross Party government in late 1944. Standing row, left to right: Dr Ferenc Rajniss, Minister for Religion and Public Education; Count Fidél Pálffy, Minister for Agriculture; Gábor Vajna, Minister for the Interior; Béla Jurcsek, Minister for Public Supply; Emil Kovarcz, Minister for Deployment and Defence Minister Ferenc Kassai, Minister for Propaganda and National Defence.

Seated row, left to right: Lajos Reményi-Schneller, Finance Minister Dr Baron Gábor Kemény, Minister of Foreign Affairs Ferenc Szálasi, Chief of State Károly Beregfy, Minister of Defence Dr Lajos Szász, Minister for Trade and Transport. László Budinszky, Minister of Justice, is absent from the picture.

The public execution of fifty-four Poles in the village of Rożki, in Radom County, in German-occupied Poland, 1942. (*Union of Fighters for Freedom and Democracy, Warsaw, 1958*)

Einsatzgruppen in Zdołbunów, Poland, shooting naked women and children from the Mizocz ghetto. The authenticity of this photograph of the shooting of Jews in connection with the liquidation of the ghetto was confirmed in a statement by Gendarmerie-Gebietsfuehrer Josef Paur in 1961. (*Gustav Hille*)

Jews captured by the SS during the suppression of the Warsaw ghetto uprising are lined up against a wall prior to being searched for weapons. Photograph taken between 19 April and 16 May 1943. (*United States Holocaust Memorial Museum, courtesy of National Archives and Records Administration, College Park*)

Mass murders were carried out by marauding Red Army soldiers during the aftermath of the Battle of Königsberg. Women and children were targeted for rape and shooting among the 3,000 victims in Metgethen, Königsberg, East Prussia, between January and February 1945. Mutilated corpses of civilians were discovered after German forces successfully recaptured Metgethen on 19 February in order to reopen the vital road and railway line between Königsberg and the Baltic Sea harbor of Pillau. (*Remo Kurka Photography*)

Polish women led to mass execution in the Kampinosa forest near Palmiry village, northwest of Warsaw. After the war the woman in the foreground was identified as Janina Skalska. Palmiry is one of the most infamous sites of German crimes in Poland, and 'one of the most notorious places of mass executions' in Poland. Along with the Katyn massacre, it has become emblematic of the martyrdom of Polish intelligentsia during World War II. (Narodowe Archiwum Cyfrowe (Sygnatura: 21-206-2) (*Polish National Digital Archive*)

Notes

Note 1: Between December 1939 and July 1941 more than 1,700 Poles and Jews – mostly inmates of Warsaw's Pawiak prison – were executed by the SS and Ordnungspolizei in a forest glade near Palmiry. The best documented of these massacres took place on 20–21 June 1940, when 358 members of the Polish political, cultural, and social elite were murdered in a single operation.

Note 2: During the Second World War, between 1939 and 1943, the village and the surrounding forest were one of the sites of the Nazi German mass executions of Jews, Polish intelligentsia, politicians and athletes, killed during the German AB-Aktion in Poland. Most of the victims were first arrested and tortured in the Pawiak prison in Warsaw, then transferred to the execution site. In total, about 1,700 Poles were murdered there in secret executions between 7 December 1939 and 17 July 1941.

Note 3: In 1946, the bodies were exhumed and reburied in a new cemetery, situated approximately five kilometres from the village itself. The reburial site has been a Polish national mausoleum since 1948.

Polish Prisoners of War being escorted by soldiers of the German Army near Lviv-Lwow, the centre of the Lwów Voivodeship in the Second Polish Republic in 1939. (*Authors collection*)

The arrival of Hungarian Jews at the Nazi death-camp Auschwitz in summer 1944. (Bundesarchiv, Bild 183-N0827-318/CC-BY-SA 3.0 (*German Federal Archives*))

Liberation by American troops in April 1945 for around 67,000 prisoners still interned in the Dachau Forced Labour Camp. More than 240,000 prisoners passed through its gates, and an estimated 41,000 never left it, having been murdered or having died from disease or ill-treatment. Dachau was the first such camp to be built in Germany. (*Colin Hepburn*)

11 May 1945: Sudeten German civilian inhabitants of Volary (in the present-day Czech Republic) are forced by US troops to walk past bodies of thirty Jewish women who starved to death on a 300-mile (500-kilometre) death march from Helmbrechts Concentration Camp (a women's subcamp of the Flossenbürg concentration camp founded near Hof, Germany) to Volary. Buried in shallow graves, the bodies had been exhumed by German civilians working under direction of Medics of the Fifth Infantry Division, US Third Army. The bodies were later placed in coffins and reburied in separate cemetery next to the cemetery of Volary. (*US Army Signal Corps*)

Above left: The Regent of Hungary Miklós Horthy and German Führer Adolf Hitler in 1938. Horthy saw his country as trapped between two stronger powers, both of them dangerous, but he considered Hitler as a bulwark against Soviet encroachment or invasion, and to be the more manageable of the two, at least at first. (*Ladislav Luppa*)

Above right: Henryk Ożarek ('Henio') on the left, and Tadeusz Przybyszewski ('Roma') on the right, from 'Anna' Company of the Gustaw Battalion in October 1994 during the Warsaw Uprising in the region of Kredytowa-Królewska Street. (*Wiesław Chrzanowski, Polish Officer and Photographer*)

Above left: British Prime Minister Winston Churchill, President Harry S. Truman, and Soviet leader Josef Stalin in the garden of Cecilienhof Palace before meeting for the Potsdam Conference in Potsdam, Germany, on 25 July 1945. (*US National Archives and Records Administration, NAID 198606*)

Above right: The Yalta Conference. British Prime Minister Winston Churchill, US President Franklin Roosevelt, and Soviet leader Joseph Stalin met at Yalta in February 1945 to discuss their joint occupation of Germany and plans for postwar Europe. Behind them stand, from the left, Field Marshal Sir Alan Brooke, Fleet Admiral Ernest King, Fleet Admiral William D. Leahy, General of the Army George Marshall, Major General Laurence S. Kuter, General Aleksei Antonov, Vice Admiral Stepan Kucherov, and Admiral of the Fleet Nikolay Kuznetsov. (*National Archives and Records Administration*)

Deportation of Polish Jews from the ghetto in Siedlce to Treblinka extermination camp in 1942. The Holocaust trains mainly comprised of locked and windowless Cattle Wagons, and were run by the Deutsche Reichsbahn National Railway, which had been placed under Reich Sovereignty in 1937. The company also had an important logistic role in supporting the rapid movement of the troops of the Wehrmacht. (*Institute of National Remembrance*)

Above left: Rudolf Hess. (*Bundesarchiv, Bild 146II-849 / CC-BY-SA 3.0*)

Above right: Hermann Göring. (*Narodowe Archiwum Cyfrowe*)

[CYPHER].

FROM BERNE TO FOREIGN OFFICE.

Mr. Norton.
No. 2851.
August 10th, 1942.

D. 4.48 p.m. August 10th, 1942.
R. 6.25 p.m. August 10th, 1942.

yyyyyy

Following from His Majesty's Consul General at Geneva No. 174 (Begins).

Following for Mr. S.S. Silverman M.P., Chairman of British Section, World Jewish Congress London from Mr. Gerhart Riegner Secretary of World Jewish Congress, Geneva.

[Begins].

Received alarming report stating that, in the Fuehrer's Headquarters, a plan has been discussed, and is under consideration, according to which all Jews in countries occupied or controlled by Germany numbering 5½ to 4 millions should, after deportation and concentration in the East, be at one blow exterminated, in order to resolve, once and for all the Jewish question in Europe. Action is reported to be planned for the autumn. Ways of execution are still being discussed including the use of prussic acid. We transmit this information with all the necessary reservation, as exactitude cannot be confirmed by us. Our informant is reported to have close connexions with the highest German authorities, and his reports are generally reliable. Please inform and consult New York. (Ends].

[INDIV].

The Riegner Telegram
This telegram from Gerhart Riegner, Secretary of the World Jewish Congress in Geneva, was received by the Foreign Office on 10 August 1942. The telegram was among the first pieces of unambiguous evidence received by the Allies that the Nazi Government planned a 'final solution' to the 'Jewish question'. (*The National Archives*)

The Barricade on the intersection of Świętokrzyska and Mazowiecka Streets viewed from Napoleon Square during the Warsaw uprising. (*Jerzy Tomaszewski*)

German civilians from the town of Hurlach move the dead bodies of Russians, Poles, French, and Jewish prisoners, starved and burned to dead by German SS troops at the Stalag #4 found in Kaufering IV to mass graves for burial. (*United States Holocaust Memorial Museum*)

Einsatzgruppen or their auxiliaries at Kovno, 1942. Einsatzgruppe Detachments and Lithuanian auxiliaries shot thousands of Jewish men, women, and children, primarily in the Ninth Fort, but also in the Fourth and Seventh forts. Within six months of the German occupation of the city, the Germans and their Lithuanian collaborators had murdered half of all Jews in Kovno. (*Forum-kenig.ru*)

Above left: Bunkbeds in Auschwitz. The dreadful overcrowded living conditions inside the barracks at Auschwitz was the main reason for outbreaks and contagious diseases among the prisoners. Several hundred three-tier wooden bunk beds were installed in each building. 12 November 2018. (*Richard Meijer*)

Above right: The defendants in their dock at the Nuremberg Trials 1945-1946. Front row, from left to right: Hermann Göring, Rudolf Hes, Joachim von Ribbentrop, Wilhelm Keitel. Second row, from left to right: Karl Dönitz, Erich Raeder, Baldur von Schirach, Fritz Sauckel.

Joseph Stalin, Winston Churchill and President Truman with their staffs around the conference table at the Potsdam Conference at Brandenburg, Germany, on 17 July 1945. No 5 Army Film & Photographic Unit. (*United States National Archives*)

Polish hostages (including Roman Catholic priests) at Old Market Square in Bydgoszcz in September 1939.

Warsaw ghetto uprising: SS troops stand near the bodies of Jews at 23 and 25 Niska Street, who committed suicide by jumping from a fourth story window rather than be captured on 22 April 1943 (*Jürgen Stroop Report*)

Warsaw uprising - Barricade on Corner of Karolkowa and Żytnia Street in Wola district, in August 1944. (*Stefan Bałuk*)

Nowolipie street looking East, near intersection with Smocza street, Warsaw in May 1943. Jews pulled from a bunker. (*Jürgen Stroop Report*)

A group of Hungarian Jews from the Tet ghetto being walked towards the gas chambers and crematoria 2 and 3 in Birkenau camp on 27 May 1944. (*United States Holocaust Memorial Museum collection*)

Jews from Carpathian Ruthenia arrive at Auschwitz in May 1944, and offloading onto the ramp at Birkenau in close proximity to the gas chambers. The chimneys in the background belong to Crematoria II and III on the left and right respectively, whose structures house subterranean undressing and gassing rooms. (*United States Holocaust Memorial Museum, Yad Vashem*)

Old Town Market Place, Warsaw, 1945. The district was damaged by the bombs of the German Luftwaffe during the Invasion of Poland in 1939, and in 1944 the tenements were mostly destroyed by the German Army after the suppression of the Warsaw uprising. (*Marek Tuszyński*)

The public execution of Polish hostages in German-occupied Szczęśliwice district of Warsaw, Poland on 16 October 1942.

A Polish priest standing among the hostages awaiting execution by the Germans in Bydgoszcz (the Prussian city annexed by Poland in 1919) in early September 1939. The executions were revenge killings for Bloody Sunday, when ethnic Germans living in the same town were subjected to a genocidal slaughter two days after the German invasion of Poland. The German Army immediately perceived the killings as a Polish-instigated massacre.

Jewish people waiting in line at the Glass House (Üvegház) in Budapest, 1944. This photograph was taken by Agnes Hirschi, Carl Lutz's daughter. (*FORTEPAN/Archiv für Zeitgeschichte ETH Zürich/Agnes Hirschi (the daughter of Carl Lutz)*)

Above left: Three SS officers, From left to right they are: Richard Baer (Commandant of Auschwitz), Dr Josef Mengele and Rudolf Hoess (the former Auschwitz Commandant) socialise on the grounds of the SS retreat outside of Auschwitz, 1944. (*Yad Vasheem*)

Above right: Reinhard Heydrich, Chief of the Reich Security Main Office, the SS and police agency, and one of the main architects of the Final Solution, 1940. (*Bundesarchiv, Bild 146-1969-054-16/Hoffmann, Heinrich/CC-BY-SA*)

Lidice Memorial 26 July 2019. (*Jorma Kontio*)

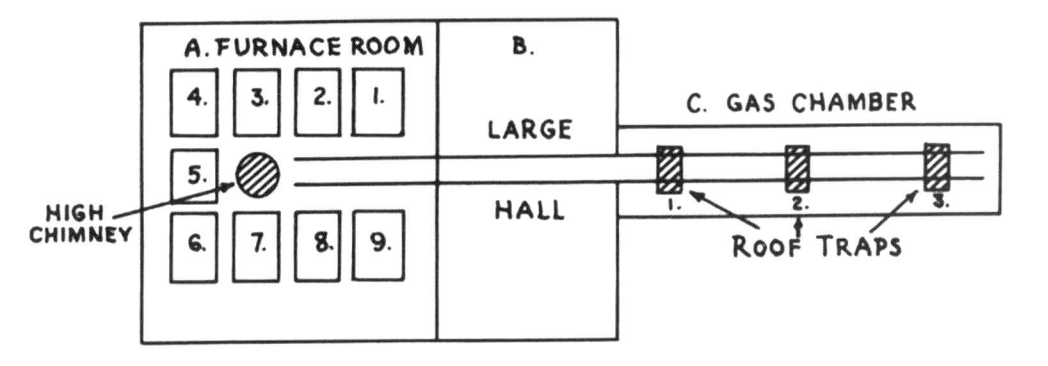

ROUGH GROUND PLAN OF CREMATORIA: TYPES I & II IN BIRKENAU

Sketch of the Auschwitz-Birkenau gas chambers and crematoria from the English-language version of the Vrba-Wetzler report. (*United States War Refugee Board, 16 November 1944*)

The Allied Occupation Zones of Germany after the Second World War.

Lviv (Lwów) during the German occupation in September 1939. (*Ireck Andreas Litzbarski*)

Field Marshall Keitel signs German surrender terms in Berlin 8 May 1945. (*Lieutenant Moore (US Army); restored by Adam Cuerden, PD-USGov-Military-Army*)

Jews captured between 19 April 1943 and 16 May 1943 at Zamenhofa Street looking north from intersection with Wołyńska streets towards Miła Street, during the Warsaw ghetto uprising, are marched to the Umschlagplatz for deportation.

SS troops arrest the Jewish department heads of the Brauer helmet factory at 28-38 Nalewki Street, which and employed 2,000 people. With the outbreak of the uprising on 19 April 1943, Hermann Brauer promised those Jewish work managers who hadn't gone into hiding, that the factory would continue to operate, and asked that they come to work. These managers received special transit passes to move freely about the ghetto, which were attached to their coat lapels. On 24 April 1943, the SS raided the factory, rounded up the managers, and conducted body searches prior to deporting them, and then setting fire to the factory.

Soldiers of the 55th Armored Infantry Battalion and tank of the 22nd Tank Battalion, 11 Armored Division, move through a smoke filled street in Wernberg, Germany, on 22 April 1945. (*National Archives and Records Administration, US Federal Government*)

Polish civilians murdered by German troops during Warsaw Uprising. Photo taken in Warsaw's district Wola where SS troops murdered about 60,000 people during so called 'Wola massacre' during the first days of August 1944. (*Miasto Nieujarzmione, Iskry, 1957*)

Members of the 405th Regiment F Company, searching the perimeter of the airfield at Gardelegen, found several bullet-riddled bodies, clad in prison striped clothing in a storage shed. (*Clifford Rentz*)

Members of the 405th Regiment F Company, searching the perimeter of the airfield at Gardelegen, opened one of the large wooden doors of a barn and were greeted with a cloud of smoke and the stench of burned flesh. There were some 300 charred and smoking bodies inside. (*Clifford Rentz*)

SS troops stand near the bodies of Jews outside 23-25 Niska Street, who committed suicide by jumping from a fourth story window rather than be captured on 22 April 1943.

The bodies of Jews executed after their capture during the Warsaw Ghetto Uprising from 19 April 1943–16 May 1943.

Above left: Edvard Beneš. (*Overseas Picture Division. Washington Division, 1944*)

Above right: A Polish insurgent fighter surrendered from his position in the sewers under Warsaw, Poland, on 27 September 1944. (*August Ahrens, German Federal Archive*) populations, or elements thereof, remaining in Poland, Czechoslovakia, and Hungary, would have to be undertaken.

The Hungarians had actively participated with the Third Reich on both the Western and Eastern fronts throughout the war, but were reluctant to accept the concept of collective responsibility for as long as it could, diverting the blame for wartime atrocities onto the Germans and the deposed Hungarian dictatorships. They also protected themselves from crippling indemnity and restitution, despite the disastrous moral and economic effects of Ferenc Szálasi's 'arrow-cross' puppet-government, during the last few months of 1944.

While serious concerns were raised about the removal of a significant productive minority from the labour force during a time of complete economic ruin and rampant unemployment, the legitimate military and political authority in Hungary, being under the strict joint control of the Allied Control Commission, ruled that the Danube Swabian community, which numbered more than 470,000 people, was to be removed from Hungary regardless of the initial compunction of the de facto ruler Mátyás Rákosi, the leader of the Hungarian Communist Party, and his government. At least 40,000 ethnic Hungarians had been forcibly expelled from Slovakia by the Czechoslovak government, along with more than 3 million Sudeten Germans, to occupied Hungary to become legally and socially accepted as citizens. In terms of numbers, the expulsion of German-speaking people from Hungary after the Second World War was not as significant as those in Poland or Czechoslovakia; the minority were not considered to be a potential political threat to the state.

Some of the Hungarian politicians who objected to the expulsion, i.e. the Smallholders Party and the Social Democrats, and repeatedly insisted upon the need to maintain the moral 'high ground' on the issue, to be able to better defend Hungarian minorities abroad (particularly those in Czechoslovakia and Romania). The threat that the expulsion of the Germans from Hungary would create a moral basis for neighbouring countries to remove their Hungarians was the main reason for the heated political debates within the government and the government's strong objection to the collective responsibility principle.

Mátyás Rákosi demanded total expulsion, but pointed out that the expulsion was a Soviet order that had to be carried out. Following a heated debate on the principle of collective responsibility, the government accepted the idea of expelling the Swabian population from Hungary. There followed a number of governmental orders restricting the rights of the German-speaking population.

The decree of 15 October suspended the autonomy of many German villages and restricted the authority of their local governments. The same decree also suspended the political rights of German nationals, including the deprivation of voting rights. The situation for the Swabian population following the Potsdam Conference in August 1945 had suddenly become one of desperation as they became the targets of the expulsion order, although no official preparations were undertaken to carry out the population transfer until December.

Despite Hungary having being occupied by German forces in 1944, and having suffered the disastrous moral and economical effects of Ferenc Szálasi's Arrow-Cross puppet government during the last few months of that year, Hungarians in general were not seeking revenge after the war, and so did not consider the German minority to be a potential political threat as it was in Czechoslovakia or Poland. President Edvard Beneš had demanded the expulsion of Hungarians alongside Germans from Czechoslovakian territory as early as 1943, and had the backing of the Soviet Union. The fact that Hungary received the text of the Potsdam decision in Russian was a clear sign of post-war power relations in the region, but it also indicated the limits of the political latitude allowed to the Hungarian government. Beneš' original plan had been to expel 600,000 Hungarians – around 90 per cent of the total Hungarian population at the time – for 'reasons of security', but the proposal was not agreed by either the United States or Great Britain. However, due to the diplomatic pressure from the Soviet Union, Article XII (the orderly transfer of German populations remaining in Czechoslovakia and Hungary) of the Potsdam treaty itself imposed an obligation that the country was bound to fulfil.

In January 1945, under Allied direct observation, 32,000 ethnic German men and women aged between 17 and 35, were arrested and, along with ethnic Germans from the other Danube Swabian communities of Yugoslavia and Romania (the Banat), were forcibly sent to Russia as part of Allied 'war reparations'; being put to work as slave labour to rebuild Stalino Oblast (now Donetsk Oblast) and to work in its coal mines. The conditions were so poor that many died from disease and malnutrition.

Beneš issued Decrees only ten days after the end of the war, which not only trampled on human rights, but disregarded the sanctity of life itself. According to the Decree of 005/1945, the Hungarians and Germans were defined as traitors, and within weeks three further decrees were issued. 012/1945: the confiscation and expedited allotment of agricultural property of Germans and Hungarians, 016/1945: the punishment of Nazi criminals, traitors and their helpers, and 017/1945: the National Court to hear trials of Protectorate public figures indicted for crimes under Act No. 16/1945 in senates consisting of seven persons. There was no possibility of appeal, and death sentence was to be carried out within two hours of sentencing, or within twenty-four hours if the court decides that the execution shall be carried out publicly. These decrees inspired unrestrained violence against Hungarians and Germans, and opened the road to mass murder.

Articles Four and Five of the Land Reform Bill, which was introduced on 15 March 1945, sparked an agrarian revolution after the lands of Volksbund members, and those who served the political, economic and military interests of German Fascism at the expense of the Hungarian people, through voluntary enlistment in the fascist, military or security units, or acting as informers, were expropriated, along with any livestock, buildings and production assets. All estates larger than 575 hectares were expropriated, and other farms were reduced to a maximum of fifty-seven hectares by confiscation. Nearly 3 million hectares of confiscated land were distributed to 725,000 landless workers and smallholders via the Resettlement Programme, which was charged with controlling and managing the settlement of waves of Hungarian refugees from the neighbouring countries during the process of the reform. This land and property redistribution noticeably hurt the Hungarian economy, since it depleted a productive minority from the economy, but was in keeping with the Allies' admonitions to make the expulsions as humane and orderly as possible. A second wave of land reform began in 1948, when 170,000 hectares of leased land was transferred from large farmers to farmworkers, small farmers and cooperative farms for low-rent payments.

The Phases of Expulsion

The expulsion of Germans from Hungary was opposed by both the government and the general population. The Hungarian government was forced into taking action by the occupying Soviet forces, and used the census carried out in 1941 to identify and select every person who had declared themselves German. The census was carried out when the influence of Nazi-Germany was at its height in Hungary, right before the country joined the war. As a result of the war, the total number of Germans decreased considerably, not only because of the number of casualties during the war itself, but because many Germans fled to Germany, and a large number were captured by the Red Army, and were transported to the Soviet Union.

On 29 December 1945, the deportations started. Mass arrests and deportations began swiftly, in most cases before the expellees had time to put any valuables together. Official Hungarian figures showed that 477,000 German speakers in Hungary, including German-speaking Jews, 303,000 of whom had declared German nationality. The German population wasn't targeted as a whole in the immediate post-war period, but under discriminative measures that were introduced, the expulsions began in phases. The first were the Nazi and Arrow Cross war criminals, who caused the Jewish community to almost be extinguished, members of the Volksbund (the pro-Nazi organisation of the German-speaking minority in Hungary) and other Nazi-organisations, and members of the Waffen SS. Around 60–70,000 Germans, mostly members of Nazi organisations who felt threatened by the unpleasant prospect of spending the rest of their lives in Siberia, fled in fear from Hungary to Germany, but a large number of these were captured by the Red Army and were transported to the Soviet Union.

Although full-scale deportations did not begin until January of 1946, departures, imprisonment, and executions were rampant following the Soviet annexation of Hungary at the end of the war. Lavrentiy Beria, the head of the Soviet secret police (NKVD), and one of Stalin's most influential secret police chiefs reported in 1945 that 23,707 Germans and Hungarians had been arrested or executed due to accusations of Nazi collaboration or far-right ideological affiliations. The majority of those arrested were deported to the Soviet Union, primarily to gulags in Siberia and the wastelands of Kazakhstan, along with 400,000 Volga Germans. Of the 40,000 Swabians deported to the USSR for use as forced labour, half of them never returned. A large number of those arrested and executed by the Soviets before 1946 were legitimate war criminals, and although thousands of Hungarians and Swabians volunteered for the Honvédség (Hungarian Defence Force) or the Waffen-SS, many civilians gradually developed diverse political beliefs as the Axis neared its inevitable defeat.

Immediately after the Second World War, the only transport available in Hungary was the railway, despite the heavy damage caused by German bombing of the tracks and rolling stock. The first Hungarian State Railways' (MÁV) train of forty wagons departed on 19 January 1946 from Budaörs, near Budapest, to Mannheim in Baden-Württemberg, Germany, carrying 1,000 people, many of whom were accommodated in bunk beds in cattle cars. On the three-day journey in sub-zero temperatures, freezing to death was a distinct possibility.

Between January and June 1946, 118,474 Swabians had been expatriated, but the programme was suspended on 4 June on orders from the US authorities in Germany, which was investigating reports of abuse against the deportees being observed in the shipping out the Swabian trains, the disorderly manner in which the programme was executed, and the inhumaneness consequent to burdening German welfare agencies with penniless and destitute people. Discussions were begun between Hungarian authorities and US authorities concerning a resumption of the programme. US authorities insisted that certain conditions be met by the Hungarian authorities to ensure that the programme would be executed in an orderly and humane manner.

After a series of conferences, an agreement on the conditions to be established for the execution of the Swabian expatriation programme was reached on 22 August 1946. The agreement provided detailed conditions concerning the execution of transfers such as amounts of food, baggage, personal possessions, and minimum amounts of money for each expellee, health requirements, rate of flow, limitation of 1,100 expellees on each train, conditions under which the movement may be suspended, and similar requirements for an orderly and humane programme. The agreement stated that the expulsions would be resumed on 1 September 1946, and provided for a rate of flow of twenty trains per month of up to 90,000 expellees to 1 April 1947. After that date, the agreement stated that the Hungarian Government would consider the programme ended if the US Zone of Germany accepted a maximum of 100,000 expellees by the end of the year. However, during September, October and November 1946, while a total of fifty-two trains were scheduled for movement of Swabians, only six trains were utilised during the latter part of November due to the inability of the Hungarian authorities to provide Reichsmarks for the Swabians, of whom only 6,090 had been expatriated up to 30 November 1946.

Until June 1948, 63,794 people are recorded to have been relocated from the territory of the directorate to the Anglo-Saxon and the Soviet zones of Germany. According to the few MÁV records, there were eight relocation trains from Baranya County, and one from Szekszárd in September 1947. According to the schedules, the trains arrived via Budapest at the Hungarian-Czechoslovakian border station in Szob. From Szekszárd, the journey lasted seventeen hours, but from Mohács or Magyarbóly, the journey lasted up to twenty-four hours. The railwaymen themselves were also hit hard by the Danubian Swabians' deportations. The chief of Bátaszék station wrote a letter in August 1947 asking the director for help, reporting a severe problem triggered by the restarted deportations. Around 200 railwaymen in the vicinity had been threatened with deportation due to their ancestry, and as a result of ongoing tensions over this situation, a proper service could not be provided by them.

Besides Hungary, Yugoslavia was also trying to get rid of its German nationals. Those who had not fled during the winter of 1944 were later put onto trains which set off to Germany via Hungary, with no food, water, or medical supplies. During the long weeks of travelling, epidemics decimated the 'passengers' due to the harsh conditions. In one case of the refusal of the Yugoslavian train from Germany, it was forced to wait at the border station of Murakeresztúr from 25 January to 10 February 1946, with 1,378 people on board waiting to be handed over to the Yugoslavian railways. Seventy-eight people died from enteritis during that time.

Until the end of 1948, 2,583 families in 118 villages of Baranya County, 366 families in twenty-four settlements in Somogy County, and 1,624 families in fifty-three villages in Tolna County were resettled. Trains carrying Hungarians from Czechoslovakian territory were recorded for the first time only in the October and November monthly reports in 1947, but only in passing, as a reason for the increase in traffic. On 21 March 1948, however, special trains were commandeered from Baranya and Tolna to carry the deported Hungarians to Pécs In the final year, the arrival of a total of 147 'settler trains' were recorded in the annual summary of the regional directorate.

Romania, which along with Hungary had initially sided with Germany, then changed sides. As part of their policy of 'German war reparations', the Soviets ordered the expulsion of Germans from Romania to the Soviet Union early in 1945, to be used as forced labour. The order, according to the 1944 secret Soviet Order 7161 issued on 6 January 1945, was given to the last non-communist government of Romania under Prime Minister Nicolae Rădescu, and applied to all males between the ages of 17 and 45, and women between 18 and 30. Only pregnant women, women with children less than a year old and persons unable to work were excluded.

Arrests had already begun in Bucharest and Braşov by 13 January. The Rădescu government feigned protest, and even raised concerns regarding the fate of the women and children left behind. But the fate of the Germans had already been planned, and the Romanian authorities had assisted the Soviets in its implementation. The state railway had begun to prepare cattle wagons weeks in advance, in readiness to transport the expellees. The mission was accomplished with the Romanian authorities, Red Army units, and Soviet Main Intelligence Directorate (GRU) agents. Rădescu did not envision expulsions and that Romanian industry would suffer following the deportation of so much of its workforce, and especially of a high percentage of its skilled workforce, warning that the Soviet Union would not allow Northern Transylvania to be awarded back to Romania if Rădescu were to remain prime minister. He resigned his position on 1 March.

The expellees were sent to eighty-five separate camps where, regardless of their previous occupations or professions, one-third of them were sent to work in mines, a fourth of the remainder in construction, and the rest in industry, agriculture or camp administration. Around 10 per cent died during transportation, and from abuse by the Russians. Some of those who were unsuitable for work were returned to Transylvania at the end of 1945, and between 1946 and 1947 about 5,100 people were sent to the Soviet occupation zone of Germany. When they were freed, a quarter of deportees were sent to Germany, of whom just one-seventh returned to Transylvania. In 1948, about half of those remaining in camps were freed and in October 1949, the camps were shut down. The last third of the expellees returned to Transylvania. From a population of 298,000 Siebenbürgen Germans in 1941, 50,000 simply vanished during the ethnic cleansing.

The second phase of expulsions was organised to completely remove the entirety of the Danube Swabian community from Hungary. The Allied

Control Commission was goaded by Soviet Marshall Kliment Voroshilov and Lieutenant General Vladimir Sviridov (acting deputy chairman of the ACC) to expel at least 500,000 Danube Swabians immediately on the generalised ethnic grounds that fancifully depicted all German people as inherently pro-Nazi proponents of atrocities.

Soldiers and volunteers carried out the removal of the Danube Swabians from their homes. A great number of families had lived and worked on the same land for generations, with some of their ancestors having settled in Hungary over 200 years ago and, despite their hybridity as ethnocultural and the relatively secluded lifestyle that it had provided for them, considered Hungary as much their home as Germany. Their ethnically diverse state was the reason behind the expulsion order as it was considered to be a threat to cohesive nationalism.

Commissioners were appointed to organise and carry out the transfer of the Swabians to Germany. Led by the communist László Rajk, the Ministry of the Interior fully supported the total expulsion of the German-speaking minority. Hungarian authorities closed down the villages designated for deportation and they were sometimes encircled at night to prevent the escape of the Swabian residents. With the lack of legal regulation and proper preparation, the expulsion process was very badly organised, and the expulsion authorities operated free of control, and there were many examples of violence, thefts and looting. The task of the Hungarian authorities was further complicated by the ambiguous attitude of the Allied Powers towards the expulsions.

The German population's loyalty to the nation was investigated and tested through four local commissions which were established in July in the German-populated districts of Hungary. Around 70,000 people were examined, of whom around 30 per cent were exempted from expulsion. The commission was dissolved in January–February 1946 when the first of the mass expulsions got under way.

The Swabians were escorted to train lines and truck convoys that were waiting to transport them to one of four internment camps established by the government, where they underwent a medical examination. The transports for Germany left from the internment camps after enough people had been gathered there. One transport train normally consisted of forty coaches, each carrying twenty-five people. Every train had at least one doctor and two nurses on them. Each expellee could carry 20kg food and 80kg clothing. The first transport left on 19 January to the

American Zone of occupied Germany, collecting the Germans in the vicinity of Budapest (from the Buda Hills and the Pilis) and by July, around 120,000 Germans had been expelled from Hungary.

At least 130,000 direct shipments of families are recorded in the first phase to the American zone, especially in Austria, Bavaria, Baden-Württemberg, and Hessen. Right behind them, more than 130,000 displaced Hungarians on their way to resettle in the vacated lands. The Hungarian statistical office stated that in 1941 there were 533,045 ethnic Germans, and in 1949 just 22,455. Those who were deported to Germany founded a discord with its people, culture and language, and the Swabians struggled to grip onto their unique cultural identity. Many subsequently immigrated to countries like the United States, Canada and Australia and established small communities, while others attempted to overtly assimilate. Many of those that remained in Hungary were frightened to outwardly express their cultural identity, which was further repressed under communist rule.

According to the request of the Soviet-dominated Allied Control Authority (ACC), the expulsions should have been completed by August 1946, with the Hungarian government carrying out the deportations as quickly as possible, but the American authorities, who had complained continuously about the physical condition of the expelled people arriving from Hungary (although the extremely high costs involved in the resettlement of expelled Germans in the occupied territories may have been the real reason), tried to slow down the expulsion process by continually holding up the transports of German expellees at the borders, as well as argue with the Hungarian Foreign Ministry against the necessity of expulsions.

The subsequent delays and pressure from both sides made it difficult for the Hungarian government to foster and maintain acceptably humane management of the expulsion process, and tensions began to rise in the internment camps, where the German nationals awaiting transportation were amassed with quite inadequate facilities. The knock-on effect of the delays was greater felt in the villages, where some of the settlers moved in to take over the confiscated lands only to find that the previous occupants had not yet been evicted by the authorities.

While the Smallholders Party wanted to suspend the expulsion process, other political parties argued for the exemption of favoured social groups. The communists wanted to retain miners and industrial workers of German nationality for its two strongest industries. Between the two world wars, the Hungarian oil men proved that, despite the unfavourable geological settings, good results could be obtained; developments made in geophysical principles enabled major units of migration and the regional zones of accumulation to be better identified, making it possible to concentrate exploration on the most promising areas. This is what Hitler had intended to do as the Reich had increased its financial and economic presence in Hungary. The timber industry, for example, was developed by joint Axis and Hungarian firms. The Aluminium industry was largely German-controlled, and they had also obtained large interests in the Hungarian oil, coal and power industries, the bauxite mines, and the aircraft works. I.G. Farben had also gained a firm foothold in Hungary's chemical industry.

The escalation of problems related to the German expulsion led to Ministry of Interior to introduce a series of modifications to the decree that ordered the population transfer. One of these, issued on 10 May 1946, limited the scope of expulsions to Germans who were members of the SS and the Volksbund during the war, or those who had re-Germanised their names. A further decree was passed in the same month which exempted Germans who had joined the SS under coercion. The amendments to the decree exacerbated the situation, and by June 1946, with only 25 per cent of the number requested by the ACC, it soon became apparent that the target number of expulsions to be carried out by August could not be met.

The combined problems with the set-backs in the resettlement of Hungarian refugees from the neighbouring countries and the serious financial and economic problems that accompanied the process, together with the delays in the population transfers, prompted the Hungarian government to restart the negotiations with the American government concerning the expulsion of the German population. A new agreement was signed on 22 August 1946 after the Hungarian government accepted the requirements of the United States, which: forbade the separation of expelled families, and raised the amount of luggage each expellee could carry to 100kg (220lb). They also limited the number of transport trains that could leave every month for Germany to twenty, but the most difficult part of the agreement for the Hungarian government was its obligation to provide every expellee with an allowance of 500 Reichsmarks.

Despite its high costs, the Hungarian Council of Ministers decided to resume the expulsion of the German-speaking population recommenced in November 1946. The Soviet Union agreed to a request by the ACC on 11 June 1947 to resettle 50,000 people in the Soviet zone of occupied Germany. The expulsions recommenced on 19 August, and by the end of the month, 10,381 people of German origin had been expelled. However, less than half of them reached the Soviet Zone of Germany, as the number of escapes increased sharply; 6,720 had escaped out of the above-mentioned figure. The Soviet zone was further away, and the Hungarian government had to negotiate with the Czechoslovakian authorities. Through the thirst of confiscating their lands and redistributing the estates among the poorest peasants, only the wealthy Germans were subsequently deported. The second wave of the expulsions became even less controlled, and with no influential political force at that time to speak up for the Germans, the number of thefts and violent actions increased.

From January 1946, around 130,000 Swabians had been shipped on trains to the American zone in Germany, when the Americans halted the whole process in late June 1947. The American administration had become overwhelmed, having to process and accommodate more than 100,000 German civilians expelled from Czechoslovakia, Yugoslavia, and the Netherlands, with housing, adequate employment and basic sustenance. One of the major challenges was to maintain public health, both for humanitarian reasons and to protect the health of the occupying forces. Bombed and partially destroyed cities and towns with badly damaged fresh water supplies, overcrowding in dwellings deemed still to be habitable, and hundreds of thousands of displaced persons, refugees, and expellees arriving and leaving daily, coupled with shortages in hospital facilities and inadequate supplies of linen, bandages, and shortages in medicines, all together produced a serious threat of epidemics – especially of Typhoid fever. Major-General Morrison C. Stayer, Chief of Public Health & Welfare Officer of the Allied Military Government in Germany, led the public health specialists attached to the teams from the military government to try to restore conducive conditions.

This task in itself was monumental, having to work with the remnants of the German health system to reopen pharmaceutical stores and hospital facilities, which was further compounded by having to denazify the various health agencies and professions. Contagious diseases such as diphtheria, tuberculosis, and typhoid fever steadily increased, but not at a rate fast enough to cause a panic or fear that it could not be controlled. Dichlorodiphenyltrichloroethane (DDT) dusting stations were established at border crossing points. Miraculously, Typhus was kept out of the American zone, and mass inoculations were quickly undertaken in the most threatened areas against the other diseases while the water supplies were repaired and chlorination provided.

Programmes were set up to tackle malnutrition, which included the periodic random selection from the 25,000 people in the Western sectors of Berlin, for weighing-in by the Americans, and later by the Germans. Poliomyelitis developed in Berlin during the autumn of 1947, and four American specialists, six respirators, and equipment for hot pack therapy (to relieve the pain and promote the relaxation of tight muscles), were rushed to Berlin by air by the 'The March of Dimes' (National Foundation for Infantile Paralysis, which had been organised in 1938 to combat Polio), and this humanitarian act was greatly appreciated by the German people. The total number of cases of poliomyelitis was 2,464, of which 218 resulted in death. The issue of venereal disease also became a problem. Through the nomadic existences of a large number of expellees, the lack of sanitation, and the lack of drugs for treatment, the disease had peaked in August 1946 with rates for syphilis of thirty, and gonorrhoea of ninety, per 10,000 population per annum. The number of cases was significantly reduced by the summer of 1949.

The Danube Swabians who had joined the Waffen-SS in 1942, had done so voluntarily, but in 1944, they were forced into the Waffen-SS against their will, and with the full sanction of the Hungarian government. The Waffen-SS, which was originally intended as a palace guard to protect Adolf Hitler, grew massively in size and scale, and had become a multi-national army, and was perceived as being the military 'elite'. This elite character of the recruits of 1942 resulted in many of them serving as guards at the concentration camps, and many of them paid the price in the punishment they received from the Allies, especially the Soviets, who sought to punish them collectively, and not for their actions as individuals. All of those who fell into Soviet hands, and were found to have the SS tattoo were beaten, starved and were put to hard labour in the Gulags. The issue was always centred on their Hungarian citizenship and German nationality. It is documented that at least 35,000 Danube Swabians were forcibly relocated on trains to Saxony alone in 1947, under far worse conditions than the first phase of expulsion. By the end of the war, at least 50,000 had been expelled to East Germany.

By January 1948, the standards of the German State Public Health departments were starting to meet the requirements in the American zone; they were functioning satisfactorily, and medical supplies had become available and stocked in the hospitals, which had undergone extensive repairs, and had created more space for beds.

After the deportations to the American zone in West Germany ended, the Soviet expulsion campaign resumed. The administration of East Germany under Soviet control, and so were unhindered by the Americans in shipping the Swabians to Soviet-occupied Saxony and Brandenburg. In complete contrast to the expulsions to the American zone, these Swabians, who were generalised as potentially perfidious, often endured ethnic violence, forced labour, imprisonment, and execution. Even after the expulsions formally ended in October 1949 under the decree of the Hungarian government via Prime Ministerial Decree No. 4274/1949, Danube Swabian families (including women and children) languished in prison and refugee camps for years under dubious conditions. Many spent years in internment camps in the remote steppes of north-eastern Hungary, especially in Tiszalök, one of four camps (Recsk, Kistarcsa, Tiszalök and Kazincbarcika) that were set up by the political police. The Mátyás Rákosi government, previously under the de facto control of the ACC, and increasingly by the Soviets, gradually asserted itself as an increasingly autonomous communist state. On 25 March 1950, the Hungarian government formally withdrew all repatriation and exile restrictions on the Swabians, allowing them to return to their homeland of Hungary from the territories within the Soviet orbit.

During his speech in parliament on 4 July 1953, Prime Minister Imre Nagy announced that according to the policy of the new period, flagrant cases of injustice, such as internment, police jurisdiction, deportation and the repression of Kulaks, would be ceased. The Presidential Council of the Hungarian People's Republic issued a Decree of Amnesty on 26 July, and the Council of Ministers subsequently passed a resolution about ceasing internment and deportation and dissolving the internment camps.

The internment camp at Tiszalök was set up on the site for a new river dam and hydro-electric power station that had been planned there. The majority of the 1,440–1,500 Swabian and ethnic German inhabitants were prisoners of war, who were handed over by the Soviet authorities in December 1950 and early 1951, but the Hungarian ÁVH did not set them free. Their clothing had been taken away and they had been issued with prison uniforms with a long red stripe across the back of the jackets, were billeted in the barracks of the camp. It was run much like a concentration camp as 'special punishment' for them being prisoners of war, or having previously served in the Waffen-SS; they served as slave labour under inhumane conditions in the construction projects. The daily food allowance for each person was 400g (14oz) of bread and potato and bean soup, and no one was allowed to speak other than in the barracks. On 4 October 1953, the prisoners demonstrated against their captivity and the harsh conditions under which they lived. Five of the men were shot as an example to the others. The prisoners were all freed by 4 December 1953.

Chapter Six

Poland

Following the 'September Campaign' – the German invasion of Poland from the west on 1 September 1939, and from the east by the Soviets sixteen days later, the territory was divided between Germany and the Soviet Union, the intention being to eradicate Polish culture and subjugate its people. Tensions had soared in Europe after Hitler's defiance of the Munich Agreement, and on the afternoon of 31 March, Prime Minister Neville Chamberlain had stated in the House of Commons that,

> His Majesty's Government would feel themselves bound at once to lend the Polish Government all support in their power. They have given the Polish Government an assurance to this effect. I may add that the French Government have authorised me to make it plain that they stand in the same position in this matter as do His Majesty's Government.[1]

France and the United Kingdom subsequently declared war on Germany on 3 September, but it was of little help to the Poles. French troops made a brief and ineffective advance toward the Siegfried Line (The Saar Offensive) on Germany's western frontier from 7 September, and in some areas, gained a foothold five miles into Germany, taking a few towns and villages along the way, but they withdrew after being met by a German counter-offensive in Saarland on 17 September. Three days later, following the Polish defeat at the Battle of Kock, German and Soviet forces gained full control over Poland. Around 650,000 Polish troops were killed in the fighting, and a further 660,000 were captured as Prisoners of War. Some 130,000 escaped to neutral Romania through the Romanian Bridgehead and Hungary, and another 20,000 to Latvia and Lithuania, with the majority eventually making their way to France or Britain.

Soviet authorities immediately started a campaign of Sovietisation – the adoption of a political system based on institutions, laws, customs, traditions, culture, and the way of life of soviets. A resident register was established of carefully selected people who still lived in the newly acquired territories Western Belarus and Western Ukraine, and Soviet citizenship was imposed upon them. Those did not receive the citizenship, or refused to accept it, were arrested or deported.

The German invasion of Poland was a primer on how Hitler intended to wage war – what would become the 'blitzkrieg' strategy. After extensive aerial bombing to incapacitate or destroy Poland's air capacity, railway networks, communications and munitions dumps, the ground offensive started, with more than 2,000 tanks and overwhelming numbers of troops and artillery breaking through Polish defences. Warsaw surrendered to the Germans on 27 September 1939, and by the end of the month, the number of Jews in and around the capital city of Warsaw had increased dramatically, with thousands of refugees escaping the Polish-German front, often on foot. In less than a year, the number of refugees had in exceeded 90,000.

In October 1939, Germany directly annexed former Polish territories along German's eastern border: West Prussia, Poznan, Upper Silesia, and the former Free City of Danzig (now Gdańsk). The remainder of German-occupied Poland (including the cities of Warsaw, Kraków, Radom, and Lublin) was organised as the so-called Generalgouvernement (General Government) under a civilian governor-general, the Nazi Party lawyer Hans Frank. Security forces were immediately set up to annihilate all enemies of his Nazi ideology, whether racial, religious, or political.

Adam Czerniaków, an engineer and politician, was appointed on 4 October to head the Judenrat (Jewish Council) – a committee of twenty-four people, who would be responsible for carrying out German orders. On 26 October, the Jews were mobilised as forced labourers to clear bomb damage and perform other hard labour. All Jewish establishments were ordered to display a Jewish star on doors and windows from 23 November, and in December all Jews older than 10 were compelled to wear a white armband and were forbidden to use public transport.

The first mass killings of civilians took place on 7-8 December 1939 in a forest glade near the village of Palmiry, in the Kampinos Forest, north-west of Warsaw, when eighty prisoners were executed by the Schutzstaffel (SS) and Ordnungspolizei (German Order Police). This was the first of a wave of executions of more than 1,700 Poles and Jews that continued until July 1941. They were mostly Jewish inmates of Warsaw's Pawiak prison, but included prisoners from Pruszków, Zakroczym, Legionowo, Henryków, and Jabłonna, as well as those who carried out retaliation murders following clashes on 28 March 1940 between German police and members of the underground organisation Wilki (The Wolves) near the home of its commander, Józef Bruckner, in Sosnowa Street, Warsaw.

Although Germans in the General Government were less adequately prepared to properly deal with Poland's elites, by the end of 1939 they murdered 5,000 members of the Intelligentsia, with the most renowned act of repression being the 'Sonderaktion Krakau', a criminal act aimed at Polish intellectuals, which was conducted on 6 November 1939, and saw 183 professors, associate professors, and assistants of the Jagiellonian University and AGH University of Science and Technology in Kraków arrested and sent to their death in the Sachsenhausen Concentration Camp in Oranienburg, Germany.

The Katyn Massacre

After the Red Army invaded Eastern Poland in September 1939, soldiers of the Polish Army and Border Defence Corps, officers of the State Police and of other Polish state services prisoners of war, were captured by the Red Army and accommodated in NKVD prison camps in Kozelsk, Starobelsk, Ostashkov, Kalinin (now Tver), as well as Polish civilians who had been arrested from other locations in the territory of the USSR by its state functionaries acting on instructions from the authorities of their state, which was then allied with the Third Reich. Between 5 March and an unspecified date in 1940, 21,768 Polish citizens were shot. The atrocity was discovered in the spring following the German invasion of Russia in July 1942, and the bodies exhumed and examined. The Russians denied all responsibility and countered the accusation by saying that the Germans had committed the massacre. When Polish Prime Minister Sikorski called for an investigation by the International Red Cross, the Russian government abruptly severed all diplomatic ties with Poland.

In April 1940, the Polish prisoners were told that they would be repatriated to Poland. On 3 April, the first 'death transport' was dispatched from the camp in Kozelsk, but the train did not travel east, but rather westward. Upon arrival at the station at Gniezdowo near Smoleńsk, the prisoners were herded into black vans which drove them to a clearing in the Katyn Forest. When they stepped out, the Russians took them to a large, previously dug pit, and forced them to kneel at its edge. Their hands were tied behind their backs, and a choke knot tied around their neck and hands so that if they struggled they would have strangled themselves. They were surrounded by dozens of armed NKVD agents who systematically shot each Pole in the back of the head. The transfers from the camp to the forest went on for several weeks. By mid-May, almost 4,500 Polish officers were murdered and buried in eight mass graves – the largest of which contained twelve layers of corpses.

The murder of the prisoners from Starobelsk began on 5 April 1940, when large groups of prisoners were sent by rail to Kharkov, and placed in an internal NKVD prison, where the victims were executed by pistol shots below the back of the head. The bodies were buried in trenches in Region Six of the forest-park zone, near the village of Pyatikhatka, near Kharkov; 3,739 prisoners from Starobelsk were executed. The same fate awaited the prisoners in Ostashkov, who were removed in large groups, from 5 April 1940 onwards, from the camp to the NKVD prison in Kalinin. They were killed in a specially prepared cell by shots to the back of the head. The bodies were buried in the village of Mednoye; 6,314 prisoners from this camp died.

Churchill and Roosevelt entertained few illusions about what happened in the Katyn Forest. Churchill, wanting to avoid Anglo-Soviet recriminations, actually criticised the Polish government-in-exile, which had been formed in France in the aftermath of the invasion of Poland in September 1939, for even having called for an investigation. They feared that the Soviets would be tempted to organise and recognise a puppet regime designed for imposition on post-war Poland – the country for which Great Britain had so nobly gone to war in 1939. He judged that the best hope of avoiding this humiliation would be to persuade Stalin to forgive the London Poles and restore diplomatic relations with them; to bring this about, he telegraphed to Stalin,

> Eden and I have pointed out to the Polish government that no resumption of friendly or working relations with the Soviets is possible while they [the Poles] make charges of

an insulting character against the Soviet government ... We earnestly hope that ... you will consider this matter in a spirit of magnanimity.[2]

Roosevelt was indifferent to the entire 'graves question', as he put it. His main concern at the time was that he might lose the Polish-American vote if they were ever to find out that Stalin had broken off diplomatic relations with Poland. The Allies ordered a media ban which prevented the public from knowing that Stalin was the one responsible for the Katyn massacre.

Kidnapped Children

Plans to kidnap or otherwise separate from their parents, racially valuable Polish children to be 'Germanised' were outlined in documents sent to Heinrich Himmler on 25 November 1939. Himmler, whose title at the time was 'Reichskomissar for the consolidation of German nationality', had been made responsible two weeks earlier after receiving a forty-page document of policies regarding the population of occupied territories, titled, 'The issue of the treatment of population in former Polish territories from a racial-political view'. From it, he defined special directives for the forcible kidnapping of children of no more than 8 or 10 years old to be placed in the care of the Reich, where they would receive educational adjustment for German plans and purposes. The directive also meant that viable children, who were either abducted from German-occupied Poland or taken away from Polish forced labourers in Germany, should be excluded from deportation and assigned German names, with an ancestry designed by a special office.

In a memorandum from Himmler titled 'Einige Gedanken ueber die Behandlung der Fremdenvoelker im Osten'[3] ('Some thoughts about the treatment of foreigners in the East') on 15 May 1940, it was outlined that in the territory of Poland, only four grade schools would remain, in which education would be strictly limited. Children would be taught to count only to 500, to write their own name, and that God commanded Poles to serve Germans. Writing was determined to be unnecessary for the Polish population, and parents who desired better education for their children would have to apply to the SS and police for a special permit.

The permit would be awarded to children deemed 'racially valuable'. The fate of each child would be determined by the loyalty and obedience to the German state of his or her parents. A child determined to be 'of little racial value' would not receive any further education, and were sent to the German death camps, where they were either murdered or forced to serve as living test subjects in German medical experiments and were often tortured or killed in the process.

Annual selection would be made every year among children according to German racial standards. Children deemed adequately German would be taken, and informed that their parents were dead even if they were not. They would then go through a selection process which included a detailed racial examination, combined with psychological tests and medical exams made by experts from the SS 'Race and Settlement Main Office' ('RuSHA', which was founded by Himmler with Richard Walther Darré, one of the leading Nazi 'blood and soil' ideologists, in 1931, and was the organisation responsible for safeguarding the racial 'purity' of the SS within Nazi Germany), or doctors from the Gesundheitsamt (the Health Department). The most important part of the process was based on the colour of eyes and hair, and the shape of the skull. Minors with blue eyes and blond hair were selected in accordance with Adolf Hitler's ideal of a pure Germanic 'Aryan' race. The plan aimed to destroy the Polish as an ethnic group, and leave within Poland, a considerable slave population to be used up over the next ten years. Within fifteen to twenty years, Poles would be completely eradicated. The SS Lebensborn Association was responsible for carrying out these actions, as well as the state-funded project to choose young women to have sex with SS officers in the hope of producing an Aryan child to counteract falling birth rates in Germany and produce a 'Master Race' in accordance with Nazi eugenics.

The successful 'candidates' would have their names altered to similar-sounding German ones, and then go through the further Germanisation, during which they were compelled to learn the German language, and were beaten if they persisted in speaking Polish. When they were deemed ready, they were placed for adoption. Prospective German foster parents would be told that children had received false Polish birth certificates to rob them of their German heritage. The successful couples would be issued with false German birth certificates.

Hitler approved Himmler's directives on 20 June, and ordered copies to be sent to chief organs of the SS, to Gauleiters in German-occupied territories in Central Europe, and the governor of General Government, commanding that the operation of kidnapping Polish children to seek Aryan descendants for Germanisation be a priority in those territories. Children were hunted in schools, parks, and markets. The Nazis also went to people's homes with guns drawn to seize children. According to official Polish estimates, approximately 200,000 Polish children were abducted by the Nazis between 1940 and 1945.

Thousands of children who did not pass harsh Nazi exams and criteria, and their racist categorisation as 'acceptable' or 'undesirable' determined their fate; whether they would be killed, or sent to concentration camps, or experience other consequences. They were transferred by railway to Garwolin, Mrozów, Sobolew, Łosice, Chełm and other cities, and over 10,000 died in camps at Zwierzyniec, Zamość, Auschwitz, and Majdanek. Many died as a result of suffocation in the summer and cold in the winter. Polish railway workers, often risking their lives, would try to get food to the imprisoned children or give them warm clothes.

A special camp was established at Zamość, Poland, where, after racial examination, children selected for Germanisation were separated from their mothers. A similar facility was opened in 1942 in the city of Łódź, located adjacent to the ghetto. There, children between the ages of 12 and 16 were processed. Those who didn't meet the requirements were sent for extermination in Auschwitz. On 23 February 1943, thirty-nine boys of ages 13 to 17, who arrived from Zamość, were murdered almost immediately. One at a time, and occasionally blindfolded with a piece of a towel, they were placed on a stool. The person performing the execution then placed one of his hands on the back of the child's neck and another behind the shoulder blade. As the child's chest was thrust out, a long needle was used to inject a toxic dose of phenol into the chest. While in the throes of death, he would be taken from the stool and thrown onto a pile of corpses in another room, while the next child took his place on the stool.

Children were also sent as test subjects for experiments in special centres, which profited greatly from the increased availability of human 'material'. Many children were sent from one such centre, a Medical Nursing Home at Lubliniec, Upper Silesia, to the Neurological Institute in Breslau, where they were examined by Hans-Joachim Scherer before experiments in a forced euthanasia programme, after which their brains were used for research by neuropathologists. One of the most prominent

German physicians and neuroscientists, Julius Hallervorden, of the Kaiser Wilhelm Institute for Brain Research (KWI), who supported the murder of the children for experiments, performed histopathological studies on a total of 697 brains.

A second special centre was located in the town of Cieszyn, on the east bank of the Olza River, where the children would be given psychoactive drugs, chemicals and other substances for medical tests. The weakest children usually succumbed to the effect of the drugs and died within a relatively short time; those who survived longer than predicted brought about greater curiosity. All side-effects were recorded as well as changes in behaviour patterns. As most died, the documentation was forged to conceal traces of experiments, for example, giving the cause of death as from a lung infection or a weak heart.

After the war, the eighth of the twelve Nuremberg Trials, the United States of America vs. Ulrich Greifelt, et al, took place from 20 October 1947 to 10 March 1948. The fourteen defendants were all officials of various SS organisations responsible for the implementation of the Nazi 'pure race' programme, including Ulrich Greifelt, the Chief of Staff of RuSHA, along with Heads of Staff Richard Hildebrandt and Fritz Schwalm of RuSHA, the Heads of Staff Konrad Meyer-Hetling, Otto Schwarzenberger, Rudolf Creutz, and Herbert Hübner of the office of the Reich Commissioner for the Consolidation of German Nationhood (RKFDV), Werner Lorenz, Heinz Brückner, and Otto Hofmann of the Repatriation Office for Ethnic Germans (VoMi), Max Sollmann, Gregor Ebner, Günther Tesch, and Inge Viermetz, of the Lebensborn society, with the charges centred on their racial cleansing and resettlement activities. All the defendants pleaded 'not guilty'.

The four Lebensborn members were not found guilty, and the tribunal considered the Lebensborn society not responsible for the kidnapping of children, which was carried out by others. Greifelt was sentenced to life imprisonment (died in 1949); Creutz, fifteen years (released in 1955 and died in 1980); Hübner, fifteen years (released 1951); Lorenz, twenty years (released in 1955, and died in 1974; Brückner, fifteen years (released in 1951); Hofmann, twenty-five years (Released in 1954, and died in 1982); Hildebrandt, twenty-five years (died in 1952); and Schwalm, ten Years (released in 1951). Meyer-Hetling, Schwarzenberger, Sollmann, Ebner, and Tesch, were released after judgement for time already served, and Viermetz was acquitted.

Poland

The Nazi kidnapping of children was kept highly secret under the leadership of the SS, and in the years after the war, some children lived and died believing themselves to be German, unaware of their hidden Polish ancestry. Today hundreds of thousands of Germans might likely be descended from kidnapped Polish children.

Deportations

The first of four mass deportations of Poles, Jews, and Byelorussians to remove the ruling classes and Germanise the lands that were incorporated into the Reich, was carried out by the Einsatzgruppen on the night of 9–10 February 1940. These were intellectuals, civil servants, priests and religious leaders, political and social workers, and landowning farmers. The Germans demanded Czerniaków to order the members of the Judenrat to assist in organising the deportations from Warsaw, but he refused. The mass deportation and extermination of Jews known as the 'Grossaktion Warsaw' commenced on 26 October 1940. Czerniaków committed suicide the following day by swallowing a cyanide pill. He left a suicide note to his wife, which read, 'They demand me to kill children of my nation with my own hands. I have nothing to do but to die.' The German SS and police personnel used violence to force Jews out of their homes or places of work, and march them to the Umschlagplatz (holding area) adjacent to the Anhalter Bahnhof railway station. There, they underwent a selection process and made to board freight cars bound for Małkinia, on the Warsaw-Bialystok rail line. When the trains arrived in Malkinia, they were diverted along a special rail spur to Treblinka. The fourth and last mass deportation ended just a few hours before the German invasion of Russia in June 1941.

The Jewish Fighting Organisation 'ŻOZOB' (Zydowska Organizacja Bojowa) was established amid the first wave of deportations, which had begun on 22 July 1942 on a massive scale, from Warsaw ghetto to the Treblinka killing centre. ŻOB, which was comprised of members of Jewish youth organisations, called for the Jews of the ghetto to resist deportation. When a document, published by the Hashomer Hatzair movement three months before the start of the deportations reached the ghetto, declaring the true fate at the Treblinka extermination camp that awaited the people who were being rounded up under the guise of the

Nazi 'Resettlement in the East' programme, the youth groups took it seriously and had no illusions about the true intentions of the Germans – to annihilate Warsaw Jewry.

During this time more than 250,000 Jews from the ghetto were deported or killed, and reports of the massacres of Jews by mobile killing units and in killing centres had already filtered back to the ghetto. It wasn't until the deportations ended in September that ŻOB was able to expand, and with 23-year-old Mordechai Anielewicz appointed as its commander, it incorporated members of underground political organisations and established contact with the Polish resistance forces who provided training, armaments and explosives. On Monday, 18 January 1943, members of the Hashomer Hatzair group, led by Mordechai Anielewicz, and armed with pistols they had received from the Polish Home Army (AK), intercepted a column of Jews being rounded for deportation by German troops, and fired upon the soldiers. During the ensuing battle, which was the first armed action to be undertaken within the ghetto, the Germans sustained casualties, but almost all of the Jewish fighters were shot. Anielewicz managed to overpower the soldier with whom he was struggling and escaped unharmed. The news of the clash spread quickly to other cells of the underground, and they too began to resist. Yitzhak Zuckerman, with a party from the Dror Youth Movement, lay in wait for the German force on Zamenhof Street, and fired a volley at them when they approached. There was shooting from within too, from several ŻOB fighters who had intentionally crept into the column of deportees.

Over four days the Germans tried to round up Jews and were met by armed resistance. The ghetto inhabitants went through a swift change. With the news of the first incident of fighting, they stopped responding to the Germans' calls that they must gather in the Umschlagplatz. They began to devise hiding places, so the Germans had to enter many buildings and ruthlessly pull out Jews. Many were killed in their homes when they refused to be taken. On the fourth day, having only managed to seize 5–6,000 Jews, the Germans withdrew from the ghetto. The remaining inhabitants believed that the armed resistance, combined with the difficulties in finding Jews in hiding, had led to the end of the AB Aktion. As a result, the armed undergrounds sought to strengthen themselves over the next months, and the vast majority of ghetto residents zealously built more and better bunkers in which to hide.

The ŻOB organisation, led by Anielewicz, became unified and organised, and a full-scale strategic revolt was planned out by the Jews. Underground shelters had been dug, including the headquarters of ŻOB, located at Ulica Miła 18 (18 Pleasant Street), and a network of roof-top passages and breaches of basement walls provided runs right through the tenements; the Jews of the Warsaw ghetto were prepared to fight to the end. The advantage was lost, however, when on the eve of Passover on 19 April, the Germans began systematically burning all of the buildings of the ghetto, trying to force the fighters to leave their hiding places.

After a month of fighting, Warsaw's Great Synagogue was razed under the orders of German Police General Jürgen Stroop, who had been in charge of the final deportations, and declared the Grossaktion, finished. Resistance continued for weeks as the Germans reduced the ghetto to rubble. Some of the resistance fighters who managed to escape the carnage joined partisan groups in the forests around Warsaw. Altogether, around 1.4 million Polish citizens were sent to the Soviet interior between 1939 and 1941, including about 400,000 Jews. Conditions for the deportees were severe; perhaps one-third died of cold, malnutrition or disease.

Beginning in October 1939, increasing numbers of Jews were forced to live in ghettos in hundreds of locations throughout Poland, where food rations were minimal, living space overtaxed, and sanitary conditions inadequate, while they were subjected to persecution, terror and exploitation. Jews from smaller towns and villages were ordered to take up residence elsewhere, but were often deported to the ghettos in nearby cities to make room for 'pure' ethnic Germans to populate the new territory. The ghettos would come to serve as staging points for Jewish slave-labour and mass-deportation centres.

Ludwig Fischer, Governor of the Warsaw District, signed an order on 2 October 1940 to officially create a Jewish district ghetto in Warsaw, and all Varsovians (residents of Warsaw) of Jewish descent were ordered to relocate to the ghetto (which was referred to as the Jewish Quarter) by 1 November, while all the non-Jews domiciled within the new boundaries were ordered to move out. After that date, it would be sealed off from the outside world. The Jews were allowed to take personal effects only with them; all remaining property was confiscated. Jewish shops and businesses outside the ghetto were closed down and sealed off.

The building firm of Schmidt & Munstermann was contracted to build the wall, which was paid for by the Jewish community. The same firm would go on to help build the Treblinka death camp two years later. Work began on 1 April 1940 of what would become the largest ghetto in Nazi-occupied Europe, at 3.4 sq. km (1.3 sq. m), and a 3-metre high brick wall topped with barbed wire was erected around the perimeter. The enormity of the task subsequently led to a postponement of the deadline to 15 November. As with the city of Łódź, the public trolleybus lines ran through the middle of the ghetto, and these were fenced off and patrolled by the police.

113,000 gentile Poles were forced to resettle to the 'Aryan' side, and a further 138,000 Jews joined them from other districts of the capital. By April 1941, 395,000 lived in the ghetto, including 4,000 Jews from Germany. At that time, it contained more Jews than all of France, and a Jewish Police force (Jüdischer Ordnungsdienst), commanded by Colonel Josef Szerynski, was established with the primary task of combatting smuggling, and to generally keep order with the ghetto. At its height, the force had 2,000 members. With very few employment opportunities available, street trading became a necessity, and anything and everything was for sale or exchange as families fought fiercely to survive. From the very beginning of the ghetto's existence, the German administration had deliberately limited food supplies to the absolute minimum. The food rations for the inhabitants of the ghetto amounted to around 1lb of bread per person weekly, with practically nothing else and as a result, prices in the ghetto averaged ten times higher than outside. Mortality due to exhaustion, starvation and disease increased on an unprecedented scale. Great efforts were made and risks were taken to run community soup kitchens, and to look after orphans whose parents had starved to death, or had died of diseases such as Typhus that raged in the overpopulated ghetto, as its inhabitants struggled with malnutrition and the lack of any healthcare.

Communal institutions and voluntary organisations strove, at great risk, to imbue life with meaning and to provide for the public's needs, such as the education of their children, preservation of religious traditions, and the fulfilment of cultural activities. Books, intellectual pursuits, music and theatre served as an escape from the harsh reality surrounding them, enabling many to rise above the degradation and humiliation they suffered. Many Jews placed themselves in grave danger in the attempts to save the lives of others, especially children, who sneaked out through holes in the wall or via underground passageways, often several times a day, and returning with goods that could weigh as much as they did. Up to 80 per cent of food consumed in the ghetto was brought in illegally. Many of the Germans themselves participated in this illicit trading, drawing considerable incomes from bribes and profits, but if a person was discovered to be smuggling, they were taken to the central lockup located on Gęsia Street, and shot.

The deceased from the ghetto, of which there were scores each day, were picked up and stacked onto by an open cart from the Funeral Home of Moti Pinkiert, which made its rounds very early each morning, and transported the corpses to be disposed of by cremation in deep pits prepared at the Okopowa Street Jewish Cemetery. More often than not, bodies would be stripped by families of the deceased relatives, so they could sell their clothing and personal items to help them survive ghetto life. Between 1940 and mid-1942, an estimated 83,000 Jews had passed away from starvation and disease.

The right of entry and exit to the ghetto was restricted to the holders of special passes issued by the German authorities. All those who left the ghetto without such a pass became liable to the sentence of death, and it is known that the German courts passed such sentences in a high number of cases. The only ties with the outside world were handled by the Transferstelle Agency, which was established to monitor the traffic of goods entering and leaving the ghetto.

On 3 May 1941, a comprehensive survey of the acts of violence perpetrated against the people of Poland, which detailed offences against religion and cultural heritage and the destruction of property in Poland, was presented by the Polish government to the governments of the Allied and Neutral Powers, in the hope that the civilised world would draw the appropriate conclusions to the renewed German efforts at mass extinction, with the employment of fresh horrifying methods.

At the conference held at St James' Palace, London, on 13 January 1942, the governments of the occupied countries placed among their principal war aims, the punishment through the channel of organised justice, of those guilty of, or responsible for, those crimes, whether they had ordered them, perpetrated them, or participated in them. Despite the solemn warnings and declarations of President Roosevelt, of the prime minister, and of Vyacheslav Molotov, the People's Commissar for

Foreign Affairs, the German government did not cease to apply its methods of violence and terror.

Poland had attempted on several occasions, both in diplomatic documents and official publications, to draw to the attention of the civilised world the conduct of the German government and the German authorities of occupation, both military and civilian, and to the methods employed by them 'in order to reduce the population to virtual slavery and ultimately exterminate the Polish nation.' These methods, which were first introduced in Poland, were subsequently applied, in varying degrees, in other countries occupied by the armed forces of the German Reich.

The German persecution had intensified against the populations, and the information received from Poland been fully authenticated that the new methods of mass slaughter, particularly of the Jewish people, confirmed that the Nazis, with systematic deliberation, was aiming at the total extermination of the Jewish population of Poland, as well as the many thousands of Jews who the German authorities had deported to Poland from the Western and Central countries, and from the German Reich itself.

The outbreak of war between Germany and Soviet Russia on 22 June 1941, and the occupation of the eastern areas of Poland by German troops, considerably increased the number of Jews in Germany's power. At the same time, the mass murders of Jews reached such dimensions that at first, people refused to give credence to the reports reaching Warsaw from the Eastern provinces, but they were confirmed again and again by reliable witnesses.

The book reported that over 50,000 Jews, with ten members of the Judenrat administrative agency among them, had been massacred in the city of Vilna on 31 August 1941, during an action referred to as 'The Great Provocation', led by SS Einsatzkommando 9 Oberscharführer Horst Schweinberger under orders from the Gebietskommissar of the Vilnius municipality Hans Christian Hingst and Franz Murer, Hingst's deputy for Jewish affairs, under 'provisional directives' of Reichskommissar for the Ostland, Hinrich Lohse.

In the city of Lwów, 40,000 were reported to have been murdered; in Równe 14,000; in Kowel 10,000, and unknown numbers of murders were carried out in Stanisławów (Stanislav), Tarnapol, Stryj, Drohobych and many other small towns in the Ukraine. At first, the executions were

Poland

carried out by shooting; subsequently, however, it was reported that the Germans applied new methods, such as poison gas, by which means the Jewish population was exterminated at Chelmo, or electrocution, for which a camp was organised in Bełżec, where during March and April 1942, tens of thousands of Jews from the provinces of Lublin, Lwów and Kielce, were exterminated.

JEWISH COUNCIL IN WARSAW
NOTICE
Warsaw, 22 July, 1942

1. By order of the German authorities all Jews living in Warsaw, without regard to age or sex, are to be deported to the East.
2. The following are exempted from the deportation order:
   a. All Jews who are employed by the German authorities or German enterprises, and can produce adequate evidence of the fact.
   b. All Jews who are members and employees of the Jewish Council according to their status on the day of publication of this order.
   c. All Jews employed in German-owned firms who can produce adequate evidence of the fact.
   d. All Jews not yet thus employed, but are capable of work. These are to be barracked in the Jewish Quarter.
   e. All Jews belonging to the Jewish Civil Police.
   f. All Jews belonging to the staffs of Jewish hospitals. Or belonging to Jewish disinfection squads.
   g. All Jews who are members of the families of persons covered by (a) to (f). Only wives and children are regarded as members of families.
   h. All Jews who on the day of deportation are patients in one of the Jewish hospitals, unless fit to be discharged. Unfitness for discharge must be attested by a doctor appointed by the Jewish Council.
3. Each Jew to be deported is entitled to take with him on the journey fifteen kilogrammes of his personal effects. Anything in excess of fifteen kilogrammes will be confiscated. All articles of value, such as money,

jewellery, gold, etc, may be retained. Sufficient food for three days' journey should be taken.
4. Deportation begins on 22 July 1942, at 11.00 am.
5. Punishments:
   a. If any Jew who is not included among persons specified under par. 2 points (a) and (c) and so far not entitled to be so included, who leaves the Jewish Quarter after the deportation has begun, will be shot.
   b. Any Jew who undertakes activities likely to frustrate or hinder the execution of the deportation orders will be shot.
   c. Any Jew who assists in any activity which might frustrate or hinder the execution of the deportation orders will be shot.
   d. Any Jew found in Warsaw, after the conclusion of the deportation of Jews, who is not included among the persons specified under par. 2 (a) to (h) will be shot.[4]

It had been reliably reported that on the occasion of his visit to the Generalgouvernement of Poland in March 1942, that Himmler issued an order for the extermination of 50 per cent of Jews by the end of that year. Himmler's second visit to Warsaw in the middle of July became the signal for the commencement of the process of liquidation, the horror of which surpasses anything known in the annals of history.

The liquidation of the occupants of the ghetto was preceded on 17 July by the registration of all foreign Jews confined there who were then removed to the Pawiak prison. From 20 July, the guarding of the ghetto was entrusted to special security battalions, formed from the scum of several Eastern European countries, while large forces of German police armed with machine guns and commanded by SS officers were posted at all the gates leading into the ghetto. Mobile German police detachments patrolled the boundaries of the ghetto day and night.

At 11.00 am on 21 July, German police cars drove up to the building of the Jewish Council of the ghetto in Grzybowska Street. The SS officers ordered the chairman of the Jewish Council, Mr Adam Czerniaków, to summon the members of the council, who were all arrested upon arrival and removed in police cars to the Pawiak prison. After a few hours of detention, the majority were allowed to return to the ghetto. Around that time, flying squads of the German police from the SS-Sturmbannführer staff of Hermann Höfle entered the ghetto and broke into houses in search of Jewish intellectuals. The better-dressed Jews were shot on the spot, without the police troubling even to identify them. Among those who were killed was a non-Jew, Professor Franciszek Paweł Raszeja, who was visiting sick Abe Gutnajer in his flat on Chłodna Street in the ghetto in the course of his medical duties and had an official pass. He was killed along with the patient, his family, his assistant Dr Kazimierz Pollak and a nurse. Hundreds of Jews were killed in this way.

On the following morning, the German police again visited the office of the Jewish Council and summoned all the members who had been released from Pawiak prison the previous day. On their assembly, they were informed that an order had been issued for the removal of the entire Jewish population of the Warsaw ghetto. Printed instructions to that effect were issued in the form of posters. Additional instructions were issued verbally. The number of people to be removed was at first fixed at 6,000 daily, who would assemble in the hospital wards and grounds in Stawki Street, the patients of which were evacuated forthwith. The railway sidings not far from Stawki Street. Persons subject to deportation were to be livered by the Jewish Police not later than 4.00 pm each day. Members of the council and other hostages were to answer for the strict fulfilment of the order. All inmates of Jewish prisons, charitable institutions, and people of old age were to be included in the first contingent.

The German police again visited the offices of the Jewish Council at 7.00 pm on 23 July, and saw the chairman, Mr Czerniaków who, after they left, committed suicide. It was reported that he did so because the Germans increased their contingent of the first day to 10,000, to be followed by 7,000 persons on each subsequent day. The people were either rounded up haphazardly in the streets or taken from their homes.

All Jews employed in German-owned undertakings were exempt, together with their families, from deportation. This produced acute competition among the inhabitants of the ghetto to secure employment in such undertakings, or, failing employment, bogus certificates to that effect. Large sums of money, running into thousands of Zlotys, were being paid for such certificates to the German owners. They did not, however, save the purchasers from deportation, which was being carried out without discrimination or identification.

The actual process of deportation was carried out with appalling brutality. At the appointed hour on each day, the German police cordoned off a block of houses selected for clearance, entered the back yard and fired their guns at random as a signal for all to leave their homes and assemble in the yard. Anyone attempting to escape or hide was killed on the spot. No attempt was made by the Germans to keep families together. Wives were torn from their husbands, and children from their parents. Those who appeared too frail or inform were carried straight to the Jewish cemetery to be killed and buried there. On average, 50–100 people were disposed of in this way daily. After the contingent was assembled, the people were forcibly packed into cattle trucks; as many as 120 in each truck which had room for forty. The trucks were then locked and sealed.

The Jews were suffocating for lack of air, and the floors of the trucks were covered with quicklime and chlorine. As far as it was known at the time, the trains were dispatched to three localities: Treblinka, Bełzec and Sobibór, to what the reports described as 'extermination camps'. The very method of transportation was deliberately calculated to cause the largest possible number of casualties among the condemned Jews. Upon arrival at the camps, the survivors were ordered to strip naked, and were then killed by various means, including poison gas and electrocution. The dead were interred in mass graves dug by machinery.

All the children from Jewish schools, orphanages, and children's homes were deported, including those from the orphanage in the charge of the celebrated educationist, Dr Janusz Korczak (the pen name of the children's author Henryk Goldszmit) who refused to abandon his charges, although he was given the alternative of remaining behind. Of the 250,000 Jews deported from the Warsaw ghetto up to 1 September 1942, only two small transports, numbering around 4,000 people, are known to have been sent eastwards in the direction of Brest-Litovsk and Malachowicze, allegedly to be employed on work behind the front line. The German Employment Office (Arbeitsamt) issued 120,000 ration cards in the Warsaw ghetto during September 1942. In October, the number of cards issued was 40,000. These were for the skilled workers who were allowed to remain in a part of the ghetto while they were employed in German war production.

The deportations from the Warsaw ghetto were interrupted for five days between 20–25 August, while the German machinery for the mass

Poland

slaughter of the Jews was employed on the liquidation of other ghettos in central Poland, including the towns of Falencia, Rembertów, Nowy Dwór, Kałuszyn, and Mińsk Mazowiecki. The Polish population repeatedly expressed, through the underground organisations, their horror with the terrible fate that had befallen their Jewish fellow-countrymen.

A book titled *The Mass Extermination of Jews in German Occupied Poland*, which contained reports and documents about the Holocaust in Poland, was published by the Polish government-in-exile in Portland Place, London, on 10 December 1942. They had been kept apprised of the events in Poland by the underground state, the secular Jewish Labour Bund, among others. Copies of the book were sent to each of the foreign ministers of the twenty-six government signatories of the Declaration by the United Nations. Though the document contained extensive information on the persecution and murder of Jews in Poland, its effect was limited because many people outside German-occupied Europe found it difficult to believe the Germans were systematically exterminating Jews.

A joint declaration was announced simultaneously on 17 December 1942, in London, Moscow, and Washington:

> The attention of the governments of Belgium, Czechoslovakia, Greece, Luxemburg, the Netherlands, Norway, Poland, the United States of America, the United Kingdom of Great Britain and Northern Ireland, the Union of Socialist Soviet Republics, Yugoslavia, and of the French National Committee, has been drawn to numerous reports from Europe that the German authorities, not content with denying to persons of Jewish race in all the territories over which their barbarous rule has been extended the most elementary human rights, are now carrying into effect Hitler's oft-repeated intention to exterminate the Jewish people in Europe. From all the occupied countries Jews are being transported, in conditions of appalling horror and brutality, to Eastern Europe. In Poland, which has been made the principle Nazi slaughter-house, the ghettos established by the German invaders are being systematically emptied of all Jews, except a few highly-skilled workers required for war industries. None of those taken away are ever heard

of again. The able-bodied are slowly worked to death in Labour camps. The infirm are left to die of exposure and starvation, or are deliberately massacred in mass executions. The number of victims of these bloody cruelties is reckoned in many hundreds of thousands of entirely innocent men, women, and children.

The above-mentioned governments and the French National Committee condemn in the strongest possible terms this bestial policy of cold-blooded extermination. They declare that such events can only strengthen the resolve of all freedom-loving people to overthrow the barbarous Hitlerite tyranny. They reaffirm their solemn resolution to ensure that those responsible for these crimes shall not escape retribution, and to press on with the necessary practical measures to this end.[5]

Count Edward Raczyński, the Polish Acting Minister for Foreign Affairs, added,

It is tragic to contemplate that this policy of extermination applied to the Jews by the German government is being carried out with the active help, or at least, support of a considerable section of the German people, while the remaining part of that people allow it to pass in silence. I know that in a totalitarian regime it is not easy to protest, but the occupied nations nevertheless find the means to manifest their will and their opposition to the barbarous methods of Germany. When I think of the German nation, so powerful in its armed might and owning so gigantic a war machine, and at the same time so cowardly accepting the destruction of an entire race, the representatives of which, such as Meine, Mendelssohn and Einstein contributed so much to the glory of Germany's civilization and, on the other hand, when I think of my own nation, which itself is being massacred and nevertheless is capable of such acts of defiance and compassion as the demolition by Polish workers of a part of the wall which surrounds the ghetto of Warsaw, then I cannot help thinking how small is this mighty German nation – and how measureless in its infamy. Civilised words and remonstrances are today of no avail where that nation is concerned. The bloody crimes call out for justice without mercy, and the assurance that even now they will receive their answer in ever more telling deeds as the might of the United Nations grows and the hour of judgment approaches apace.[6]

On 6 September 1941, the Jews of Vilna were forced into two ghettos. Around 30,000 Jews were forced into the larger ghetto, known as 'Ghetto I', and another 11,000 Jews into the smaller ghetto, known as 'Ghetto II'. During the resettlement programme, around 6,000 Jews were deported to the Lukiškės prison, and from there to Ponary. The Łódź Ghetto was originally intended as a preliminary step upon a more extensive plan of creating the Judenfrei province of Warthegau. It was the second-largest ghetto in Nazi-occupied Poland. More than 165,000 Jews were forced into an area of less than 4 sq. km (1.54 sq. m). Deportations from the ghettoes began in 1942, and Lódz was the last ghetto to be liquidated when its surviving inhabitants were sent to Auschwitz-Birkenau in summer 1944.

There were over 200,000 Jews living in Lwów when it was occupied by the Soviet Union in 1939, but after it was subsequently occupied by the Germans following the invasion of Russia, Ukrainians began campaigns of violence against the Jewish population. In early June 1941, 4,000 Jews were slaughtered, and at the end of that month, a programme known as the Petliura Days (named after Simon Petliura, who had organised anti-Jewish pogroms in the Ukraine after the First World War) went on for three days, during which Ukrainian militants went on a rampage through the Jewish districts of Lwów, murdering 2,000 and injuring thousands more.

The Germans published an order on 8 November 1941, which gave the Jews until 15 December to move into a ghetto which had been established in the Zamarstynow and Kleparow quarters. In the course of the move to the ghetto, 5,000 elderly and sick Jews were killed as they were about to cross the bridge on Peltewna Street. The move was not completed by the allotted time, but many thousands of Jews were herded into the ghetto. In March 1942, the Germans began deporting Jews from the ghetto to the Bełżec killing centre. By August 1942, more than 65,000 Jews had been deported from the Lwów ghetto and murdered. Thousands of Jews were sent for forced labour to the nearby Janowska concentration camp. In early June 1943, the Germans destroyed the ghetto, killing thousands of Jews in the process. The remaining ghetto residents were sent to the Janowska and Bełżec camps.

The scale of the killing that took place in the Nazi camps made it impossible for them to keep the operation a secret. Eyewitness accounts brought reports of Nazi atrocities in Poland to the attention of the Allied governments, who were harshly criticised after the war for their failure to respond, or even to publicise news of the mass slaughter. At Auschwitz alone, more than 2 million people were murdered in a process resembling a large-scale industrial operation. A large population of Jewish and non-Jewish inmates worked in the labour camp there, and although only Jews were gassed, thousands of others died of starvation or disease. In 1943, battalion medical officer Josef Mengele arrived at Auschwitz where he saw the opportunity to conduct genetic research on human subjects: the Jewish prisoners. He began conducting medical experiments on twins, injecting them with everything from petrol to chloroform under the guise of giving them medical treatment. His actions earned him the nickname 'the Angel of Death'.

In the autumn of 1944, German forces had begun evacuating many of the death camps, sending inmates under armed guard to march further from the advancing enemy's front line. The 'Death Marches', as they became known, continued until the German surrender on 7 May 1945, and resulted in the deaths of some 250,000 to 375,000 people. The German leadership had been dissolving amid internal dissent by spring of 1945, with Goering and Himmler both seeking to distance themselves from Hitler and take power. Hitler, in his last will and political testament, dictated in a German bunker on 29 April, blamed the war on 'International Jewry and its helpers', and urged the German leaders and people to follow 'the strict observance of the racial laws and with merciless resistance against the universal poisoners of all peoples' – the Jews. The following day, Hitler committed suicide.

The Nazi policy on Jews moved from expulsion to containment, and to commanders being ordered to systematically murder the Jews of Europe. Methods of mass murder evolved at local levels as well as being decreed from the Nazi high command. Killing squads rounded up and shot entire Jewish communities. In Kiev, 33,771 Jews were shot over just two days. The murder of Jews rapidly escalated, in part because local Nazi leaders didn't have any room left to place them in the ghettos.

As left-wing groups started to form in Poland, General Sikorski, the Polish leader in London, instructed the AK to cooperate with the Russians through negotiations with the newly formed Polish Worker's Party and its private army, the Peoples Guards, but the Katyn massacre relit fears about a future of a Soviet-dominated Poland. Sikorski was killed in mid-1943, and General Stefan 'Grot' Roweski, the first commander of the Home Army, was captured by the Nazis after being betrayed by three of the AKs members who collaborated with the Gestapo, and sent to Berlin. Roweski was replaced by General Tadeusz 'Bór' Komorowski, an ex-Cavalryman. Bór' continued with the 'fly' sabotage raids started by his predecessor, and the bold exploits against the railway network. German troop trains were derailed, and guns and ammunition hijacked. The frequency and amount of damage caused by the attacks reached such a stage that on 30 June 1944, the Germans announced that, 'anyone coming within 500 m of the rails will be shot'.

The Polish Underground State was a covert administrative, political, and military structure that was established by, and responsible to, the London-based Polish government-in-exile, which Allied governments recognised as the legitimate government of Poland. It operated in occupied Poland throughout the whole of the Second World War and conducted many operations, including the sabotage and destruction of war-related factories, warehouses, machinery, and the disruption of transportation infrastructure to impede the German operations. The railroad system between Germany and the Eastern front was especially targeted. Gestapo agents, gendarmes, and Nazi collaborators were targeted in reprisal killings, such as that of the assassination of SS General Franz Kutschera, Chief of the SS and police in the Warsaw District, for their exceptional brutality.

The Home Army (Armia Krajowa – AK), which was the military wing of the Underground State, and had 380,000 soldiers at its peak, fought against massive German colonisation efforts combined with the expulsion of Polish farmers. The AK maintained regular contact with the government-in-exile through clandestine radio stations and dozens of couriers and emissaries. Jan Karski, the most famous courier, took to Allied leaders Roosevelt and Eden, an eyewitness account of conditions in occupied Poland and particularly about the German terror and extermination of the Jews. Even though helping

Jews in occupied Poland was punishable by death, in 1942 various help committees were integrated into the Zegota (the Relief Council for Jews in Poland) organisation with the express purpose of helping Jews. It organised and provided accommodations, financial aid, medical care, and procured forged identity documents for Jews in hiding on the 'Aryan' side. Among others, Zegota was responsible for saving 2,500 Jewish children from the Warsaw ghetto. Additionally, through its couriers and radio transmissions, the Polish underground had been informing the free world about the plight of the Jews under German occupation.

The weapons of the AK were mostly pre-1939 Polish arms, captured or purchased from Germans, airdropped by the British, and those produced by the underground in clandestine shops where machine guns (based on a British Sten design), revolvers, grenades, and flame-throwers were manufactured. Among its biggest successes were the obtaining of information about German preparations for the invasion of the Soviet Union in 1941, and the development of the secret weapon (V-1) in Peenemunde which resulted in Allied aerial bombardment of the facility in 1943, the capture of an unexploded V-1 rocket and its transfer to England.

The Home Army was dissolved by General Leopold Okulicki on 19 January 1945, and underground administrative structures on 1 July 1945. With it, the Polish Underground State reached its end. The Home Army's losses during the five-year struggle, including the Warsaw Uprising, were more than 72,000 soldiers killed. During the entire German occupation, over 1,120 different periodicals were published. The highest circulation was achieved by the Home Army's weekly Information Bulletin with 50,000 copies. Seventeen publications managed to sustain publication throughout the entire occupation period of 1939–45. In addition to Polish and Action 'N' German-language publications, there were twenty-five periodicals in Hebrew and Yiddish (in the Warsaw ghetto), one in French, and one in English designed for POWs held in the German camps on Polish territory.

The Warsaw Ghetto Uprising

The order for Jewish people living in the ghetto to be moved to extermination camps under a 'resettlement programme' was given by Heinrich Himmler, the Reichsfuhrer of the Schutzstaffel (SS) in

Poland

July 1942, and by the autumn, more than 300,000 people were deported from the Warsaw ghetto alone.

The inhabitants of the ghetto rose in armed revolt against the deportations, disease and constant hunger.

Underground resistance groups had been formed in many ghettos across Eastern Europe between 1941 and 1943, stocking up smuggled-in and homemade weapons to use against the Germans. The everyday round-ups and random executions by the Nazis Pawiak, Palmiry, Oświęcim, Madjanek and Treblinka led the citizens of Warsaw to act with extreme determination in what would come to be acknowledged as the most famous attempt being made by the Jews in armed fighting against the Germans. The uprising of Jewish Resistance began on 19 April 1943, after German troops and police entered the ghetto to deport its surviving inhabitants. The ghetto fighters took on the more heavily armed and well-trained Germans and 750 of them were able to hold out for almost a month, but their resistance was slowly being crushed, until the revolt ended on 16 May 1943. Of the more than 56,000 Jews who were captured, around 7,000 were shot, and the remainder were deported to camps. The Warsaw ghetto uprising inspired revolts in other ghettos and in killing centres such as Treblinka, and although many of them knew they were bound to lose against overwhelmingly superior German forces, they chose to die fighting.

General Komorowski had radioed his plans to the Polish government-in-exile in London on 20 November 1943, asking that German airfields near Warsaw be bombed, and airlifts of arms and ammunition begin to be made to Polish insurgents, and that the 1st Parachute Brigade and the Polish fighter squadron be dispatched to Warsaw, ahead of the launch of an uprising with a series of military operations that were code-named 'Burza' (Tempest), confident in the indication that they would be liberated by the Red Army. The British government responded that Polish troops had already been deployed to the D-Day operations, and to Monte Cassino, that it did not have sufficient aircraft to carry out an emergency airlift, and the RAF would not relinquish any part of the Polish squadrons. On 26 July 1944, the Polish government-in-exile, still believing that the Allies would provide supplies and military reinforcements, authorised the Delegatura in Poland to make its decision on the date and time for the start of the Warsaw Uprising.

In December 1944 the Germans still occupied western Poland, while the Soviets were advancing on Germany from the south. Increasingly better equipped and more mobile, they assembled a huge force along the front between the Baltic Sea and the Carpathian Mountains, but Hitler was sceptical of their capabilities and failed to reinforce Germany's eastern defences. The Soviets under Marshall Zhukov launched their assault on 12 January 1945, with Marshall Konev's forces attacking in the south from Sandomierz and Marshall Rokossovsky's in the north, encircling Warsaw. By 19 January, Zhukov had taken Lódz and Konev had reached Silesia. By the end of the month, Konev had crossed the River Oder, Zhukov had reached Brandenburg and Pomerania, and Rokossovsky had taken Danzig, leaving twenty-five German divisions in the north isolated and trapped. By 13 February, the Soviet forces were halted at the Oder-Neisse line, less than 160km (100 miles) from Berlin, and German civilians, in panic, were evacuating from the city. On the Western Front, Allied troops had broken through the Normandy defences, and news of the attempted assassination of Hitler was announced. The time for the uprising was now.

The Warsaw ghetto uprising of 1944 was a major battle and the largest single operation prepared and executed by a partisan organisation during the Second World War. On 27 July 1944, around 100,000 people were summoned to begin constructing fortifications for the Germans, which would have created a very disadvantageous situation for the Red Army when they entered the city and engaged the Germans.

On 1 August, the order was sent out to its groups to begin an uprising which, in later years, would be described as 'the greatest act of resistance of any occupied country'. For the morale of the Polish soldiers and civilians who had been preparing for battle, this was the optimum time to strike back. The Red Army was standing at the line of the Vistula River, but were held back from intervention. Soviet leader Josef Stalin ordered the Red Army to stay out of the fighting because he did not want the Resistance to lay the foundations of an independent post-war Poland.

During the afternoon rush hour of that day, the troops, armed only with small weapons from local caches, what they had managed to steal from the Germans and what had been dropped by the RAF, moved to pre-designated posts. They paralysed German communications on the left bank of the Vistula River and attacked German-occupied buildings. The civilians started to build barricades in the streets, and the national red and white flags were mounted and displayed in liberated areas. The smaller Armia Ludowa, Gwardia Ludiwa, and Narodowe Siły Zbrojne resistance groups joined in the uprising. Warsaw's sewer system was used throughout the uprising to move across German-held territory in-between areas of the city under Polish control. One of the frequently used systems ran from the city centre to Malczewskiego Street in the southern Mokotów district. During the first few hours, the Germans were expelled from Napoleon Square, and the Victoria Hotel on Jasna Street, and the sixteen-storey-high Prudential Insurance Company skyscraper on Świętokrzyska Street, were taken over and used as the stop-over and headquarters for Brigadier-General Antoni Chruściel (codenamed 'Monter'), the commander of the armed forces of the uprising.

Overnight, the General Post Office was liberated after a heavy battle, and the national flag raised upon its roof. During attacks on the Polish posts the next day, the Germans drove men, women and children in front of their tanks to shield themselves from the Home Army snipers. There was no anti-tank weaponry, and escalating bombing attacks by the Germans increased the number of homeless each day. Rebels conquered the intensely defended stronghold at the Ciepłe and Grzybowska Street intersection, which frequently changed hands.

By 3 August, Polish fighters successfully captured a series of complexes in Warsaw's most important boroughs: Śródmieście, Powiśle, part of Czerniaków, Żoliborz, Mokotów, the Old Town, Wola, Sadyba, and parts of Ochota and Praga, but could not overcome the German strongholds because of the lack of weapons and ammunition. On 3 August, Stalin promised the Polish Prime Minister Stanisław Mikołajczyk that the Red Army would fight the Germans if the uprising would last for at least six days. The Soviets did nothing to help the Polish fighters throughout the whole of the battle. The next day, the Underground Command ordered that the offensive be restricted to only a few areas and subsequently, the Germans recaptured each district one by one and gained control of the major streets. From 4 to 11 August, the Germans reclaimed Wola and Ochota, and in the process slaughtered over 40,000 Polish inhabitants.

On 5 August, the Germans, having regained territories, began to systematically destroy all buildings and monuments, and annihilate all Polish military and civilian resistance. Of the 1,100 buildings, the Germans completely destroyed over 400, and burned out over 300 more. The SS Brigade, composed of common criminals, went on a killing frenzy massacring thousands of Polish men, women and children. SS and police units went on a house-to-house rampage, herding Polish citizens into the streets and executing them by machine-gun fire, shooting babies in their carriages, looting, murdering, and raping. The Nazis targeted hospitals with terrible ferocity – shooting patients in their beds. The streets were covered with dead bodies, piled on and buried in the rubble. By the end of the day, over 10,000 citizens had been slaughtered. The mass killings went on for several days.

The insurrectionists were gradually evacuated from their homes and hiding places and captured as the German forces methodically worked their way, street by street, and estate by estate, through Ochota. On 11 August, the resistance positions along Wawelska Street, including its stronghold, were attacked and emptied after fierce gun battles. Survivors were driven to the Zieleniak camp. The bodies of the murdered and deceased prisoners were moved by civilians conscripted into the Verbrennungskommando who were ordered to lay them in piles in the gymnasium of the Hugo Kołłątaj Secondary School in Grójecka Street, after which RONA soldiers doused the bodies with alcohol and set them on fire. Three boy scouts of the Gustaw battalion of the AK were captured on 12 August, and as they were ordered to help to lower corpses into an evacuated pit, were shot in the back their heads by a German officer. The final evacuation of civilians to the Pruszków transit camp began on 13 August, while the Verbrennungskommando continued burning the bodies of the victims of the massacre.

The staff of RONA set up their headquarters in a building of the Wolna Wszechnica Polska (Polish Free University) at No 2a Opaczewska Street (today No 2 Banacha Street), where most of the other buildings had been looted and burned, while the 1,700 soldiers under its command took over the building of the 21st Hugo Kołłątaj Secondary School, at 93 Grójecka Street, close to where they had killed the residents of No 104 with grenades as they were hiding in the cellar. The gravest of the atrocities were committed in the local hospitals, in the Maria Skłodowska-Curie Radium Institute, where around 170 patients and staff were brutally murdered by the members of RONA. After robbing the staff and patients, and destroying the food stock, pharmacy and much of the hospital equipment, the nurses were gang-raped, and the building was looted and set on fire. Around sixty people avoided death by seeking shelter in the building's cellar and chimneys, but some were found the next day, 19 August, when members of RONA returned to the institute to set light to what didn't burn the previous day. Fifty critically ill patients were killed on the spot, and the others were sent to the Zieleniak camp, which had become a place of mass crimes.

Warsaw's sewers, which were designed by the English engineer William Lindley, were used as a means of transportation between separated districts from the early weeks of 1939. The clearances in the passages varied between those tall enough to enable adults to walk upright (although the sludge level was quite high and aggravated by a strong current, to smaller ones, which, at 3ft high and 2ft wide, could not be easily negotiated. All the sewers had domed floors which were slippery and thick with debris. Since all traffic was one-way, and passing was impossible, the partisans controlled sewer traffic by issuing permits on a scheduled basis to organise the flow, while guarding the manhole entry points.

It was due to the existence of the sewer system that the remnants of the Old Town's defenders and its civil population disappeared mysteriously at the end of August 1944 during the Warsaw Uprising. The sewers used are under Bonifraterska Street, the Gdanski Railway Station, Stoleczna Street, and the sewer junction under the tracks of the Gdanski Railway Station where the main sewer lines of the city converge: A1 and A2 which run under Okopowa Street; B runs underneath Marszalkowska Street; and C from underneath the New Town district and Miodowa Street.

At that time, around 6,000 people were able to use the system as the final evacuation route to retreat to Warsaw's downtown district, and about a 1,000 managed to make it to the Zoliborz district. It was only at the end of August that the Germans realised that the sewers were being used by the insurgents, and immediately tried to disrupt the flow of traffic by throwing in hand grenades, pouring in acrid gas, laying mines, building obstacles, and dumping and igniting gasoline. At the end of September, 150 evacuating Mokotow defenders accidentally exited into a German-held area and were executed on the spot.

The sewers remained in sole use by the Polish underground fighters, and from that point on, 'sewer paranoia' developed among the German forces in Warsaw. The Germans lived in constant anxiety until the very end of the uprising, when the resistance fighters were able to come out of the sewers unexpectedly and strike at German positions from the rear.

On the eleventh day of the uprising, Warsaw was in flames. Under the heavy shelling and gunfire, burning houses collapsed, and people sought shelter anywhere they could find it, in dens, burrows or makeshift shacks built from the rubble, carrying with them what possessions they could. Moving between buildings was safer using the basements, crawling through holes they had made. Without anti-tank weapons, they could only watch as the German war machines rumbled past.

The German raids intensified on the town over the next few days. Having occupied the Ateneum Theatre on Czerwony Krzyz (Red Cross) Street, the Germans used it as a stronghold from which to control the area between the Średnicowy Bridge that spanned the Vistula River, and the Poniatowski Bridge to the south.

The skyscraper on Napoleon Square was ablaze on 16 August, as was the famous Gebethner and Wolff Publishing House, but attempts to douse the flames were futile as the underground water pipes had been smashed during the bombings, and the only water available was from wells people had dug. The water situation was made even worse after the insurgents cut off what supplies remained, along with the gas and electricity supplies to the city.

The Home Army troops were ready to fight again on 19 August, but had to fight on two fronts: The eight-storey-tall telephone exchange building on Zielna Street, which had been occupied by a strong, well-armed garrison, as a vantage point to shell nearby streets and buildings, and also an attacking force from the direction of Saxon Gardens, less than 200 metres (650ft) away. Polish storm troops of the 'Kilinski' paramilitary Battalion attacked the tall building using grenades, makeshift flame-throwers, and Błyskawica sub-machine guns, with grim fighting waged on every stairway and every floor. Tanks from the Gestapo headquarters on Szucha Street were hurried in via Aleje Ujazdowskie to Pius XI Street, but as they got between Aleje Ujazdowskie and Mokotowska Street, they were bombarded with a hail of Molotov cocktails. The leading tanks stopped, ablaze, and as their crews climbed out to escape, they were mown down with sub-machine gunfire. The remaining tanks hastily withdrew. The garrison was forced to surrender by the following afternoon; 115 prisoners were taken, including six Gestapo officers (who were transferred to special camps) and six wounded men, who were taken to a field hospital.

While the Poles succeeded in destroying most of the German strongholds in the city, the Germans regrouped and began to systematically attack one section of the city at a time, supported by air attacks by German Junkers Ju-87 Stukas, with building after building, and street after street, razed by the German bombers. The Home Army had no air force, and the Stukas swooped in low and unchallenged, over each of their targets. Over the next three months, the Germans proceeded to demolish what was left of the city. Demolition groups used explosives and flame-throwers to destroy the houses that were still standing, as well as historical monuments and places of interest, reducing Poland's capital to a vast desert of hollow-shelled buildings and rubble.

The uprising was a heroic and tragic sixty-three-day struggle to liberate the capital of Poland, and was the longest and bloodiest urban insurgency of the war. Polish losses included 150,000 civilians dead, around 18,000 AK soldiers killed, and around 7,000 wounded. The German forces lost around 10,000. Its ultimate failure was because of the lack of support from the Allies. When the AK requested airdrops of arms and supplies into Warsaw, the Soviets refused permission for Allied planes to land and refuel on airfields under their control. The Allied airdrops had to be carried out from faraway Brindisi in Italy, which reduced both their carrying weight and the number of sorties. The only air-support operation which ran continuously for the duration of the rising were limited night supply drops by long-range planes of the RAF, other British Commonwealth air forces and units of the Polish Air Force in the West which had to use distant airfields.

Angry at their failure to end the uprising, and humiliated by the Polish underground's military achievements, the Nazi collaborationist formation SS Sturmbrigade Dirlewanger (the 36th Waffen Grenadier Division of the SS), and their fellow Axis collaborators in the Russian National Liberation Army (RONA, also known as the 'Kaminski Brigade') forces under the command of Bronislav Kaminski, turned on Warsaw's civilian population, brutally massacring up to 200,000 of them in unspeakable monstrous acts of cruelty and barbarity. The most notorious of these was what is known as the 'Wola massacre' where, from 5 to 12 August 1944, Nazi units commanded by SS Gruppenführer Heinz Reinefarth and SS Oberführer Oskar Dirlewanger, executed around 60,000 Polish civilians. In one of his reports to the commander of the German 9th Army, Reinefarth stated that, 'We have more prisoners than ammunition to kill them.'[7] On 12 August, Erich von dem Bach ordered a stop to the indiscriminate killing of Polish civilians in Wola, and issued a new directive stating that captured civilians were to be evacuated from the city, and deported to concentration or labour camps.

Due to the ever-growing number of people being expelled from their homes, the Germans created a transitional camp over the brick-walled and cobbled area of a former vegetable market called Zieleniak, and from 6 October, people could be gathered before being transported to Durchgangslager 121 (Dulag 121), the transit camp in Pruszków (today the area of Hale Banacha), outside Warsaw. Crimes against the local population continued during the round-ups carried out by RONA troops, who often beat and shot their prisoners while herding them towards the camp, pulling women out of the crowd to rape them, and often killing them afterwards.

The camp was inspected on the day of its inception by Erich von dem Bach-Zelewski, the commander of all German armed forces in Warsaw during the uprising, and concluded that, 'there was nothing wrong there, everything was in order'.[8] The victims were searched for valuables, jewels and money at the gate to the camp, and then forced inside. While interned, a small amount of mouldy bread was sometimes given out, but there was no fresh drinking water, no sanitary facilities, and no medicine or medical aid was available. The camp was filled to overflowing by 7 October. The RONA soldiers sometimes shot at the imprisoned people for fun, and the corpses laid in piles along the camp wall or buried in a makeshift manner. Several hundred people of non-Polish descent were escorted away on the same day to a Labour camp in Okęcie.

Over 1,000 died while interned in the Zieleniak camp, which was closed down in 19 August. Many other sites were used for mass executions, some of which are now marked with memorial plaques to commemorate the victims. RONA units withdrew from Ochota between 22–25 August 1944, although the looting of property in the district continued until the beginning of October. The German occupational administration organised a systematic campaign of pillaging; booty was loaded into goods trains in the Warszawa Zachodnia railway station and sent to Germany. After this, the Vernichtungskommando systematically set the remaining streets of houses and building on fire, thus affecting the final destruction of the city district. Over 600,000 starved and utterly exhausted civilians were deported from Warsaw via Zieleniak camp by the end of the uprising, of whom over 55,000 were deported on to other concentration camps.

From the post-war stance of the communist administrations installed in Soviet-occupied Europe, the remaining German populations outside post-war Germany were seen as a potentially troublesome 'fifth column' that would, because of its social structure, interfere with the envisioned 'Sovietisation' of the respective countries. Stalin saw the expulsions as a means of creating antagonism between the Soviet satellite states and their neighbours; the satellite states would then need the protection of the Soviet Union. The Western allies also saw the threat of a potential 'fifth column' and hoped to secure a more lasting peace by eliminating the German minorities, the idea of which had been supported by Winston Churchill and Anthony Eden since 1942, and which they thought could be done humanely.

The creation of ethnically homogeneous nation-states in Central and Eastern Europe had been presented as the key reason for the official decisions of the Potsdam and previous Allied conferences, as well as the resulting expulsions. The compulsory population exchange between Greece and Turkey in 1923 lent legitimacy to the concept, and Churchill cited the operation in which approximately 1.3 million Orthodox Greeks of the Ottoman Empire relocating to Greece, in exchange for roughly 355,635 Muslims living in Greece going to Turkey, as a success in a speech discussing the German expulsions.

As early as 9 September 1944, Soviet leader Joseph Stalin and Polish communist Edward Osóbka-Morawski of the Polish Committee of National Liberation had signed a treaty in Lublin on population exchanges of Ukrainians and Poles living on the 'wrong' side of the Curzon Line. Many of the 2.1 million ethnic Poles expelled from the Soviet-annexed Kresy to other areas of the Soviet Union including Siberia and Kazakhstan, as a consequence of the Molotov–Ribbentrop Pact, on 17 September 1939.

Driven by a desire for retribution, and the belief that the majority of Germans had acted in full support of Hitler, none of the expellees were checked for their political attitudes or their activities, and even in the few cases when this happened, and expellees were proven to have been bystanders, opponents or even victims of the Nazi regime, they were rarely spared from expulsion. There was an expressed fear of disloyalty of Germans. To the Poles, the expulsion of Germans was seen as an effort to avoid such events in the future. Karol Świerczewski, the ex-Soviet Army General who became the commander of the Second Polish Army, briefed his soldiers to 'exact on the Germans what they enacted on us, so they will flee on their own and thank God they saved their lives'. The Polish underground resistance fighter-soldier Jan Karski had journeyed to Washington to warn President Roosevelt during a 'secret' meeting in July 1943 of the possibility of Polish reprisals, describing them as 'unavoidable'[9] and 'an encouragement for all the Germans in Poland to go west, to Germany proper, where they belong.'[10]

The map of Poland changed again as a result of the German defeat. Soviet troops re-entered the eastern borderlands in January 1944 and took control of what was to become Western Belorussia and Western Ukraine during the following month. In July of that year, the German occupiers were expelled from the area between the new Polish–Soviet boundary and the Vistula River. Joseph Stalin set the post-war borders between Poland and the USSR in 1945 without consultation with, or reference to, the Western Allies or their politics. Until 1939, there were few opportunities for Stalin to move the international border with Poland, but by the time the Second World War came to an end, he used the raw military might of the Soviet Union to make various adjustments that he saw fit to the western borders, all to the benefit of Moscow. Between 1944–46, Stalin negotiated territorial and other advantages from border issues along his periphery, creating systemic territorial buffers in both the East and West. The United States and Britain ultimately sanctioned the changes at the expense of Poland, Hungary, Czechoslovakia and China to the benefit of Romania, Mongolia and the USSR. The territories west of the Vistula (including Warsaw) came under Red Army control in January and February 1945. The Polish Committee of National Liberation, a civilian regime, was established under Soviet patronage in the latter two regions immediately upon liberation. Polish rule was extended de facto to Lower Silesia and Pomerania shortly thereafter.

Flight and Expulsions

The Red Army advanced into the eastern parts of post-war Poland in the Lublin–Brest Offensive, launched on 18 July 1944, and the Soviet spearheads first reached eastern German territory on 4 August 1944, in north-eastern East Prussia and Memelland, causing a spontaneous mass flight of Germans from Poland, driven by the rumours of Soviet atrocities. In 1945, the eastern territories of Germany, as well as Polish areas that had been annexed by Germany, were occupied by the Soviet Red Army and Polish communist military forces. German civilians from the area were also sent as 'reparations labour' to the USSR. The devastation of the Polish economy and elites (the latter, additionally, engaged in the post-war death-and-life struggle between communists and anti-communists) made the task of defining who were Germans to be expelled and who were Poles to be retained anything but easy. The administration of Poland's German Eastern territories was handed over to the Ministry of the Regained Territories (Ministerstwo Ziem Odzyskanych, MZO), whose activities were complicated by the presence of Soviet administration (until 1946), and of the Red Army administration.

The Act on Expulsion of Enemy Elements from Poland was issued by the authorities in Warsaw on 3 May 1945, which gave local authorities a legal basis for the wild expulsions that had already been occurring. The forced expulsions of the German minority were ordered and encouraged by the Polish post-war government as well as the Soviet occupying forces initially implemented the expulsions, but before long, direct violence against civilians was exacerbated by a variety of Polish militia, especially the Volunteer Reserve of the Citizens' Militia (ORMO). These militia groups included many Polish men who had joined them upon returning from forced labour in Germany to take revenge for the injustices they had suffered. In the general atmosphere of lawlessness and impunity further facilitated violent excesses. The first phase of the expulsions thus have to be considered in the context of the displaced, death and destruction suffered by the Polish population under German occupation during the Second World War.

The head of the Central Committee, Władysław Gomułka, ordered, 'There has to be a border patrol at the border [Oder-Neisse line] and the Germans have to be driven out. The main objective has to be the cleansing of the terrain of Germans, the building of a nation-state.'[11] To ensure the Oder-Neisse line would be accepted as the new Polish border at a future Allied conference (Potsdam Conference), up to 300,000 Germans living close to the river's eastern bank were subsequently expelled. On 26 May 1945, the Central Committee ordered all Germans to be expelled within one year and the area settled with some 3.5 million ethnic Poles; 2.5 million of them were already resettled by summer.

Although the Allies had already endorsed the principle of a population transfer, Polish authorities unilaterally initiated forced expulsions from spring 1945, and did not fully comply with the decisions taken in Potsdam, and continued with forced expulsions into the Soviet zone of occupation until the end of 1945. These were aimed at legitimising Polish control over former German territories east of the Oder-Neisse line before the Allied forces could come to a formal decision regarding the German minority in the East. Before 1 June 1945, around 400,000 Germans had managed to cross the Oder and Neisse rivers eastward before Polish authorities closed the river crossings, another 800,000 entered Silesia from Czechoslovakia, which raised Silesia's population to 50 per cent of the pre-war level. This led to the odd situation of treks of Germans moving about in all directions, to the east as well as to the west, each warning the others of what would await them at their destination.

International public opinion was generally relieved by the announcement at Potsdam that the Allied governments were proposing to assume control of the expulsion process. The destinations of the expellees designated between representatives of the Polish and Czechoslovak governments and the Allied Control Council (ACC), which was formed by the United States, the Soviet Union, France and Great Britain, as the occupying countries' temporary governing body for Germany. An agreement was reached on 20 November 1945, from which a timetable was set out for the transfer of expellees to each of the four zones of occupation.

Amid the transfers, local conflicts and ethnic hatreds took a turn for the worse. German citizens or Polish citizens of German descent were deprived of their Polish citizenship, their property was expropriated and their livestock confiscated often accompanied by violence, pillaging and rapes. Civilians were often forced to leave on short notice and transported in unheated freight cars without access to food or water, with the weakest and the sick dying from exhaustion. Germans were charged for immunisation, and deaths due to oedema and typhus reached epidemic proportions by early 1946.

The British launched 'Operation Swallow' at the end of February 1946, aimed at fulfilling the obligations set out by the ACC. Some 6,500 Germans were shipped towards the British Zone from Poland each day, while the daily total from Czechoslovakia in the direction of the American zone was at least four trains with 1,200 deportees in each. The launch of a British-run sea link from the Baltic Sea port of Danzig to the port of Lübeck increased these numbers by an additional 43,000 during its period of operation from late March until June 1946.

One of the transports from Poland was met on 3 March 1946 by a correspondent from the *Manchester Guardian*, who discovered that two of the expellees had been found dead on arrival, and that 250 were so seriously ill that they required immediate hospitalisation. The women bore marks of systematic maltreatment over a long period, with the scars of physical and sexual abuse much in evidence. A British medical officer who examined the German expellees determined that, 'most of the women had been violated, among them a girl of ten and another of sixteen'.

Reports about the systematic maltreatment of the German expellees from Poland subsequently began to flood in from Allied reception centres. Of 4,100 expellees on three 'Swallow' trains, 524 were admitted directly to the hospital. The camp commandant reported that most of the women in these transports were multiple rape victims, as were some of the children. The officials in the reception areas had begun to press for its immediate suspension of the transports, but although officials in London noted the deplorable condition in which the expellees were arriving, they did not seek to restrict the intake of expellees to a level that could be accommodated, as it would have prolonged the transfer operation into the indefinite future. Instead, they agreed to a Polish request at the end of April 1946 to increase the daily rate of transfers from 5,000 to 8,000. The result was a perpetual state of crisis, with increased suffering, and higher mortality among the German expellees from the Recovered Territories.

The census of February 1946 was the only one carried out in communist Poland that asked the question about one's nationality, and the returns were used to compile the expulsion lists of who were the Germans to be expelled, and who were the Poles to be retained. 2,288,000 people from the population of 'indubitable Germans', pre-war citizens of German ethnicity and pre-war Polish citizens of German ethnicity, with their descendants, was the first group slated for expulsion, with the temporary exclusion of 'indispensable Germans', held back for their professional skills, along with their families. A second group, numbering 417,400 people, was formed from 'autochthons' – indigenous inhabitants subject to verification: the Szlonzoks, who were either German citizens or Polish ones who acquired citizenship of Germany through the DVL, the Kashubs (citizens of Germany or the Free City of Danzig who became German citizens) and the similar Slavic-Germanic ethnic group of the Mazurs from Germany's southern East Prussia. The Polish authorities saw the autochthons as 'poloniseable', or 'unconscious Poles', who needed to be reminded of their 'dormant Polishness'. Deprived of any citizen rights, around 500,000 Germans in Poland, East Prussia, and Silesia, who collaborated with the German occupiers were considered 'traitors of the nation' and were employed as forced labour in communist-administered camps at Glatz, Mielęcin, Gronów, Sikawa, Central Labour Camp Jaworzno, Central Labour Camp Potulice, Łambinowice (run by Czesław Gęborski), Zgoda labour camp, and others, before being expelled from Poland.

Thirty camps were established to hold some 50–60,000 German war prisoners, but they also imprisoned members of the anti-communist Polish partisan movement and almost 100,000 ethnic Germans or Volksdeutsche. Of these German concentration camps, the camps in Majdanek, Skrobów and Jaworzno were reopened by the Soviet Army to intern anti-communist partisans who had become enemies of the established people's democratic system. The largest camps in Poland operated in Jaworzno, Chrusty, Sikawa, Mysłowice, Libiaż and Mielęcin. Between 1945 and 1951, one of the largest camps was the one in Jaworzno, where over 7,000 people died between 1945 and 1947. Between 1947 and the spring of 1949, some 3,800 Ukrainians – men, women and children – were interned to this camp, which was reorganised as a correctional camp in 1951, and every trace of the horrors of previous years was completely erased. Over 10,000 people had been sent to this camp until its abolishment after 1956.

In 1974, the German Federal Archives estimated that more than 200,000 German civilians were interned in Polish camps, and that over 60,000 perished. In many internment camps, no relief from outside was permitted, although in some camps the Polish guards would receive packages from relatives of the prisoners, and plunder them before passing on any remains. Internees who came to claim their packages were mistreated by the guards if they did not speak in Polish – even if they were Germans born in German-speaking Silesia or Pomerania. Frequently, the relatives were so ill-treated when they tried to deliver packages that they never returned.

Poland

The authorities rightly predicted that the number of the incoming Polish expellees from the Kresy (Eastern territories) and settlers from Central Poland would be lower than that of the Germans who fled or would be expelled. From 1945–48, the parallel process of 'national rehabilitation' was applied to those who acquired German citizenship via the DVL. Few were eventually expelled. By 1950, 3,155,000 German civilians had been expelled, and 1,043,550 were naturalised as Polish citizens.

Chapter Seven

The Removal of Germans from Eastern Europe

On 20 November 1945, the Allied Control Council (ACC) agreed to the removal of 6,650,000 Germans from Eastern Europe to the various occupied zones of Germany. In what later came to be part of 'Operation Swallow', Britain and Russia agreed to split 3.5 million Western Poland expellees between their respective zones, in the hope that it would help stem the massive tide of expellees arriving in Britain's zone, of which it took occupancy on 5 June, but the operation did not eventually start until 20 February 1946.

It had been agreed at Potsdam that 15 per cent of all equipment dismantled in the Western zones of former Nazi Germany, especially from the metallurgical, chemical, and machine manufacturing industries – would be transferred to the Soviets in return for food, coal, potash, timber, clay products, and petroleum products. The deliveries started in 1946, but the exchange deal for food, heat and basic necessities, and to increase agricultural production in the remaining cultivation area, did not materialise. As a consequence, the American military administrator, General Lucius D. Clay, stopped the transfer of supplies. As a result of the halt of deliveries from the Western zones, the Soviet Union had established central administration in their zone for nutrition, transport, jurisdiction, finance, and other areas already in July 1945, began a public relations campaign against American policy and began to obstruct the administrative work of all four zones.

In Britain, Benjamin Smith, the Minister for Food, along with other politicians serving under the premiership of Clement Atlee, as well as the Press, categorically rejected the idea of giving rations to Germans because the British people were the top priority. In October 1945 he stated that, 'While I hold this job, unless there are shortages over which no one has control, I will not be a party to reducing rations to this country below their present standard'.[1] The *Lancashire Evening Post* supported Smith, describing him as 'a doughty champion of the interests of the common people', who placed British post-war recovery over that of Germany. This incited growing public anger at rationing, scarcity, controls, austerity and government bureaucracy. Some aspects of rationing in Britain became stricter than during wartime for some years after the war. While some senior politicians tried to play down Britain's responsibility to help the Germans, and complained about the failure of other countries, which had exacerbated the problems beyond Britain's control, both Ernest Bevin and the Deputy Prime Minister Herbert Morrison blamed Russia directly for the German peoples' plight: if the expulsions had not taken place at the time they should have, they claimed, then the food problem 'would not have been so tragic, and that Britain had done more than enough to help the Germans, while North and South America had done very little'.[2]

The British zone in Germany was overwhelmed by the arrival of expellees; between February and July 1946, around 8,000 were arriving daily from Poland. The 'illegal' arrival of expellees, many from the Soviet zone as well as Jewish victims of the 1944–46 Jewish pogroms in Poland, caused this number to rapidly rise to 25,000 per week until October. At this time, only 1,200 people were being processed and leaving the British zone each week. Food, shelter, medicine, clothing and water were all in short supply. Concurrently, Britain was under pressure not only to rebuild its own country and ensure the British people survived, but to also provide for its increasingly overcrowded zone in Germany as it tried to rebuild German infrastructure and democracy. Hitler's scorched earth policy during the retreat of the Wehrmacht and SS retreat in 1945, as well as heavy rainfall right through the summer of 1945, gave rise to famine-stricken areas across the zone. By early 1946, the food crisis had grown so great that in March, Field Marshal Montgomery was forced to cut German rations to 1,000 calories a day – only twenty more than that allowed for the refugees and expellees of the various Nazi internment camps during the war. Fears grew further after cases of oedema, caused by severe malnutrition, became regular occurrences across the zone. The British Foreign Secretary, Ernest Bevin, and his American counterpart James F. Byrnes met in New York on 2 December 1946, to discuss the acute food shortage, and agreed on the economic unification of the American and British zones, creating the 'Bizone', which became effective from 1 January 1947.

A strong element within British politics and media were unwilling to help the Germans, but it was not necessarily out of spite or anger, but in the belief that a recovered and healthy Britain could only protect Europe from Russia's communism and a resurgent, violent Germany once it had rebuilt itself. They needed the country to be in a better position mentally, physically and financially, to respond to the significant threat posed by Russia through its attitude towards Occupied Germany during the food crisis, and its post-war westward expansion. Communism's spectre and the Eastern Bloc's formation overtook British concerns about a resurgent Germany.

Chapter Eight

Germany

The intensive British area-bombing campaign from May 1942 onwards, targeted large industrial cities with incendiary bombs and, not distinguishing between military and civilian targets, created thousands of refugees as whole cities were flattened or burnt down. On 30/31 May 1942, the first of three British 'thousand bomber raids' was launched against Cologne. Over the next three years, sixty-one German cities were attacked. Dresden and Hamburg suffered the most; in Dresden alone, 70 per cent of buildings were destroyed, and 150,000 people were killed. Overall in Germany 3.6 million homes were destroyed, 7.5 million people were made homeless and 300,000–400,000 civilians were killed with twice that number being wounded in the air raids.

The war had been going badly for Germany since the end of 1941. The USA had joined the war on the side of the Allies, and 'Operation Barbarossa', the Nazi invasion of the Soviet Union, was in stalemate. In February 1943, as the pressure on the home front increased, Goebbels announced the Universal Labour Service and the closure of non-essential businesses, and both the economy and the whole of society were mobilised for war production. The Allied air raids on the cities had a limited impact on the morale of the German population, as Nazi propaganda downplayed their destruction as well as the number of deaths. The biggest concern for the citizens was that the massive destruction of houses led to severe overcrowding in the buildings that were left still habitable. While 12 per cent of bombs fell on factories, 50 per cent fell on residential areas. Thus, German industrial production continued to increase until mid-1944, but the war had brought total misery to the German civilians. The production of civilian clothing had been suspended, and no ration cards were issued for clothes – exchange centres were set up so that people could swap clothing and furniture, and Food ration cards were no longer always honoured.

The Volkssturm (People's Home Guard) was set up by the Nazis on 18 October 1944, partly to act as a defence force as the Allies advanced, but mainly to raise morale. Staffed by conscripting males between the ages of 16 and 60 years who were not already serving in any military unit, it had some marginal effect on morale, but it was undermined by the recruits' visible lack of uniforms and weaponry. During the Battle for Berlin (16 April – 2 May 1945), the Volkssturm had a strength of around 60,000 in the Berlin area, formed into ninety-two battalions, of which thirty battalions (those with some weapons) were sent to forward positions, while those without weapons remained in the inner city. Despite their efforts, the last four months of the war were an exercise in futility for the Volkssturm, and the Nazi leadership's insistence to continue the fight to the bitter end contributed to around an additional 1.23 million deaths, half of them being German military personnel and the other half from the Volkssturm.

The Yalta Conference, which was held in the resort town in the Crimea from 4 to 11 February 1945, had determined that Germany and Berlin would be divided into four zones of occupation, so the Western allies left Eastern Germany and the city of Berlin to the Red Army. Following the Normandy landings on 6 June, the allied forces moved swiftly and decisively to take Western cities in France, and then moved on to liberate Paris. By September, they had reached the German border, and while the failure of Operation Market garden prevented a decisive breakthrough into the heart of Germany being obtained by the end of the year, the United States Army General, Dwight Eisenhower, In an effort to avoid a diplomatic issue with the Soviets, ordered his forces into the south of Germany to cut off and wipe out other pieces of the Wehrmacht and to avoid the possibility that the Nazi government might attempt to escape through the Alpine passes into Austria or entrench in any mountain redoubt.

By April 1945, both sides knew who was going to lose the Second World War. The allied invasion of Normandy on 6 June 1944, while immensely significant, was not the critical turning point of the war, but it signalled the beginning of the final push to liberate Europe from Nazi rule. The Nazis could no longer hold back the enemy, and the active Allies – largely American, British, and Soviet troops, who knew as they closed in with a succession of victories across the occupied countries of the Third Reich, that the expulsions, which had been planned long

Germany

before the war came to an end, and would inevitably cause death and hardship on a very large scale.

After 8 May 1945, human dignity played a very small part in the treatment of Germans when the fears of retaliation had passed. The victors from the East and the West, who occupied the conquered lands applied all means of degradation and violations of dignity onto the people. Cruel tortures of imprisoned German soldiers went on daily, with no right of appeal or hearing. Germany had committed unspeakable atrocities against Russia in the early years of the war, and was now being repaid in an orgy of killing, raping, and looting its civilian population.

The Soviet writer and Bolshevik revolutionary Ilya Ehrenburg's leaflet titled 'Kill' was delivered among soviet soldiers before the Red Army entering East Germany. It incited Soviet soldiers to treat Germans as sub-human and made no distinction between soldiers and civilians. The last paragraph declared that,

> The Germans are not human beings. From now on the word German means to use the most terrible oath. From now on the word German strikes us to the quick. We shall not speak any more. We shall not get excited. We shall kill. If you have not killed at least one German a day, you have wasted that day. If you cannot kill your German with a bullet, kill him with your bayonet. If there is calm on your part of the front, or if you are waiting for the fighting, kill a German in the meantime. If you leave a German alive, the German will hang a Russian and rape a Russian woman. If you kill one German, kill another – there is nothing more amusing for us than a heap of German corpses. Do not count days, do not count kilometres. Count only the number of Germans killed by you. Kill the German – that is your grandmother's request. Kill the German – that is your child's prayer. Kill the German – that is your motherland's loud request. Do not miss. Do not let through. Kill.[1]

Ehrenburg's incendiary leaflet played no small part in the orgy of murder and rape by Soviet soldiers against German civilians.

Allied control saw many indigenous Moroccan soldiers fight on Allied behalf as part of French forces. Their 1st Group fought through the Siegfried Line in the forested area of Bienwald, in the southern Pfalz region of Germany, from 20 to 25 March 1945. In April 1945, the 1st and 4th Groups took part in the fighting to seize Pforzheim. During the last weeks of the war, the 2nd Group fought in the Black Forest and pushed southeast to Germany's Austrian border. During the same period, the 1st and 4th Groups advanced with other French forces on Stuttgart and Tübingen. By mid-1946, all three groups had been repatriated to Morocco.

In Stuttgart, German women and girls were also considered 'fair game' by the French, and rampaged through the bombed-out city and shelters and committed an orgy of rape. Scenes of sexual depravity and horror spread throughout the Eastern regions as rampantly as the diseases the criminals left behind. The local police verified 1,198 cases of rape. The ages of the victims ranged from 14 to 74. According to police reports, most of them were attacked in their homes by turbaned thugs who broke down the doors in looting forays. Four of the women were killed by their attackers, and four others committed suicide. One of the victims was killed by her husband who then killed himself. They committed 385 rapes in the Constance area, 600 in Bruchsal and 500 in Freudenstadt. They moved in gangs relentlessly from home to home in Karlsruhe, threatening, raping and stealing all they could carry. In the County Women's Clinic in Karlsruhe alone, 276 terminations of pregnancies after rape were performed in April and May of 1945.

Stalin sent in two waves to capture Berlin. Marshal Georgy Zhukov, who has been responsible for the defence of Moscow, Stalingrad, and Leningrad against German forces, and Ivan Konev, who had commanded forces in major Soviet offensives at Kursk, in the Dnieper-Carpathian and Vistula-Oder offensives competed to be the first to enter Berlin. The four-day Belorussian Front Campaign that followed from 16 to 19 April 1945, ended with depleted German formations withdrawing as the troops of Zhukov's 1st Belorussian Front, who were greatly aided by Marshal Konstantin Rokossovsky's 2nd Belorussian Front by further reducing the enemy resistance, breaking through the defensive lines. It was at a high cost in casualties, but it provided the opportunity to advance on Berlin, which was only 90km (56 miles) to the west.

On 20 April, the 1st Belorussian Front started shelling Berlin's city centre as they advanced from the east and north, while Konev's forces broke through the strategic Army Group front, which included the

River Neisse, with a short but massive bombardment by tens of thousands of artillery pieces, and advanced towards the southern suburbs of Berlin. The weight of ordnance delivered by Soviet artillery during the battle was greater than the total tonnage dropped on the city by Western Allied bombers. Russians were given three days to do what they wanted as a reward for taking Berlin. Rape, looting, and burning what houses and buildings were still standing. More than 2 million German women and children were raped, with many dying or killing themselves as a result.

Berlin, one of the largest and most modern cities of Europe, was left a wasteland after the war. Around one-third of the city, especially the inner city, was in ruins. Vast piles of rubble and rows of building exteriors with collapsed interiors; hideous skeletons of a destroyed city; 600,000 apartments had been destroyed, and only 2.8 million of the city's original population of 4.5 million still lived in the city. The irreplaceable architectural gems of the Schlüter, Knobelsdorf, Schadow and Schinkel were annihilated. Palaces, museums, churches, monuments and cultural sites all fell victim to the intense Allied bombing raids. Over 68,500 tons of bombs had been dropped by the US and British bombers alone. It had also been attacked by the French Armee de l'Air between 1944 and 1945 as part of the Allied campaign of strategic bombing of Germany, and by aircraft of the Red Air Force, especially in 1945 as Soviet forces closed in on the city.

The post-apocalyptic scene was described as a ghost town by the Soviets, who were the first occupying power. While all women aged between 15 and 65 were conscripted on 29 May as 'rubble women', the Soviets estimated that even with this 60,000-strong workforce, the clean-up would take twelve years. The biggest problem that the Berliners had to face was the threat of starvation; German wartime ration cards were no longer valid. Any remaining rations had been either used to feed Russian troops or had been stolen by hungry Germans.

On 15 May, the Russians introduced a five-tier ration-card system: The highest tier was reserved for intellectuals and artists; rubble women and manual workers received the second-tier card, which was more valuable to them than the twelve Reichsmark per thousand bricks they were being paid as they cleared up; the lowest card, nicknamed the 'ticket to the cemetery', was issued to housewives and the elderly. During this period, the average Berliner was around 6–9kg (13–20lb) underweight.

The Potsdam Conference, so-called because it was held at Cecilienhof, the home of Crown Prince Wilhelm in Potsdam in occupied Germany, took place from 17 July to 2 August 1945. It brought together President Harry S. Truman from the United States, the Communist Party General Secretary Joseph Stalin from the Soviet Union, and from the United Kingdom, Prime Ministers Winston Churchill and Clement Attlee (Attlee participated alongside Churchill while awaiting the outcome of the General Election on 5 July, and then replaced him as prime minister after the Labour Party's defeat of the Conservatives), to decide how to administer Germany, which had agreed to unconditional surrender nine weeks earlier.

It was decided at the Conference to fully disarm and demilitarise Germany.

> The Nazi Party was outlawed, and all German land, naval and air forces, the Schutzstaffel (SS), Sturmabteilung (SA), Sicherheitsdienst (SD), and Gestapo, with all their organisations, staffs and institutions, including the General Staff, the Officers' Corps, Reserve Corps, military schools, war veterans' organisations and all other military and semi-military organisations, together with all clubs and associations which serve to keep alive the military tradition in Germany, shall be completely and finally abolished in such manner as permanently to prevent the revival or reorganisation of German militarism and Nazism.[2]

The German Navy was divided equally between the three powers, as was the German merchant marine, with some of the ships being distributed to other Allies. Germany was also banned from building war materials, with the reduction or destruction of all civilian heavy-industry with war-potential, such as shipbuilding, machine production and chemical factories. Restructuring of the economy was to be geared towards agriculture and light industry.

Bertrand Russell wrote in *The Times* of 19 October 1945,

> It was decreed by the Potsdam agreement that expulsions of Germans should be carried out 'in a humane and orderly manner,' it is well known, both through published accounts and through letters received in the numerous British families which have relatives or friends in the armies of occupation,

Germany

that this proviso had not been observed by the Russian and Polish allies. It is right that expression should be given to the immense public indignation that has resulted, and that our allies should know that British friendship may well be completely alienated by the continuation of this policy. [...] In Eastern Europe now mass deportations are being carried out by our allies on an unprecedented scale, and an apparently deliberate attempt is being made to exterminate many millions of Germans, not by gas, but by depriving them of their homes and of food, leaving them to die by slow and agonising starvation. This is not done as an act of war, but as a part of a deliberate policy of peace.[3]

The problem of what to do about Germany was not successfully addressed at the Potsdam Conference in July 1945. After the end of the war, the only decision of significance that emerged from wartime planning was the agreement of zones of occupation, which placed the future of post-war Germany into jeopardy through divisions within and between Allied powers.

Each of the different zones of Germany coped with this massive influx of people in its own way: Britain took control of its occupation zone in Western Germany, which included Lower Saxony, Schleswig-Holstein, North West-Rhine and the Ruhr, on 5 June 1945. Hamburg was a broken city where the streets were dotted with the uneven and scorched skeletal building facades from the bombs and firestorms that had rained down upon it for five long years, and during one of the last battles of the war, was where the remaining troops of the German 1st Parachute Army fought the British VIII Corps for the control between 18 April and 3 May 1945. Now dispossessed, the former main port and industrial centre was desperately short of food, shelter, medicine, clothing and fresh water for the inhabitants who had lost everything through no fault of their own. And the situation went from bad to worse as more expellees and refugees streamed in from the East. The British used their colonial model of indirect rule, whereby the local, regional, and state administrations served as an extension of the British occupation authorities. They placed Germans whom they felt were politically uncompromised in positions of power within the administration. Germans who had been closely associated with Nazi organisations or had been functionaries often ended up on the 'automatic-arrest list'; by the end of 1946 British had officials arrested and interned around 68,500 Germans.

The drastic shortage of housing in the British Zone often strained relations between the occupied and occupiers, and the situation was further exacerbated by the presence of millions of displaced Eastern Germans who sought shelter for themselves and their families in a war-torn Germany. Those Germans who fled before the capitulation frequently encountered Nazi functionaries who generally welcomed the incoming Germans, and arranged for accommodations in private houses, and used police force if the owners of those houses rejected their new lodgers. The initial refugees who arrived in the autumn months of 1944 even reported that the local population welcomed them with gifts. The refugees and expellees who came into the British Zone legally under the code-name of Operation Swallow, often ended up in overcrowded and unsanitary camps while officials processed them, checked them for diseases and sometimes deloused them, and located relatives or accommodations. Some of the camps used were previously Nazi military camps, POW camps, or concentration camps for political prisoners.

Between February 1946 and October 1947, eight trains plied their way back and forth between Szczecin and Lübeck, each composed of covered freight wagons with a total capacity of 2,000 people. Other trains took refugees from Kaławska to Mariental, Alversdorf and Friedland; and from April 1946, refugees were also transported to Lübeck by sea. In this way, some 6,000 'eastern' Germans were transported into the British zone almost every single day for a full year-and-a-half. By the end of the decade, more than 4.25 million new people had settled there.

The American Zone received refugees from Czechoslovakia, Hungary, Romania and Yugoslavia – more than 3.5 million of them in total. The effect this had on all parts of Germany (except for the French zone, which received relatively few refugees) was verging on the catastrophic. Even after their arrival, refugees continued to die in their thousands because they were unable to find the shelter, the medical aid or the food to sustain them after their westward odyssey. The authorities struggled to cope, and hundreds of thousands were still languishing in refugee camps at the start of the 1950s.

The Soviet Zone was probably the worst prepared of all of the zones. The towns and cities were among the most comprehensively destroyed by the war, and which was in the process of being stripped of everything of value for Soviet war reparations. Many Red Army soldiers perceived the destruction of German cities, material goods, and lives to be a form of 'sacred vengeance'. A flood of refugees arrived in the aftermath of the war, mostly from the new Poland, but also from Czechoslovakia. By the end of November 1945, there were already a million of them trying to scratch a living in the zone, disoriented and virtually destitute. During four years from the end of the war, at least 3.2 million refugees had settled. Around 3 million more stayed temporarily before moving on to other parts of Germany.

1947 saw major shifts in occupation policy in Germany. On 1 January, the United States and the United Kingdom unified their respective zones and formed Bizonia, which caused tensions between East and West to escalate. In March, the breakdown of the Moscow Conference of Foreign Ministers and the enunciation of the Truman Doctrine served to harden the lines of an increasingly bipolar international order. In June, Secretary of State George Marshall announced the European Recovery Programme. The purpose of the 'Marshall Plan', as it came to be known, was not only to support economic recovery in Western Europe, but also to create a bulwark against communism by drawing participating states into the United States' economic orbit. In June 1948, without informing the Soviets, US and British policymakers introduced the new Deutschmark to Bizonia and West Berlin. The purpose of the currency reform was to wrest economic control of the city from the Soviets, enable the introduction of the Marshall Plan aid, and curb the city's black market.

The Berlin Airlift

In May 1946, the Americans stopped reparations shipments from their zone to the Soviets. In December, the British and Americans combined their zones; the French joined some months later. The Soviets viewed these actions as a threat and issued more demands for a say in the economic future of Germany. Negotiations between the Soviets, Americans, and British finally broke down on 22 June 1948, and two days later, Soviet forces blocked all access to Berlin by rail, road and river into West Berlin.

Panic began to set in as the population of West Berlin worried about shortages of food, water, and medical aid. On 26 May, the response from the United States and Britain was to start what was to become one of the greatest humanitarian efforts of the time, a massive airlift of supplies into West Berlin – the Berlin Airlift (US 'Operation Vittles' and British 'Operation Plainfare'). The airlift became ever more efficient and the number of aircraft increased, and at the height of the campaign, one plane landed every forty-five seconds at Tempelhof Airport. The joint operation transported more than 2.3 million tons of supplies and 227,655 passengers by 189,963 flights in the fifteen months of the airlift. It saved the city without war, but the cost was 126 accidents, seventy of them major, and the USAF lost twenty-eight airmen during the operation.

At the same time, the Allied counter-blockade on Eastern Germany was causing severe shortages, which, Moscow feared, might lead to political upheaval. The Soviets, fearing that the Western powers would force the creation of a single capitalist Germany by joining their zones together and overpowering the East, officially ended the blockade on 12 May 1949. The Allies continued the Berlin Airlift through to 30 September to stockpile fuel, food, and medicine in Berlin in case Stalin changed his mind. The Soviets had sought huge reparations from Germany in the form of money, industrial equipment, and resources. The blockade imposed by Stalin turned out to be a terrible diplomatic move, while the United States emerged from the confrontation with renewed purpose and confidence.

The Berlin Crisis of 1948–49 solidified the division of Europe. Shortly before the end of the blockade, the Western Allies created the North Atlantic Treaty Organisation (NATO). Two weeks after the end of the blockade, the state of West Germany was established, soon followed by the creation of East Germany. The incident solidified the demarcation between East and West in Europe; it was one of the few places on earth that the US and Soviet armed forces stood face-to-face. It also transformed Berlin, once equated with Prussian militarism and Nazism, into a symbol of democracy and freedom in the fight against communism.

The Holocaust Trains

The Holocaust trains were operated by the Deutsche Reichsbahn National Railway System under the strict supervision of the German

Nazis and their allies, for the purpose of forcible deportation of Jews and other victims of the Holocaust, to the German Nazi forced labour, concentration, and extermination camps.

The first forcible eviction of German Jews with Polish citizenship occurred less than a year before the outbreak of war under the 'Kristallnacht' or the 'Night of Broken Glass', also called the 'November Pogrom', which was carried out by the Sturmabteilung (the Nazi Party's original paramilitary forces) and civilians throughout Nazi Germany on 9/10 November 1938. Around 30,000 Jews were rounded up and sent via rail to refugee camps.

After the Évian Conference at Évian-les-Bains in France in mid-July 1938, when both the United States and Britain refused to accept any more Jewish immigrants, the British Government agreed to take in the shipment of children arranged by the 'Kindertransport' scheme, with some 10,000 eventually arriving in the UK, it left all of the remaining European Jews trapped under the Nazi regime to become the target of Hitler's 'Final Solution to the Jewish Question'.

By the end of 1941, around 3.5 million Polish Jews had been segregated and ghettoized by the German SS in a massive deportation action involving the use of freight trains, which were referred to as Sonderzüge (special trains). The liquidation of the ghettos started in 1942, and trains were used to transport the condemned populations to the death camps, making the Deutsche Reichsbahn an indispensable element of the mass extermination machine. The fully enclosed windowless cattle wagons greatly reduced the number of troops required to transport the condemned Jews to their destinations. The Nazi propaganda machine described the movements as part of a 'resettlement to the east' programme, while more efficient gassing facilities were constructed which required limited supervision.

Some of the trains that had already transported goods to the Eastern front carried human cargo bound for extermination camps on the return journeys. The standard means of delivery was in 30ft long freight cars or cattle wagons, although third-class passenger carriages were used when the SS wanted to keep up the appearances of the mythical resettlement programme, particularly in the Netherlands and in Belgium. Each car was routinely loaded up to 200 per cent over its design capacity (100 people per car), and with the steam locomotives pulling up to the maximum of fifty-five cars, resulting in an average of 5,000 people per trainset.

The people deported in sealed freight cars suffered from intense heat in summer, or from freezing temperatures in winter. No food was provided, but two buckets were normally provided in each car, one for water and another to use as a toilet, but with the prisoners so tightly packed into their transport, it was usually impossible to sit or kneel to access either, so the buckets were pushed around by foot for their use, and were quickly filled to overflowing. The constant stench of vomit, urine and excrement would have been overpowering. A small barred window provided irregular ventilation, which sometimes resulted in deaths from either suffocation or the exposure to the elements, and without food or water, many deportees died of starvation or dehydration before the trains reached their destinations. When there were not enough cars to make it worth their while to do a major shipment of Jews to the camps, the victims were held in a switching yard – sometimes for days, and the armed guards would shoot anyone trying to escape.

The Sonderzüge had a low priority in the movement of rail traffic, and would proceed to the mainline only after all other transports, such as more important military trains had gone through, inevitably extending transportation times beyond expectations. The average transport took about 4½ days to reach the camps, and many deportees died in transit due to delays and cramped conditions. On 18 August 1942, when forty-five wagons with 6,700 Jews arrived at Belzec from Lwów Ghetto, less than 100km (62 miles) away, 1,450 of them were already dead.

Most of the Jews had been forced to pay for their transport via charges levied for their accommodation in the ghettos. Adult Jews paid full price for the one-way tickets, while children under 12 years of age paid half price, and those under 4 went free. Jews who had run out of money were the first to be deported. Part of the revenue was forwarded by the SS to the German Transport Authority to pay the German Railways for the transportation of the Jews, and the Reichsbahn was paid the equivalent of a third-class railway ticket for every prisoner transported to his or her destination: 8 million passengers at four Pfennig per track kilometre, times 600km (average voyage length), equalled 240 million Reichsmarks. The Reichsbahn pocketed both this money and its own share of the cash paid by the transported Jews after the SS fees had been settled.

The German Transport Ministry organised the trains, and the number of journeys were logged (mainly) by the Polish State Railway company that had been taken over by Germany. Between 1941 and December 1944, when the Auschwitz-Birkenau camp officially closed, over 1,600 trains had been used to transport condemned populations to the camps. The last train left on 13 September 1944, shortly before a large part of the NS staff went on strike in an attempt to hasten the end of the German occupation.

According to an expert report established on behalf of the German 'Train of Commemoration' project, the receipts taken in by the state-owned Deutsche Reichsbahn for mass deportations in the period between 1938 and 1945 reached a sum of £536,405242.18 ($664,525,820.34). Hans-Rüdiger Minow, a spokesperson for the Board of Directors of the project, advised Polish and other Eastern European victims' organisations, which had convened in Warsaw in 2010 to quantify their reparations claims that, 'Our expert assessment calculated Berlin's revenues, alone for the victims of the mass deportations by the Reichsbahn to forced labour and extermination camps, to be around half a billion euros – interest not included.'

Nederlandse Spoorwegen (NS) provided transport from Camp Westerbork, in the Drenthe province of north-eastern Netherlands (which was a transit camp set up by the Dutch government in the summer of 1939) as far as the village of Nieuweschans, on the border of Netherlands and Germany, and from there, the Deutsche Reichsbahn Gesellschaft (German National Railroad Alliance) took over transport to Auschwitz. In June 2019, The Netherlands' state-run rail company announced that it will pay tens of millions of euros in compensation to Holocaust victims and their families after a recommendation that it pay up to £45m (€50m) to around 500 survivors of the camps and 5,500 next of kin of the thousands of people it transported to Nazi death camps during the Second World War. Roger van Boxtel, the chief executive of NS, said it was time for the company to make a gesture to those 'directly involved' as he reiterated an apology first made in 2005, but at that time only set up a commission to decide how much to pay.

The French National Railway Company (SNCF) under the Vichy Government was requisitioned for the transport of German armed forces and armaments, from which the invading German troops were responsible for the destruction of nearly 350 French railway bridges and tunnels. According to differing estimates, SNCF surrendered between 125,000 and 213,000 wagons and 1,000–2,000 locomotives.

German occupying forces in France also requisitioned SNCF to transport nearly 77,000 Jews as well as thousands of other so-called undesirables, without food or water (pleaded for in vain by the Red Cross), to Nazi extermination camps. These deportations have been the subject of historical controversy and lawsuits in France as well as in the United States to the present day. In December 2014, SNCF agreed to pay up to $60 million (GBP 45.8967) worth of compensation to Holocaust survivors in the United States, corresponding to approximately $100,000 (£ 76,332.86) per survivor.

All railway lines leading to death camps built in occupied Poland are ceremonially cut off from the existing railway system in the country, similar to the well-preserved arrival point at Auschwitz known as the 'Judenrampe' platform. Commemorative monuments were traditionally erected at collection points elsewhere.

The Yalta Conference

The Yalta Conference was the second of three wartime conferences among the Big Three, preceded by the Tehran Conference in 1943 and followed by the Potsdam Conference in July 1945. Code-named the 'Argonaut Conference', the Yalta Conference, was convened in the Livadia Palace near Yalta, from 4 to 11 February 1945. The meeting comprised the heads of government of the United States, the United Kingdom, and the Soviet Union, represented by President Franklin D. Roosevelt, Prime Minister Winston Churchill, and Premier Joseph Stalin, respectively, to discuss agendas for Europe's post-war reorganisation, and how to keep the peace between post-war countries. France's leader, Charles de Gaulle, was not invited to the Yalta Conference, and Stalin agreed to include France in the post-war governing of Germany only if France's zone of occupation was taken from the American and British zones.

At the time of the conference, the war in Europe was practically won. All of France and Belgium had been liberated. The German Army had been pushed back from the Western Front towards its border with France following the D-day landings of June 1944, and on the Eastern Front, the Red Army had turned the tide of the war inexorably in the favour of the Allies, and were within 70km (43 miles) of the German capital, Berlin. Although Hitler was unwilling to surrender, his military was on its knees and the final capitulation was beyond doubt. But the differences between East and West would inevitably return to the surface.

The representatives of the three powers at the conference were not natural allies; Britain and America had broadly similar concerns and aims for world peace and order based on capitalist democracy, while Stalin and his USSR had an entirely different world view based on Soviet communism and dictatorship. Churchill pressed for free elections and democratic governments in Eastern and Central Europe, and specifically Poland. Roosevelt wanted Soviet support in the US Pacific War against Japan, specifically for 'Operation Storm', the planned invasion of Japan. Stalin demanded a Soviet sphere of political influence in Eastern and Central Europe, an essential aspect of the USSR's national security strategy, with Poland being the first item on the Soviet agenda, stating that, 'For the Soviet government, the question of Poland was one of honour'[4] and security because Poland had served as a historical corridor for forces attempting to invade Russia, and added that, 'because the Russians had greatly sinned against Poland, the Soviet government was trying to atone for those sins.'[5] He concluded with, 'Poland must be strong' and that, 'the Soviet Union is interested in the creation of a mighty, free and independent Poland.'[6]

The main objectives of the USSR were to secure their position and interests through political domination of Eastern Europe, ensuring that Germany would no longer pose a threat to their power and achieving reparations for their huge losses. Their material and human sacrifices far outweighed that of the Western allies, and Stalin was keen to be compensated accordingly. Going further, and not wanting to leave the countries which he had saved from Nazism open to capitalist democracy, he wanted a ring of totalitarian satellite countries to protect the Soviet Union.

After the war, Germany and Berlin would be split into four occupied zones. Stalin agreed that France would have a fourth occupation zone in Germany, but it would have to be formed out of the American and British zones.

The Nuremberg Trials

The Nuremberg trials were a series of thirteen trials carried out in Nuremberg, Germany, between 1945 and 1949, to bring Nazi war criminals to justice. The choice of the German city was significant for it was there that the National Socialist Party had held its annual rallies. Although the legal justifications for the trials and their procedural innovations were controversial at the time, the Nuremberg trials are now regarded as a milestone toward the establishment of a permanent international court, and an important precedent for dealing with later instances of genocide and other crimes against humanity.

Each of the four Allied powers supplied two judges – a main judge and an alternate. There were prosecutors and defence attorneys according to British and American law, but the decisions and sentences were imposed by a tribunal (panel of judges) rather than a single judge and a jury. The Trial of Major War Criminals was held from 20 November 1945 to 1 October 1946. Twenty-four individuals were indicted, along with six Nazi organisations determined to be criminal (such as the Gestapo or secret state police). The chief American prosecutor was Robert H. Jackson (1892–1954), an associate justice of the US Supreme Court.

The inclination of the British government and the prime minister, Winston Churchill, in December 1942, had originally been simply to shoot Axis leaders out-of-hand as outlaws, once they were caught, and even in May 1945, this was still the preferred option. The plan was to allow senior officers in the field to confirm the identity of the 'war criminals', and then to execute them by firing squad within six hours. Anthony Eden, Britain's foreign secretary, had announced in 1942 that, 'The guilt of such individuals is so black that they fall outside and go beyond the scope of any judicial process.'[7] The Americans and Russians, however, preferred a public show trial which would dispense with preordained capital punishment.

The International Military Tribunal (IMT) was constituted on 8 August 1945 to cope with the unique situation faced by the court, and while the Western powers knew that Stalin's regime was guilty of many of the crimes against humanity laid out against the German prisoners (the dissection of Poland in September 1939 and attacking Finland three months later, which would have been in the dock as well), it was forced to keep silent to maintain a public face of collaboration and accept the Soviet insistence that only Axis aggression was covered by the new legal body of international law. The surviving Italian fascist leaders were later tried by Italian courts.

The twenty-four Nazis in positions of political influence including Hans Frank (Governor-General of Occupied Poland), Wilhelm Frick

(Minister of the Interior), Julius Streicher (radical Nazi antisemitic publisher), Alfred Rosenberg (Minister for Occupied Eastern Territories), Ernst Kaltenbrunner (Head of Security Forces), Joachim von Ribbentrop (Foreign Minister), Fritz Sauckel (Head of Forced-Labour Allocation), Alfred Jodl (Armed Forces Command), Wilhelm Keitel (Head of the Armed Forces), and Arthur Seyss-Inquart (Reich Commissioner for the Occupied Netherlands) were charged with the four counts falling within the jurisdiction of the court: crimes against peace; planning and waging aggressive war; war crimes; and crimes against humanity (genocide and persecutions of civilian populations). The Nazi leader Adolf Hitler committed suicide on 30 July 1945 and was never brought to trial. Heinrich Himmler and Joseph Goebbels had already killed themselves rather than face capture and trial.

As the accused men and judges spoke four different languages, the trial saw the introduction of a technological innovation taken for granted today: instantaneous translation. The International Business machines Corporation (IBM) provided the technology, and recruited men and women from international telephone exchanges to provide on-the-spot translations through headphones in English, French, German and Russian.

After 216 court sessions, the IMT announced its verdicts on 1 October 1946: eighteen were found guilty and three were acquitted. Twelve were sentenced to death by hanging, including Hermann Göring (Hitler's former deputy and the most senior surviving Nazi) but committed suicide the night before he was due to hang. The executions of the ten were carried out on 16 October. Rudolf Hess (Deputy Leader of the Nazi Party) was sentenced to life in Spandau Prison, as were Walther Funk (Reich Minister for Economic Affairs) and Erich Raeder (Head of the German Navy). Hess committed suicide while in prison on 17 August 1987. Four were sentenced to terms of imprisonment ranging from ten to twenty years: Karl Doenitz (Erich Raeder's successor as Head of the German Navy), Baldur von Schirach (Head of the Hitler Youth), Albert Speer (Armaments Minister), and Konstantin von Neurath (Governor of Bohemia and Moravia). Martin Bormann (Hitler's Adjutant) was sentenced to death in absentia (he remained missing). Albert Speer, the 'Decent Nazi' and Hitler's personal architect, was released in 1966 after being given a twenty-year sentence for being responsible for the mass exploitation of forced foreign labour. He spent his remaining years writing about the Nazi regime, donating most of his royalties to Jewish charities.

Following the Trial of Major War Criminals, an additional twelve trials were held at Nuremberg, and lasted from December 1946 to April 1949, and were grouped together as the Subsequent Nuremberg Proceedings. They were conducted before US military tribunals rather than the international tribunal that decided the fate of the major Nazi leaders. Growing differences among the four Allied powers had made other joint trials impossible.

These proceedings included the Doctors' Trial, from 9 December 1946 to 20 August 1947, in which twenty-three defendants were accused of crimes against humanity, including medical experiments on prisoners of war. The Judges' Trial of sixteen lawyers and judges who were charged with furthering the Nazi plan for racial purity by implementing the eugenics laws of the Third Reich, was held between 5 March and 4 December 1947. Other subsequent trials dealt with German industrialists accused of using slave labour and plundering occupied countries; high-ranking army officers accused of atrocities against prisoners of war; and SS officers accused of violence against concentration-camp inmates. In all, 199 defendants were tried at Nuremberg; 161 were convicted and thirty-seven were sentenced to death, including twelve of those tried by the IMT. Eight others were given life in prison and an additional seventy-seven people received prison terms of varying lengths. Authorities later reduced a number of the sentences.

The findings at Nuremberg led directly to the United Nations Genocide Convention (1948) and Universal Declaration of Human Rights (1948), as well as the Geneva Convention on the Laws and Customs of War (1949). In addition, the International Military Tribunal supplied a useful precedent for the trials of Japanese war criminals in Tokyo between 1946 and 1948, the 1961 trial of Nazi leader Adolf Eichmann in 1962, and the establishment of tribunals for war crimes committed in the former Yugoslavia (1993) and in Rwanda (1994).

The Red Cross

The Red Cross has long acknowledged its awareness of the treatment of Jews during the Second World War, but maintains that if it had disclosed what it knew, it would have lost its ability to inspect prisoner of war camps on both sides of the front. In his book *Une Mission Impossible*, Jean-Claude Favez, having gained unrivalled access to its archives, presented a fundamental reappraisal of the role of the world's most famous charity in the Second World War. The book was published in France in 1988, and later translated into German but didn't appear in English until 1999 as *The Red Cross and the Holocaust*.

For the most part, however, the Red Cross's assistance came late in the war and beneficiaries were relatively few compared with the millions of people who died in the camps. Files containing 25,000 microfilmed pages were turned over to the United States Holocaust Memorial Museum. Radu Ioanid, the museum's specialist on Holocaust survivors, saw that the Red Cross, which is supposed to maintain neutrality, had rescued thousands of Jews in Hungary and Romania and had assisted Jews at a concentration camp in Ravensbruck, Germany. The documents are in two groups, one dealing with Jewish prisoners and the other with hostages and political detainees, and both groups of files contained many first-hand accounts and reports on the persecution of Jews and political prisoners from 1939 to 1945.

Another scholar at the museum, Randolph L. Braham, Distinguished Professor Emeritus in Political Science at the City University of New York, wrote in his book, *The Politics of Genocide* (Columbia University Press, 1994): 'The International Red Cross feared that intervention in support of the Jews might jeopardize its traditional activities on behalf of prisoners of war.'

Mr Ioanid said, 'There is no doubt that the Red Cross let itself be used by the Nazis.'[8] But to its credit added, 'The Red Cross took 3,000 to 3,500 Jewish orphans from Romania to Palestine on ships in 1944, when the Romanians realised that their German allies were going to lose the war, and relaxed their anti-Jewish campaign. By then, however, half of Romania's 760,000 Jews had already been killed.'[9] Giving an example, the 'positive reports' that Red Cross inspectors wrote about the concentration camp at Terezin, Czechoslovakia, he said the organisation had been 'clearly manipulated'. To all outward appearances, Terezin, also known as Theresienstadt, was an unthreatening, model camp that even had its own symphony orchestra. In reality, it was a way station for Jews and other prisoners headed to the death camp at Auschwitz.

Notes

Adam Czerniaków was made head of the twenty-four member Jewish Council (Judenrat) on 4 October 1939, and was responsible for implementing German orders in the new Jewish Ghetto in Warsaw. As the German authorities began preparing for mass deportations of Jews from the Warsaw ghetto to the newly built Treblinka extermination camp in July 1942, the Jewish Council was ordered to provide lists of Jews and maps of their residences. The orders stated that deportations would begin immediately at the rate of 6,000 people per day, to be supplied by the Jewish Council and the Ghetto Police. Failure would result in the execution of 100 hostages, including Council employees and Czerniaków's wife. Realizing that deportation meant death, Czerniaków went to plead for the orphans on 23 July. When he failed, he returned to his office in the council building at 26/28 Grzybowska Street, and killed himself by taking a cyanide capsule. He left a suicide note to his wife, which read, 'They demand me to kill children of my nation with my own hands. I have nothing to do but to die,' and a note to one to his fellow members of the Council, explaining, 'I can no longer bear all this. My act will prove to everyone what the right thing is to do.' He was succeeded by his deputy Marek Lichtenbaum.

Adolf Eichmann the SS-Obersturmbannführer, was captured in San Fernando, Buenos Aires, on 11 May 1960 by Mossad agents in Argentina in 1960. He stood trial at the Beit Ha'am (today known as the Gerard Behar Centre) in central Jerusalem before a special tribunal of the Jerusalem District Court in Israel where, on 12 December 1961, he was convicted on fifteen counts of crimes against humanity, war crimes, crimes against the Jewish people, and membership in a criminal organisation. He was sentenced to death by hanging on 15 December. Following failed appeal hearings, the sentence was carried out on 1 June 1962.

Notes

Alois Brunner was an Austrian SS officer held responsible for sending over 100,000 European Jews to ghettos and concentration camps in Eastern Europe. He was renowned for his exceptional brutality while he was commander of the Drancy internment camp outside Paris from June 1943 to August 1944, from which nearly 24,000 people were deported. He was also the man responsible for the creation of gas vans, which were the antecedents of the Nazi death camps. Post-war, he fled to Syria where the Assad regime sheltered him for decades, going by the name of Abu Hussein, but his notoriety meant he was practically kept as a prisoner. Convicted and sentenced to death by French courts in absentia, Israeli agents attempted to kill him on two occasions by sending him parcel bombs, the second of which caused him to lose and eye and four fingers, but did not kill him. Brunner spent his last years in miserable conditions underneath an apartment block in Damascus. He died in 2001 at the age of 89.

Andrey Vlasov was a top Soviet general. He fought in the Battle of Moscow (30 September 1941 – 20 April 1942) and later, as commander of the Soviet 2nd Shock Army, he was captured during an attempt to lift the withering Siege of Leningrad. During his time as a German prisoner, he affirmed his anti-Bolshevism and switched sides, and headed the Russian Liberation Army, which was comprised mostly former Soviet prisoners of war. At the end of the war, he changed sides again, and ordered the ROA to aid the Prague uprising against the Germans. Vlasov and a group of the ROA then tried to escape to the Western Front, but fell into the hands of American soldiers. The Americans later handed him and other ROA members over to the Soviets in a prisoner exchange. Vlasov was subsequently tried for treason, and hanged on 1 August 1946. The Russian historian Kirill Aleksandrov said, during an interview in 2015 on Radio Prague International that, 'Without the Vlasov army fighters the Prague [fighters] would have suffered colossal human losses. The number of victims was still high, some 1,500 victims, but it could have been worse, much worse.'

Bruno Tesch was a German chemist and entrepreneur, and one of two partners in a leading pest control company, Tesch and Stabenow (Testa). Together with Karl Weinbacher, Testa distributed Zyklon B, a pesticide consisting of inert adsorbents saturated with hydrogen cyanide, a volatile liquid extremely toxic to animals and humans. For legitimate use as a pesticide, Zyklon B included a warning odorant as not everyone can smell cyanide or recognize its faint almond-like odour. The company sold Zyklon B to the Wehrmacht and the SS in Auschwitz-Birkenau without the odorant, clearly showing that it was intended for use on humans; 4.5 million people were gassed to death by the use of Zyklon B in the Auschwitz/Birkenau alone. Tesch and Weinbacher were convicted by a British war tribunal, and executed by hanging in Hameln prison, Germany, on 16 May 1946. The company continued in Hamburg after the war as Testa GmbH until 1979, when it merged with Heerdt-Lingler GmbH (HeLi).

Döme Sztójay was responsible for the deportation of the entire Jewish population of Hungary outside of Budapest by the time Sztójay had fallen ill in July 1944, and was forced to give up his position as prime minister. He fled Hungary with the Nazis as the Soviet army approached Budapest. He was caught by American troops who returned him to Hungary in October 1945. On 22 March 1946, Sztójay, who had legalised Ferenc Szálasi's Arrow Cross Party, was found guilty by a People's Tribunal of war crimes and crimes against the people, and sentenced to death. On 22 August, he was executed by a firing squad in Budapest.

Ferenc Szálasi was the leader of the Arrow Cross Party and, after Miklós Horthys' forced removal by the Germans, became both Head of State and prime minister of the Kingdom of Hungary's 'Government of National Unity' (Nemzeti Összefogás Kormánya) for the final six months of Hungary's participation in the Second World War. During his brief rule, Szálasi's men murdered 10,000–15,000 Jews. Szálasi fled ahead of the Arrow Cross Party's cabinet, which was dissolved on 7 May 1945, a day before Germany's surrender. Szálasi was captured by American troops in Mattsee, Saltzburg, Austria, on 6 May, and was tried by the People's Tribunal in Budapest for war crimes and high treason. He was hanged on 12 March 1946 in Budapest, along with two of his former ministers, Gábor Vajna and Károly Beregfy, and the party ideologist József Gera. The method of hanging was unusual. A large post had a rope attached to a hook at the top. Szálasi was marched up steps, placed with his back to the post, his legs and arms were tied, the noose placed around his neck, the rope tightened, and the steps were removed. With the post only leaving a couple feet between Szálasi and the ground it is likely that he died slowly due to strangulation rather than being instantaneously rendered unconscious and dying shortly after as would happen when utilising the standard drop. This would also explain why his arms and legs were bound as to prevent struggle during the process.

Friedrich Jeckeln the SS General was taken prisoner by Soviet troops near Halbe on 28 April 1945. He, along with other German personnel, was tried before a Soviet military tribunal in the Riga Trial in Latvia from 26 January 1946 to 3 February 1946. Jeckeln and the other defendants were found guilty, sentenced to death and hanged in Riga on 3 February 1946 in front of some 4,000 spectators. Against popular misconception, the execution did not happen in the territory of the former Riga Ghetto, but in Victory Square (Uzvaras laukums).

Hans Christian Hingst was the head of the German occupation administration, and responsible for the organisation of the robbery, persecution, and ghettoization of the Jews in the city of Vilna from August 1941 to July 1944.

Hans Michael Frank, the German politician and lawyer who served as head of the General Government in Poland during the Second World War, instituted a reign of terror against the civilian population and became directly involved in the mass murder of Jews. He engaged in the use of forced labour and oversaw four of the extermination camps; the policies of enslavement and extermination would later be used extensively in conquered territories of the Soviet Union. Frank was captured by American troops on 4 May 1945, at Tegernsee in southern Bavaria. Following two failed suicide attempts, he was indicted for war crimes and crimes against humanity, and tried before the International Military Tribunal in Nuremberg. After being found guilty on 1 October 1946, he was sentenced to death by hanging, which was carried out at Nuremberg Prison on 16 October.

Heinz Reinefarth was assigned to be SS and Police Leader in Reichsgau Wartheland, which comprised the region of Greater Poland and adjacent areas, in January 1944. At the outbreak of the Warsaw uprising, Reinefarth was ordered to organise a military unit consisting of personnel from various security units and head for Warsaw. From 5 August 1944, Reinefarth's group took part in fighting in the Wola area. In two days, the units of Reinefarth and SS-Oberführer Oskar Dirlewanger executed approximately 60,000 civilian inhabitants of Warsaw in what is known as the Wola Massacre. After the war, Reinefarth was taken into custody by the British and American authorities, but due to the lack of evidence, he was never prosecuted for his actions in Warsaw, despite Polish requests for his extradition. After a West German court released him citing a lack of evidence, Reinefarth enjoyed a successful post-war career as a lawyer, becoming mayor of the wealthy resort town of Westerland, on the isle of Sylt, and a member of the Landtag, the state parliament of Schleswig-Holstein. The West German government also gave the former SS-Obergruppenführer a general's pension before he died in 1979.

Hermann Höfle was an Austrian-born SS commander and Holocaust perpetrator during the Nazi era. He was deputy to Odilo Globočnik in the Aktion Reinhard programme, serving as his main deportation and extermination expert. Höfle was arrested in 1961 in connection with these crimes, but he committed suicide in prison before he could be tried.

Hinrich Lohse was a Nazi politician and was appointed the Reichskommissar for the Ostland on 17 July 1941, after the German occupation of Baltic States from the Soviet Union. He shared many of the responsibilities for the ghettoization of the Jews of Latvia. He retained his functions in Schleswig-Holstein, and shuttled between his two seats of Riga and Kiel until the autumn of 1944, when he fled during the time when Nazi Germany was losing power. He was seized by the British Army around May 1945, and was sentenced in 1948 to ten years in prison, but was released in 1951 due to illness. Lohse spent his twilight years in Mühlenbarbek, Schleswig-Holstein, Germany.

Ilya Ehrenburg was a Soviet writer, Bolshevik revolutionary, journalist and historian, and was active in war journalism throughout the Second World War. His much criticised article 'Kill' was published in 1942, when German troops were deeply within Soviet territory, murdering, raping, and plundering. His work was read like the fire-and-brimstone passages from the Bible by the Soviet troops, inciting them to treat Germans as sub-human. The final paragraph concludes:

The Germans are not human beings. From now on the word German means to use the most terrible oath. From now on the word German strikes us to the quick. We shall not speak any more. We shall not get excited. We shall kill. If you have not killed at least one German a day, you have wasted that day ... If you cannot kill your German with a bullet, kill him with your bayonet. If there is calm on your part of the front, or if you are waiting for the fighting, kill a German in the meantime. If you leave a German alive, the German will hang a Russian and rape a Russian woman. If you kill one German, kill another – there is nothing more amusing for us than a heap of German corpses. Do not count days, do not count kilometers. Count only the number of Germans killed by you. Kill the German – that is your grandmother's request. Kill the German – that is your child's prayer. Kill the German – that is your motherland's loud request. Do not miss. Do not let through. Kill.

Ion Antonescu Serving as prime minster as well as his own foreign minister and defence minister of Romania, he presided over two successive wartime dictatorships. Antonescu enforced policies that were independently responsible for the deaths of as many as 400,000 people, most of them Bessarabian, Ukrainian and Romanian Jews, as well as Romanian Romani. He stood trial in May 1946 and was prosecuted at the first in a series of People's Tribunals, on charges of war crimes, crimes against the peace and treason. Despite two appeals, Antonescu was found guilty of the charges and on 1 June 1946, he was executed by a military firing squad near Jilava, Romania.

Josef Horák Following the German occupation of Czechoslovakia in March 1939, Josef, who served in the Czechoslovak Air Force, decided to smuggle himself out of the country, and fight for his homeland abroad. He served as a pilot with the Royal Air Force's Czechoslovak 311 bomber squadron. His family was massacred along with every inhabitant of the village of Lidice, Czechoslovakia, which was afterwards razed to the ground by the Nazis on 9 June 1942, as an alleged response to the assassination of Reinhard Heydrich a few days earlier.

Josef Szerynski was a Polish police colonel, whose name had been Sheinkman, before his conversion to Catholicism, and commanded the Jüdischer Ordnungsdienst which was tasked with combatting smuggling in and out of the Warsaw ghetto as well as keeping order. Szerynski was arrested by the Gestapo on 1 May 1942, for smuggling furs out of the ghetto for personal gain. He was released on the condition that he led the deportation action to Treblinka extermination camp in July 1942. He survived an assassination attempt by the Jewish underground in June, and remained in charge of the Ghetto Police until the end of the Grossaktion Warsaw on 21 September 1942, by which time it had claimed the lives of over 254,000 men, women and children from the ghetto. He committed suicide right after the next wave of deportations in January 1943.

Joseph Stalin was born in Georgia and was the revolutionary and Soviet politician who led the Soviet Union from the mid-1920s until 1953 as the general secretary of the Communist Party of the Soviet Union.
He was found semi-conscious by staff on the bedroom floor of his Volynskoe dacha, having suffered a cerebral haemorrhage. He was moved onto a couch and remained there for three days, being hand-fed using a spoon, and given various medicines and injections. Stalin died on 5 March 1953; an autopsy revealed that he had died of a cerebral haemorrhage, and that he also suffered from severe damage to his cerebral arteries due to atherosclerosis, which can occur through arsenic poisoning, and although no firm evidence has ever appeared, it raises the possibility that Stalin was murdered.

Jürgen Stroop was a German SS commander during the Nazi era, who served as SS and police leader in occupied Poland. He was involved in the suppression of the Warsaw ghetto uprising, taking over from the SS Functionary Ferdinand von Sammern-Frankenegg, following the latter's failure to suppress the uprising at the onset. The action cost the lives of over 50,000 people. Following the defeat of Germany, Stroop was prosecuted during the Dachau Trials and convicted of liquidating the Warsaw ghetto, which led to the murder of more than 50,000 people and the deportation of hundreds of thousands of other Jews to the death camps, ordering the shooting of one hundred Poles on 16 July 1943, and participating in the mass murder of Polish civilians in the Warthegau. He was hanged at Mokotów Prison on 6 March 1952.

Notes

Karl Hermann Frank was a prominent Sudeten German Nazi official in command of the Nazi police apparatus in the Protectorate, including the Gestapo, the Intelligence Agency (SD), and the Criminal Police (Kripo), was publicly hanged on 22 May 1946 by the Austro-Hungarian 'pole-drop' method, for his role in organising the massacres of the people of the Czech villages of Lidice and Ležáky. The execution drew a crowd of over five thousand onlookers and sparked a frenzy against all Germans.

Karol Pazúr initiated the murder of 265 Carpathian Germans and Hungarians near Přerov on 18 June 1945. He was arrested after the details of the massacre were published by the press two years later, was brought to trial in 1947 by the High Military Court in Bratislava, and was sentenced to seven years and six months in prison. He appealed, and the case was heard again in 1949 by the Supreme Military Court in Prague, who raised his sentence to twenty years. However, in 1951, his sentence was reduced by half by the then communist president, Klement Gottwald, who, two years later, granted him amnesty. Karol Pazúr died in Slovakia in 1979. The broad public only heard of the massacre after the 1989 fall of the communist regime.

Karl Weinbacher (see Bruno Tesch)

Ludvik Svoboda was a Czechoslovak general and politician who in 1938, following the accession of the Sudetenland to Germany, he was one of the founders of the Obrana Národa (Defence of the Nation) – A Czech insurgent guerrilla organisation that fought against the German occupation from 1939 to 1945. In 1946 he was awarded the title People's Hero of Yugoslavia. Svoboda was also awarded the title Hero of the Soviet Union on 24 November 1965, and Hero of the Czechoslovak Socialist Republic (a title he was awarded again in 1970 and 1975). He had been elected as president of Czechoslovakia on 30 March 1968 to 1975, during which time, in 1970, he was awarded the Lenin Peace Prize. He died in Prague on 20 September 1979.

Oskar Dirlewanger served as the founder and commander of the 36th Waffen Grenadier Division of the SS, also known as the 'Dirlewanger Brigade', during the Second World War. It was composed of violent criminals convicted of major crimes such as premeditated murder, rape, arson and burglary who were expected to die fighting on the front line. During operations, the unit engaged in pillaging and mass murder of civilians. Dirlewanger presided over and personally participated in many of the worst acts of violence during the Wola and the Ochota massacres in Warsaw was arrested on 1 June 1945 by French occupation troops while hiding under a false name near the town of Altshausen in Upper Swabia. He died on 7 June 1945 in a French prison camp at Altshausen. It has been speculated that he probably died as a result of ill-treatment by his Polish guards.

Rezső Kasztner, who had been directly instrumental in the negotiated release of Jews from Budapest in late 1944, moved to Palestine after the end of the war, and became a civil servant working in the Israeli government. He was later accused by the journalist Malkiel Grunwald of collaborating with the Nazis to secure the release of his relatives and friends on the Kasztner Train, and by not doing enough to warn Hungarian Jews about their fate. Despite the judge summing up the trial by saying that Kasztner had 'sold his soul to the devil', the Israeli Supreme Court cleared Kasztner of all wrongdoing. However, before the new decision could be announced, Kasztner was assassinated on 3 March 1957 at Tel-Aviv by Zeev Eckstein, part of a three-man squad from a group of veterans from the pre-state Zionist militia Lehi, led by Yosef Menkes and Yaakov Heruti, and died of his injuries twelve days later.

Walter Herman Julius Rauff was a SS colonel who was involved in the development and modification of trucks by diverting their exhaust fumes into airtight chambers in the back of the vehicles, which would then be used as mobile gas chambers. Rauff was responsible for the deaths of nearly 100,000 communists, Jews, Roma and the physically and mentally ill in this way. He was also responsible for the indiscriminate execution of both Jews and local Partisans in Tunisia and Northern Italy during the war. Post-war, he sought refuge in Santiago, Chile, which harboured him for twenty-three years. There had been numerous international efforts to bring him to trial since 1961. The last request to extradite Rauff to West Germany, by the renowned Franco-German journalist and Nazi hunter Beate Klarsfeld in 1983, was flatly rejected by the Pinochet regime. Amid a campaign for his extradition by Israel, West Germany and other nations, 77-year-old Rauff died of a heart attack at his home on 14 May 1984.

Glossary

AB Aktion was a second stage of the Nazi German campaign of violence which was aimed to eliminate the intellectuals and the upper classes of the Second Polish Republic across the territories slated for eventual annexation.

Aktion T4 was a post-war name for mass murder through involuntary euthanasia in Nazi Germany. The name T4 is an abbreviation of Tiergartenstraße 4, a street address of the Chancellery department set up in early 1940, in the Berlin borough of Tiergarten, which recruited and paid personnel associated with the early experiments.

Allied Control Authority replaced the extinct civil government of Nazi Germany as the governing body of the Allied Occupation Zones in Germany and Austria after the end of the Second World War in Europe. The members were the Soviet Union, the United Kingdom, the United States and France. The Allied Control Council was constituted the sole legal sovereign authority for Germany.

Arrow Cross was a far-right Hungarist movement led by Ferenc Szálasi, which formed a government in Hungary known as the Government of National Unity. They were recorded as having around 300,000 members in 1939, and following the result of the National Elections in May of that year, had become second most popular party. They were in power from 15 October 1944 to 28 March 1945.

Delegatura was an anti-communist resistance organisation formed on 7 May 1945, and acted as underground representatives of the Polish government-in-exile, and was active in Poland until 8 August 1945.

Einsatzgruppen established by Reichsführer SS and Chief of the German Police Heinrich Himmler, were units of the Nazi security forces composed of members of the SS and the Order Police (Orpo) that acted as mobile killing units during the German invasions of Poland in 1939, and the Soviet Union in 1941. Operating along the entire front, the Einsatzgruppen murdered an estimated 1.5 million Jews in large and small-scale operations, including the massacre of almost 34,000 Jews at Babi Yar in Ukraine, in September 1941.

Einsatzkommandos were a sub-group of five mobile killing squads of up to 3,000 men, usually composed of 500–1,000 functionaries of the SS and Gestapo, whose mission was to exterminate Jews, Polish intellectuals, Romani, homosexuals, communists and the NKVD collaborators in the captured territories, often far behind the advancing German front.

Ethnic cleansing is the systematic forced removal of ethnic, racial and/or religious groups from a given territory by a more powerful ethnic group. The forces applied may be various forms of forced migration (deportation, population transfer), intimidation, as well as genocide and genocidal rape. Ethnic cleansing is usually accompanied with efforts to remove physical and cultural evidence of the targeted group in the territory through the destruction of homes, social centres, farms, and infrastructure, and by the desecration of monuments, cemeteries, and places of worship.

Gebietskommissar (Territorial Commissioner) is the German designation for a type of administrative entity headed by a government official known (in English) as a Reich Commissioner.

Government-in-exile The Polish government-in-exile in London played an important role in exposing Nazi atrocities. Through the press and diplomatic channels, it tried constantly to inform the international community and Allied and neutral governments about what was happening in Auschwitz and other camps, the occupation reign of terror in Poland, the killing of Poles, and the extermination of the Jews.

Judenrat (Jewish Council) was an administrative agency imposed by Nazi Germany during the Second World War on Jewish communities across occupied Europe, principally within the ghettos, including those of German-occupied Poland.

Glossary

KdF – Kanzlei des Führers der NSDAP was a Nazi Party organisation and served as the private chancellery of Adolf Hitler. It handled different issues pertaining to matters such as complaints against party officials, appeals from party courts, official judgments, and clemency petitions, and also played a key role in the Nazi euthanasia programme.

Lwów Voivodeship was an administrative unit of interwar Poland. Because of the Nazi-Soviet invasion of Poland in accordance with the secret Molotov-Ribbentrop Pact, it became occupied by both the Wehrmacht and the Red Army in September 1939.

Molotov–Ribbentrop Pact on 24 December 1989, the Congress of the USSR People's Deputies officially recognised the secret protocols and condemned them as illegal and invalid from their inception. The protocols to split up territories between Germany and the Soviet Union. According to these protocols, Finland, Estonia, Latvia and Bessarabia were within the Soviet sphere of interest, and Poland and Lithuania fell into the German sphere of interest.

Oberscharführer (Translated as Senior Leader) was a Nazi Party paramilitary rank that existed between 1932 and 1945. Oberscharführer was first used as a rank of the Sturmabteilung and was created due to an expansion of the enlisted positions required by growing SA membership in the late 1920s and early 1930s.

Operation Reinhard was the codename of the secretive German plan to exterminate Poland's Jews in the General Government district of German-occupied Poland during the Second World War. This deadliest phase of the Holocaust was marked by the introduction of extermination camps.

Pogrom is a Russian word which, when directly translated, means 'to wreak havoc'. Pogroms typically describe violence by Russian authorities against Jewish people, particularly officially-mandated slaughter, though the word has been extended to the massacres of other groups as well.

Pole-Drop is a variation of the short-drop method of hanging, but instead of the noose being connected to a movable object which is then pulled away, the prisoner is lifted up and held while the noose is attached to a metal hook or eye bolt at the top of a stout post. The body is then allowed to drop a few inches, and their suspended bodyweight and physical struggling causes the noose to tighten, normally resulting in death by strangulation or carotid or Vagal reflex.

Reichsmark was the German currency from 1924 until 20 June 1948 in West Germany, where it was replaced with the Deutsche Mark, and until 23 June in East Germany, when it was replaced by the East German mark.

Rożki lies in the district of Gmina Kowala in Radom County, Masovian Voivodeship, in east-central Poland.

Serov Instructions an undated top secret document, signed by General Ivan Serov, Deputy People's Commissar for State Security of the Soviet Union (NKGB), which detailed procedures on how to carry out the mass deportations to Siberia of 13–14 June 1941, which occurred throughout the Baltic States during the first Soviet occupation, in 1940–41.

Schutzstaffel (SS) was originally an adjunct to the SA, was placed under the control of Heinrich Himmler and evolved to be more than a bodyguard unit for Hitler. It was split into two groups: the Allgemeine SS (General SS) and Waffen-SS (Armed SS). The Allgemeine SS was responsible for enforcing the racial policy of Nazi Germany and general policing, whereas the Waffen-SS consisted of combat units within Nazi Germany's military. A third component of the SS, the SS-Totenkopfverbände (SS-TV), ran the concentration camps and extermination camps.

Sturmabteilung (SA) (literally 'Storm Detachment'), was the Nazi Party's original paramilitary, and played a significant role in Adolf Hitler's rise to power in the 1920s and 1930s.

Sturmbannführer (translated as Assault Leader) was a Nazi Party paramilitary rank equivalent to major that was used in several Nazi organisations, such as the SA, SS, and the NSFK.

Subcarpathian Ruthenia was the eastern region of Czechoslovakia until March 1939, when it was immediately annexed by Hungary following the dismemberment of the Czechoslovak state. In 1946 it was incorporated into the Soviet republic of Ukraine.

Glossary

Sudetendeutsche Heimatfront (The Sudeten German Party) was created by Konrad Henlein on 1 October 1933, some months after the First Czechoslovak Republic had outlawed the German National Socialist Workers' Party.

Umschlagplatz were holding areas adjacent to railway stations in occupied Poland where Jews from ghettos were assembled for deportation to Nazi death camps.

White Mountain was a cataclysmic battle fought on 8 November 1620 between the Roman Catholic Habsburgs and the Protestant Union, that eradicated Bohemian independence, decimated Czech culture, and threw Bohemia into what the Czechs term 'its dark age'. Although the battle lasted for less than two hours, its consequences were felt for centuries.

Bibliography

Allatson, Paul, McCormack, Jo, *Portal Journal of Multidisciplinary International Studies Vol. 2, No. 1,* (January 2005)

Annas, George J., *The Nazi Doctors and the Nuremberg Code,* (Oxford University Press, 1995)

Apor, Balázs., *The Expulsion of the German Speaking Population of Hungary,* (2004)

Bank, Barbara, *Internment and Labor Camps of Former Socialist Countries – Czechoslovakia, Poland and Yugoslavia (1945–1956)* (2013)

Bankier, David; Michman, Dan (eds.) Holocaust and Justice. (Berghahn Books, 2011)

Baume, Maïa De La, French Railway Formally Apologizes to Holocaust Victims, (The New York Times, 25 January 2011)

Berger, Ronald J., *Fathoming the Holocaust: A Social Problems Approach,* (Transaction, 2002)

Black, Edwin, *IBM and the Holocaust,* (Dialog Press, 2002)

Braham, Robert L, *Politics of Genocide – The Holocaust in Hungary Vols 1-2,* (Downtown Publishing, 1997)

Braham, Randolph L., *The Politics of Genocide: The Holocaust in Hungary, Volume 1* (East European Monographs, 2016)

Bray, Charles, *London Daily Herald,* (24 August 1945)

Browning, Christopher R., *The Path to Genocide: Essays on launching the Final Solution,* (Cambridge University Press, 1992)

Brunnbauer, Ulf, Sundhaussen, Holm, *Power of Definition: Ethnic Cleansing in Eastern Europe in the 20th Century,* (LIT Verlag Münster, 2006)

Bryant, Chad, *Prague in Black: Nazi Rule and Czech Nationalism,* (Harvard University Press, 30 Sept 2009)

Bullivant, Keith; Giles, Geoffrey J; Pape, Walter, Germany and Eastern Europe: Cultural Identities and Cultural Differences, (1999)

Bibliography

Buresova, Jana, *The Homecoming: The Reception and Treatment of Repatriates to Post-war Czechoslovakia*, (Rodophi, B.V. 2014)

Carlton, David, *Churchill and the Soviet Union* (Manchester University Press, 2000)

CBC News, French railway must pay for transporting family to Nazis, (7 June 2006)

Csapody, Tamás, *Labour Servicemen at Bor*, (Vince Publishing, 2014)

de Zayas, Alfred-Maurice, *A Terrible Revenge*, (Palgrave Macmillan, 2Rev Ed, 2006)

de Zayas, Alfred-Maurice, *Nemesis at Potsdam* (Roudedge & Kegan Paul, 2nd edition, 1979)

de Zayas, Alfred-Maurice, *The German Expellees: Victims in War and Peace*, (Palgrave Macmillan, 1993)

Pressac, Jean-Claude, *Auschwitz Crematoria: The Machinery of Mass Murder* (in French) (CNRS Editions, 1993)

Death Marches (US Holocaust Memorial Museum, 2014)

De Balliel-Lawrora, Johannes Rammund, *The Myriad Chronicles*, (Xlibris, Corp., 2010)

Deforest, Walter R. *American Journal of Public Health*, (September, 1950)

Deforest, Walter R. *Public Health Practices in Germany under US Occupation (1945–1949)*, (1950)

Dejmek Jindřich, *Historical Roots: The Sudeten Problem in the Czech Lands to 1938,* (1998)

Douglas, R.M., *Orderly and Humane: The Expulsion of the Germans after the Second World War*, (New Haven & London: Yale University Press, 2012)

Eberhardt, Pitor, *Political Migrations in Poland 1939–1948* (Didactica, 2006)

Ehrenburg, Ilya, *Vojna (The War)* (Moscow, 1943)

Feis, Herbert, Between War and Peace: The Potsdam Conference, (Princeton University Press, 1960)

Felak, James Roman, *After Hitler, Before Stalin: Catholics, Communists, and Democrats in Slovakia, 1945- 1948*, (University of Pittsburgh Press; 1st ed, 16 July 2009)

Fleming, Gerald, *Hitler and the Final Solution,* (Berkley, 1984)

Fosse, Marit, Fox, John, Sean Lester: The Guardian of a Small Flickering Light, (Hamilton Books, 2016)

Friedlander, Henry, *The Origins of Nazi Genocide: From Euthanasia to the Final Solution*, (University of North Carolina Press, Chapel Hill, 1995)

Friss, Ivan, *Negotiations in Prague*, (14 August 1947)

Gerlach, Christian, *War, Food, Genocide: Research on German Extermination Policy in the Second World War,* (Hamburg, 1998)

Gillespie, Alexander, *A History of the Laws of War: Volume 3 The Customs and Laws of War with Regards to Arms Control*, (Hart Publishing, 2011)

Glenthöj, Jörgen, Kabitz, Ulrich, Krötke, Wolf, *Konspiration und Haft 1940-1945*, (Gütersloher Verlagshaus, 18 July, 2019)

Gollancz, Victor, *In Darkest Germany* (London, 1947)

Goodrich, Thomas, *Hellstorm: The Death of Nazi Germany 1944-1947,* (CreateSpace Independent Publishing Platform, 18 Aug. 2014)

Hilberg, Raul, *The Destruction of the European Jews,* (Chicago, 1961)

Hitler's speech to the Commanders in Chief on 22 August 1939 (document No. 798-PS) translated by Virginia von Schon, 15 November 1945

Hrabar, Roman Zbigniew, Nazi robbery of Polish children: Abduction and Germanization of Polish children in 1939-1945, (in Polish) (Silesian Publishing House, *1960)*

Hungarian State Railways (MÁV) Arch. *DNR. Document No: 113241* (1947)

Hungarian State Railways (MÁV) Arch. (*Operational Records, March–May 1948)*

Jones, Joseph, *The Politics of Transport in Twentieth-Century France,* (McGill Queens University Press, 1984)

Kacowicz, Arie Marcelo, Lutomski, Pawel, *Population resettlement in international conflicts: a comparative study*, (Lexington Books, 2007)

Kahan, Lazar, *The Slaughter of the Jews in Chelm,* (Yizkor Book Project, 1954)

Kaplan, Jan, Nosarzewska, Krystyna, *Prague: The Turbulent Century,* (Konemann, 1999)

Kaplan, Karel, The short March: the Communist takeover in Czechoslovakia, 1945–1948, (C. Hurst & Co. Publishers, 1987)

Kittel, Manfred, Moller, Horst, *Deutschsprachige Minderheiten 1945,* (in German), (De Gruyter Oldenbourg, 2006)

Kleiner, Rose, *Archives to throw new light on Ehrenburg* (Canadian Jewish News (Toronto), 17 March 1988)

Bibliography

Klessman, Christoph, *Die doppelte Staatsgründung: Deutsche Geschichte 1945–1955*, (Vandenhoeck & Ruprecht, 1982)

Kogon, Eugen; Langbein, Hermann; Rückerl, Adalbert; eds. *Nazi Mass Murder*, (Yale University Press, New Haven and London, 1993)

Kopka, Bogusław, *Gułag nad Wisłą. Komunistyczne obozy pracy w Polsce 1944–1956,* (in Polish) (Kraków, Wydawnictwo Literackie, 2019)

Kopka, Bogusław, *The Concentration Camp Warsaw: the History and Repercussions*, (Warsaw, Instytut Pamięci Narodowej, (2007)

Krupička, Miroslav, *History of Radio Prague, (Radio Prague,* Retrieved 17 June 2018)

Lancashire Evening Post, (27 October 1945)

Lifton, Robert Jay. *The Nazi Doctors: Medical Killing and the Psychology of Genocide*, (Papermac, 1990)

Lukas, Richard C., *Forgotten Holocaust,* (Hippocrene Books 2013)

Lukas, Richard C., *Germanization: Did the Children Cry? Hitler's War against Jewish and Polish Children, 1939–1945,* (Hippocrene Books, 2001)

MacDonogh, Giles, *After the Reich: The Brutal History of the Allied Occupation*, (New York: Basic Books, 2007)

MacIntyre, Alasdair, *Against the Self-Images of the Age: Essays in Ideology and Philosophy* (Duckworth, 1971)

Madajczyk, Czesław, *General Governorate in the Nazi plans*, (in Polish), (Polish Scientific Publisher, Warsaw, 1961)

Magocsi, Paul Robert, *Historical Atlas of East Central Europe*, (Seattle WA and London, 1995)

Majewski, Piotr M., *Edvard Beneš and the German question in the Czech Republic,* (Institute of National Remembrance Commission for the Prosecution of Crimes against the Polish Nation 2001)

Marasek, Jan, *Speaking to My Country*, (Lincolns-Prager Ltd; First ed., 1944)

Marrus, Michael R., *Chapter 12: The Case of the French Railways and the Deportation of Jews in 1944, In*

Rozett, Robert, *Conscripted Slaves, Hungarian Jewish Forced Laborers on the Eastern Front during the Second World War,* (Yad Vashem Publications, 2013)

Mierzejewski, Alfred, *The Most Valuable Asset of the Reich: A History of the German National Railway Volume 2, 1933–1945,* (The University of North Carolina Press, 2000)

Molotsky, Irvin, *The New York Times*, (19 December 1996)
Moses, Dirk A., *Genocide and Settler Society: Frontier Violence and Stolen Indigenous Children in Australian History,* (Berghahn Books, 2005)
Müller, Rolf-Dieter, *Hitler's Ostkrieg and the German settlement policy: The cooperation of Wehrmacht, economy and SS*, (in German), (Fischer, 1991)
Naimark, Norman, *Fires of Hatred,* (Harvard University Press, 2002)
Neugebauer, Wolfgang, Czech, Herwig, *Action T4 in Austria*, (2010)
New Encyclopedia Universal PWN (PWN Publishing House, Warsaw, 2004)
Orwell, George, *Politics and the English Language*, (Horizon, 1946)
Paikert, C.G., *The Danube Swabians. Germans Populations in Hungary and Yugoslavia and Hitler's impact on their Patterns,* (Martinus Nijhoff, The Hague, 1967)
Péterffy, Gergely, *Railway Traffic in Southwest Hungary after World War II* (Pro&Contra, 2018)
Piotrowski, Tadeusz, *Poland's Holocaust*, (McFarland & Co, 1998)
Polian, Pavel, *Against Their Will: The History and Geography of Forced Migrations in the USSR* (Central European University Press, 2003)
Polish Fortnightly Review, *The Real Terror, Part 2*, (15 November, 1941)
Quigley, Carroll, *Tragedy & Hope: A History of the World in Our Time*, (GSG and Associates, 2004)
Remme, Tilman, *The Battle for Berlin in World War Two*, (BBC, 2007)
Reiber, Alfred J, *Forced Migration in Central and Eastern Europe, 1939-1950*, Routledge; 1st ed., 2000)
Reynolds, David, *America, Empire of Liberty: A New History*, (Penguin, 2010)
Reynolds, David, Pechatnov, Vladimir, *The Kremlin Letters: Stalin's Wartime Correspondence with Churchill and Roosevelt,* (Yale University Press, 2 Oct. 2018)
Ruane, Michael E., *The Washington Post, (9 February 2018)*
Rummel, Rudolph Joseph, *Statistics of Democide, Ch.7,* (Transaction Publishers, 1997)
Rummel, Rudolph Joseph, *Death by Government: Genocide and Mass Murder since 1900*, (Transaction Publishers, 1997)
Russell, Bertrand, *The Times,* (19 October 1945, edit)
Sampson, Jobim, *Battle of Berlin: Lost Evidence,* (Flashback Television Limited for the History Channel, 2004)

Bibliography

Selwyn Ilan Troen, Benjamin Pinkus, Merkaz le-moreshet Ben-Guryon, *Organizing Rescue: National Jewish Solidarity in the Modern Period,* (Routledge, 1992)

Schechtman, Joseph B., *Postwar Population Transfers in Europe 1945–1955*, (University of Pennsylvania Press, Philadelphia, 1962)

Schmidt, Ulf, *Karl Brandt: The Nazi Doctor* (Hambledon, 2007)

Shaver, Katherine, *Holocaust group faults VRE contract,* (*The Washington Post,* 7 July 2010)

Sofsky, Wolfgang, *The Order of Terror: The Concentration Camp*, (Princeton University Press, Princeton, 1997)

Spieler, Silke, *Expulsion and eviction crime 1945–1948*, (Cultural Foundation of the German Expellees, Bonn, 1989)

Staněk, Tomáš, *Post-war excesses in the Czech lands in 1945 and their Investigation*, (Institute for Contemporary History of the Academy of Sciences, Prague, 2005)

Szabolcs, Szita, *Haláleröd. A History of the Military Labour Service 1944–1945,* (Kossuth Könyvkiadó, 1989)

Szurovy, G. *Hungarian-German Mineral Oil Ltd. (MANAT) activities from 1940 to 1944* (1987)

The Mass Extermination of Jews in German Occupied Poland, (Hutchinson & Company, Ltd, 1942)

Ther, Philipp, *German and Polish Expellees*: *Society and Expellee Policy in the SBZ/GDR and in Poland* 1945– 1956, (Vandenhoeck & Ruprecht, 1998)

Thompson, D., *The Nazi Euthanasia Programme*, (Axis History Forum, 14 March 2004)

Thompson, Dorothy, *Life Magazine*, (Andrew Heiskell, 22 March 1948)

Toth, Agnes, *Settlements in Hungary between 1945 and 1948: Relation of the Germans, the Internal Population Movements and the Slovak-Hungarian Population Exchange*, (in German) (Kecskemét, 1993)

Uzarczyk, Kamila, The Ideological basis of Breed Hygiene, (Adam Marszałek Publishing House, 2002)

Vaughan, David, *The Battle of the Airwaves: the extraordinary story of Czechoslovak Radio and the 1945 Prague Uprising*, (Radio Prague, Retrieved 10 June 2018)

Vidal-Naquet, Pierre, *Les assassins de la Mémoire*, (in French) (Seuil, 1995)

Wardzyńska, Dr Maria, *It was 1939. Occupation of the German Security Police in Poland Intelligenzaktion,* (Commission for the Prosecution of Crimes against the Polish Nation, 2009)

Wilson, Erin, *The Forced Expulsion of Ethnic Germans from Czechoslovakia after World War II:*

Memory, Identity, and History, (Connecticut College, New London, Connecticut 25 April, 2011)

Ziemer, Gerhard, *Deutscher Exodus: Expulsion and integration of 15 million East Germans*, (Seewald, 1973)

Strategic Review, Vol XII, (United States Strategic Institute, Winter 1984)

Holocaust Encyclopedia Killing Centres, (United States Holocaust Memorial Museum)

The staff of the Hungarian Jewish Relief Organisation, National Committee for Attending Deportees (DEGOB)

Socha, Paweł, *The Nazi Labour Camp on 7 Lipowa Street,* (Sztetl.org.pl)

The National Archives at Kew, Richmond, Surrey

https://chechar.wordpress.com/2019/06/19/summer-1945

http://faroutliers.blogspot.com

https://lumenlearning.com

http://munkataborok.hu

https://polishgreatness.com

https://theholocaustexplained.org

https://thelocal.de

http://uncensoredhistory.blogspot.com

https://wintersonnenwende.com

https://yivoencyclopedia.org

www.churchillarchiveforschools.com

www.eafund.org

www.globalpolicy.org

history.state.gov

www.zug-der-erinnerung.eu

Credits:

Professor James Mayfield, Concordia University/Institute for Research of Expelled Germans.

http://expelledgermans.org

Endnotes

Introduction

1. From Documents on British Foreign Policy. 1919-1939. eds. E.L. Woodward and Rohan Riftlep; 3rd series (London: HMSO, 1954), 7:258-260.
2. Konspiration und Haft 1940–1945, p378, Jörgen Glenthöj, Ulrich Kabitz, Wolf Krötke Gütersloher Verlagshaus, 18 Jul 2019.
3. Konspiration und Haft 1940–1945, p378, Jörgen Glenthöj, Ulrich Kabitz, Wolf Krötke Gütersloher Verlagshaus, 18 Jul 2019.
4. Konspiration und Haft 1940–1945, p378, Jörgen Glenthöj, Ulrich Kabitz, Wolf Krötke Gütersloher Verlagshaus, 18 Jul 2019.
5. Speech by the Führer to the Commanders in Chief on August 22, 1939, in United States Department of State, Documents on German Foreign Policy: From the Archives of the German Foreign Ministry. Washington, DC: United States Government Printing Office, 1957–1964. Series D (1937–1945), The Last Days of Peace, Volume 7: August 9 –September 3, 1939. Document192, pp. 200-04.
6. Speech by the Führer to the Commanders in Chief on August 22, 1939, in United States Department of State, Documents on German Foreign Policy: From the Archives of the German Foreign Ministry. Washington, DC: United States Government Printing Office, 1957–1964. Series D (1937–1945), The Last Days of Peace, Volume 7: August 9 –September 3, 1939. Document192, pp. 200-04.

Chapter One – Hitler's Final Solution

1. https://www.jpost.com/blogs/the-jewish-problem---from-anti-judaism-to-anti-semitism/chapter-11-the-final-solution-from-decision-to-execution-364523.

2. Sweeney, Kevin P. (2012) "We Will Never Speak of It: Evidence of Hitler's Direct Responsibility for the Premeditation and Implementation of the Nazi Final Solution" Constructing the Past: Vol. 13: Iss. 1, Article 7.
3. by Gotz Aly; translated by Gordon McFee (from the German edition of the Berliner Zeitung, December 13th, 1997).
4. Sweeney, Kevin P. (2012) "We Will Never Speak of It: Evidence of Hitler's Direct Responsibility for the Premeditation and Implementation of the Nazi Final Solution" Constructing the Past: Vol. 13: Iss. 1, Article 7.

Chapter Two – The Nazi Camps

1. http://www.holocaustresearchproject.org/euthan/14f13.html
2. http://www.holocaustresearchproject.org/euthan/14f13.html

Chapter Three – The Death Marches

1. *A History of the Laws of War: Volume 3 The Customs and Laws of War with Regards to Arms Control*, Alexander Gillespie, Hart Publishing, 2011.

Chapter Four – Czechoslovakia

1. *Sean Lester: The Guardian of a Small Flickering Light*, Marit Fosse, John Fox, Hamilton Books, 2016.
2. Amendments to the Federal Tort Claims Act, S. 2117: Joint Hearing Before the Subcommittee on Citizens and Shareholders Rights and Remedies and the Subcommittee on Administrative Practice and Procedure of the Committee on the Judiciary, United States Senate, Ninety-fifth Congress, Second Session, U.S. Government Printing Office, 1978.
3. De Balliel-Lawrora, Johannes Rammund, *The Myriad Chronicles*, (Xlibris, Corp., 2010)
4. https://www.inconvenienthistory.com/11/2/6785

Endnotes

5. De Balliel-Lawrora, Johannes Rammund, *The Myriad Chronicles*, (Xlibris, Corp., 2010)
6. Speaking to My Country, Jan Masarek, Lincolns-Prager (Publishers) Limited; First ed, (1944)
7. Radio Prague International, Jan Velinger, 12 May 2004.
8. Radio Prague International, Jan Velinger, 12 May 2004.
9. Radio Prague International, Jan Velinger, 12 May 2004.
10. Forced Migration in Central and Eastern Europe, 1939–1950, Alfred J. Reiber, Routledge; 1st ed, (31 Oct. 2000)
11. Prague in Black: Nazi Rule and Czech Nationalism, Chad Bryant, Harvard University Press, 30 Sept 2009.
12. After Hitler, Before Stalin: Catholics, Communists, and Democrats in Slovakia, 1945–1948, James Ramon Felak, University of Pittsburgh Press; 1 edition (16 July 2009)
13. De Balliel-Lawrora, Johannes Rammund, *The Myriad Chronicles*, (Xlibris, Corp., 2010)
14. *Forgotten Voices: The Expulsion of the Germans from Eastern Europe After World War II*, Ulrich Merten, Routledge; 1st ed, (31 Jan. 2012)
15. *Hellstorm: The Death of Nazi Germany 1944–1947*, Thomas Goodrich, CreateSpace Independent Publishing Platform (18 Aug. 2014)
16. *Hellstorm: The Death of Nazi Germany 1944–1947*, Thomas Goodrich, CreateSpace Independent Publishing Platform (18 Aug. 2014)
17. *Orderly and Humane: The Expulsion of the Germans after the Second World War*, RM Douglas (New Haven & London: Yale University Press, 2012)
18. *Orderly and Humane: The Expulsion of the Germans after the Second World War*, RM Douglas (New Haven & London: Yale University Press, 2012)
19. *Iron Curtain: The Crushing of Eastern Europe 1944–56*, Anne Applebaum, Penguin (4 Oct. 2012)
20. Stalin, Czechoslovalia, and the Marshall Plan: New Documentation from Czechoslovak Archives, Karol Kaplan, Vojtech Mastny, Translated by John M. Deasy.
21. The Brussels and North Atlantic Treaties 1947–1949: Documents on British Policy Overseas, Series 1, Vol X, eds. Tony Insall, Patrick Salmon, Whitehall History Publishing, 2015.

22. The Brussels and North Atlantic Treaties 1947–1949: Documents on British Policy Overseas, Series 1, Vol X, eds. Tony Insall, Patrick Salmon, Whitehall History Publishing, 2015.
23. https://www.muzeuminternetu.cz/offwebs/czech/348.htm

Chapter Six – Poland

1. The House of Commons Sitting of 31 March 1939: The European Situation, Series 5, vol. 345 cc2415-20.
2. *The Kremlin Letters: Stalin's Wartime Correspondence with Churchill and Roosevelt, David Reynolds*, Vladimir Pechatnov, Yale University Press (2 Oct. 2018).
3. Heinrich Himmler on the Treatment of Foreign Ethnic Groups in the East, 15 May 1940, Reinhard Kühnl, German fascism in sources and documents, 3rd edition, Cologne 1978, pp. 328ff.
4. Documents on the Holocaust, Selected Sources on the Destruction of the Jews of Germany and Austria, Poland and the Soviet Union, Yad Vashem, Jerusalem, 1981, Document no.128.
5. *Auschwitz, the Allies and Censorship of the Holocaust*, Michael Fleming, Cambridge University Press (17 April 2014).
6. The Mass Extermination of Jews in German Occupied Poland, Polish Ministry of Foreign Affairs, Hutchinson & Co., Ltd, 10th December 1942.
7. Ciche lata kata, Tebinka, Jacek, nr 32 (2362), 10 September 2002, page 66.
8. *The Story of the SS: Hitler's Infamous Legions of Death*, Al Cimino, Arcturus Publishing, 2017.
9. *Death by Government: Genocide and Mass Murder Since 1900*, Rudolph Joseph Rummel, Transaction Publishers; 1st ed., 30 Jan, 1997.
10. *Death by Government: Genocide and Mass Murder Since 1900*, Rudolph Joseph Rummel, Transaction Publishers; 1st ed., 30 Jan, 1997.
11. Deutsche Und Polnische Vertriebene: Gesellschaft und Vertriebenenpolitik in SBZ/ddr und in Polen 1945–1956, Philipp Ther, Vandenhoeck & Ruprecht, December 31, 1998, p. 56.

Chapter Seven – The Removal of Germans from Eastern Europe

1. *Lancashire Evening Post*, 27 Oct. 1945
2. *Lancashire Evening Post*, 27 Oct. 1945

Chapter Eight – Germany

1. Alfred de Zayas, *Nemesis at Potsdam* (London: Roudedge & Kegan Paul, 2nd edition, 1979), pp. 6546, 201; Erich Kern (ed.), Verheimlichte Dokumente (Munich: FZ- Verlag, 1988), pp. 260-61, 353-55.
2. The Conference at Malta and Yalta, 1945, vol 1, US Department of State, Greenwood Press (1976)
3. *The German Expellees: Victims in War and Peace*, Alfred-Maurice De Zayas, Palgrave Macmillan UK, 1993.
4. *Warlords: An Extraordinary Re-creation of World War II Through the Eyes and Minds of Hitler, Churchill, Roosevelt, and Stalin*, Simon Berthon, Joanna Potts, Da Capo Press, 2007.
5. *Warlords: An Extraordinary Re-creation of World War II Through the Eyes and Minds of Hitler, Churchill, Roosevelt, and Stalin*, Simon Berthon, Joanna Potts, Da Capo Press, 2007.
6. *Warlords: An Extraordinary Re-creation of World War II Through the Eyes and Minds of Hitler, Churchill, Roosevelt, and Stalin*, Simon Berthon, Joanna Potts, Da Capo Press, 2007.
7. *Stay the Hand of Vengeance: The Politics of War Crimes Tribunals*, Gary Jonathan Bass, Princeton University Press (28 April 2014).
8. *The New York Times*, Irvin Molotsky, 19 December 1996.
9. *The New York Times*, Irvin Molotsky, 19 December 1996.

Index

Adam Czerniaków, 96, 110, 156
Adolf Eichmann, 154, 156
Adolf Hitler, vii, viii, 24, 26, 69, 92, 100, 153, 167, 168
Aktion T4, 12, 165
Albania, xiii, 71
Albert Speer, 79, 153,
Alfred Jodl, 38, 153
Allied Control Authority, 89, 165
Andrey Vlasov, 35, 157
Antoni Chruściel, 121
Antonín Hron, 28
Antonín Zápotocký, 66
Armia Krajowa, 117
Armistice, 74, 76, 77, 78
Arrow Cross Party, 70, 77, 158
Arthur W. Tedder, 39
Aryan, 29, 30, 100, 101, 106, 118
Auschwitz-Birkenau, 9, 18, 75, 115, 149, 158
Austria, 6 , 7, 12, 14, 17, 19, 21, 24, 29, 51, 52, 53, 55, 56, 59, 60, 69, 89, 138, 158, 165
Ebensee, 14
Hartheim Castle, 6
Mauthausen-Gusen, 8, 14, 22
Baden-Württemberg, 85

Bavaria, viii, 9, 17, 23, 26, 77, 89, 159
Obersalzberg, viii
Tegernsee, 23, 159
Béla Horváth, 76
Béla Imredy, 69
Béla Miklós, 78
Berlin Airlift, 145, 146
Bertrand Russell, 142
Bizone, 136
Bohuslav Marek, 61
Bolsheviks, 139, 160
Bronislav Kaminski, 125
Buchenwald, 14, 22, 23, 80
Carl Lutz, 79
Comecon, 64
Cominform, 64
Comintern, 64
Communist Party, 35, 40, 45, 59, 62, 63, 64, 65, 81, 142, 162
Croatia, 17, 71
Bačka and Baranja, 71, 73, 75
Sajmište, 71
Zemun, 71

Czechoslovakia, vii, x, xi, 12, 24, 69, 72, 80, 81, 82, 91, 113, 128, 130, 144, 145, 155, 161, 163, 168

Index

Balbínova Street, 36, 38
Moravia, 17, 27, 30, 36, 51
Czech Republic, vii, 19, 54, 55
Czernin Palace, 66
Dejvice, 39
Dobšinej, 55
Fochova Třída, 36, 37
Gelnica, 55
Horní Moštěnice, 54
Janova Lehota, 55
Kežmarok, 55
Konstantinovy Lázně, 41
Krásné Březno, 60
Ležáky, 31, 32, 163
Lidice, 12, 31, 32, 48, 161, 163
Mikulov, 51, 52, 56
Młynice, 55
Můstek, 33
Na Smetance, 38
Pankrác, 39
Postelberg, 61
Postoloprty, 61
Přerov, 42, 54, 163
Ruzyně Airport, 28, 33
Strašnice, 37, 38
Švédské šance, 55
Svitava, 55
Svratka, 55
Terezin, 31, 155
Ústí nad Labem, 60
Vinohradská Street, 36
Žatec, 61
Zbrojovka, 56
Žiar nad Hronom, 55
Žižkov, 37, 38

Dachau, 8, 9, 22, 23, 43, 80, 162
Daily Mail, 51

Deutschmark, 145
Diphtheria, 92
Disease, 15, 21, 52, 60, 70, 73, 77, 79, 82, 92, 105, 106, 107, 116, 119
Döme Sztójay, 74
Draža Mihailović, ix
Dror Youth Movement, 104
Ede Marányi, 79
Edmund Veesenmayer, 74
Eduard Weiter, 23
Einsatzgruppen, 3, 72, 103, 165, 166
Edvard Beneš, 25, 27, 28, 32, 33, 40, 41, 46, 47, 48, 62, 64, 65, 66, 67, 82, 83
Emanuel Moravec, 28, 33, 34
Emil Hácha, 28
Ernest Bevin, 135
Euthanasia, 2, 3, 5, 6, 10, 11, 12, 15, 18, 101, 165, 167
Ferenc Szálasi, 77, 78, 81, 82, 158, 159, 165
Field Marshal Montgomery, 135
František Moravec, 28
František Chvalkovský, 1, 28
František Weidmann, 29
Franciszek Paweł Raszeja, 111
Franz Kutschera, 117
Franz Murer, 108
Friedrich Jeckeln, 72, 159
Fritz Schwalm, 102
Fritz Todt, 79
Führer, xiv, xvi, 1, 2, 28
Gas van, 6, 71
Georgy Zhukov, 38, 120, 140
Gerhard Kretschmar, 2
German 1st Panzer Army, 78

183

Germany, vii, viii, ix, x, xi, xiii,
 1, 3, 6, 8, 10, 12, 14, 15, 17,
 19, 21, 22, 23, 24, 25, 26, 27,
 28, 29, 39, 43, 47, 49, 52, 53,
 57, 59, 60, 65, 66, 67, 69, 70,
 71, 74, 76, 77, 78, 79, 80, 84,
 85, 86, 87, 88, 89, 90, 91, 93,
 95, 96, 97, 99, 100, 106, 108,
 114, 117, 119, 120, 126, 127,
 128, 129, 130, 131, 132, 134,
 135, 136, 137, 138, 139, 140,
 141, 142, 143, 144, 145, 146,
 147, 149, 150, 151, 155, 158,
 160, 162, 163, 164, 165, 166,
 167, 168
Bad Köstritz, 23
Baden-Württemberg, 85
Bergen-Belsen, 20, 76
Berlin, 3, 5, 13, 27, 28, 57, 74, 92,
 117, 120, 138, 140, 141, 145,
 146, 149, 150, 151, 165
Bernburg, 6
Bienwald, 140
Brandenburg, 5, 6, 12, 93, 120
Buchenwald, 14, 22, 23, 80
Eisenberg, 23
Flensburg, 23
Flossenbürg, 22, 23, 80
Gera, 23
Grabow, 20
Gross-Rosen, 22
Hadamar, 6
Hamburg, 20, 23, 137, 143, 158
Hessen, 89
Jena, 23
Lauenburg, 22
Leipzig, 2
Lübeck, 23, 131, 144
Ludwigslust, 20
Mannheim, 85
Mauthausen–Gusen, 8, 14, 22
Neuengamme, 8, 20, 23
Nuremberg, 25, 29, 72, 102, 151,
 152, 154, 159
Obersalzberg, viii
Sachsenhausen, 8, 10, 13, 22, 80, 97
Saxony, 76, 92, 93, 143
Sonnenstein, 6
Stuttgart, 140
Thuringen, 14
Tübingen, 140
Wöbbelin, 20
Württemberg, 85

Germanisation, 29, 31, 32, 100,
 101
Gesundheitsamt, 100
Gregor Ebner, 102
Georgy Zhukov, 38, 120, 140
Günther Tesch, 102,
Hans Christian Hingst, 108, 159
Hans Georg von Friedeburg, 38
Hans-Joachim Scherer, 101
Hans-Jürgen Stumpff, 38
Hashomer Hatzair, 103, 104
Harry S. Truman, xi, 38, 41, 66,
 142, 145
Heinz Brückner, 102
Helmut Kohl, 2
Henryk Goldszmit, 112
Herbert Hübner, 102
Herbert Linden, 3
Hinrich Lohse, 108, 160
Hlinka Guard, 27, 63
Honvédség, 85
Horst Schweinberger, 108

Index

Hungary, vii, x, xiii, 18, 21, 27, 28, 40, 41, 46, 69, 70, 71, 72, 73, 74, 75, 76, 77, 78, 79, 80, 81, 82, 83, 84, 85, 86, 87, 88, 89, 90, 93, 95, 128, 144, 155, 158, 165, 168
Abda, 80
Bácsalmás, 75
Baranya, 86
Buda Hills, 89
Budaörs, 85
Debrecen-Apafa, 80
Kazincbarcika, 93
Kiskunhalas, 80
Kistarcsa, 79, 93
Lake Balton, 80
Murakeresztúr, 86
Pilis, 89
Pozsonyi Road, 77
Pusztavám, 80
Recsk, 93
Smallholders Party, 81, 83, 89
Somogy, 86
Szent István Park, 77
Tiszalök, 93
Tolna, 86
Volksbund, 83, 84, 90

IBM, 8, 153
I.G. Farben, 18, 90
Ilya Ehrenburg, 139, 160
Imre Nagy, 93
Inge Viermetz, 102
Ion Antonescu, 80, 161
Ivan Konev, 120, 140
Jakob Edelstein, 29
James F. Byrnes, 135
Jan Karski, 117, 128
Jan Kubiš, 31
Jan Masaryk, 62, 63, 64, 66
János Gyöngyösi, 41
Janusz Korczak, 112
Jaroslav Záruba, 39
Jewish Labour Bund, 113
Jewish Police Force, 106, 111
Joel Brand, 76
Johannes Blaskowitz, 28
Josef Vondra, 61
Jozef Gabčík, 31
Josef Szerynski, 106, 162
Joseph Stalin, viii, ix, x, xi, xv, xvi, 32, 41, 49, 63, 64, 65, 84, 98, 99, 120, 121, 127, 128, 140, 142, 146, 150, 151, 152, 162
Judenrat, 96, 103, 108, 156, 166
Julius Hallervorden, 102
Jürgen Stroop, 105, 162
Kaminski Brigade, 125
Karl Brandt, 2, 3
Karlsbad Programme, 26
Karol Pazúr, 55, 163
Karol Świerczewski, 127
Kazimierz Pollak, 111
Kirill Aleksandrov, 157
Klement Gottwald, 40, 59, 62, 63, 64, 65, 66, 163
Kliment Voroshilov, 88
Konrad Henlein, 24, 25, 26, 27, 40, 44, 53, 169
Konrad Meyer-Hetling, 102
Konstantin von Neurath, 153
Košice Programme, 40, 44
László Bárdossy, 72, 73
László Rajk, 88
Laurence Steinhardt, 62
Lavrentiy Beria, 84

Lebensborn Association, 100, 102
Leopold Okulicki, 118

Lithuania, 17, 95, 167
Ponary, 115

Lubyanka, 75
Ludvik Svoboda, 35, 63, 163
Malmö (Sweden), 23
Manchester Guardian, 131
Martin Gottfried Weiss, 23
Mátyás Rákosi, 81, 93
Max Sollmann, 102
Meshchansky District, 75
Miklós Horthy, 73, 74, 76, 77
Miklós Kállay, 74
Mordechai Anielewicz, 104
Morrison C. Stayer, 91
Munkaszolgálat, 69, 70
National Front, 40, 62
Nazi Party, 24, 25, 96, 142, 147, 153, 167, 168
Netherlands, 17, 91, 113, 147, 149, 153
NSDAP, 24, 25, 67, 167
NKVD, x, 14, 84, 97, 98, 166
Nuremberg, 25, 29, 72, 102, 151, 152, 154, 159
Oder-Neisse, ix, 129, 130
Operation Barbarossa, 12, 72, 137
Operation Bernhard, 13, 14
Operation Margarethe, 74
Operation Plainfare, 146
Operation Reinhard, 12, 15, 19, 167
Operation Swallow, 130, 131, 134, 144
Operation Vittles, 146

Otto Hofmann, 102
Otto Schwarzenberger, 102
Pál Teleki, 69, 73
Paul Molnar, 55
People's Militia, 65, 129
Philipp Bouhler, 3, 10

Poland, vii, viii, ix, x, xi, xii, xiii, xiv, xv, xvi, 4, 5, 6, 9, 11, 12, 13, 14, 16, 17, 18, 19, 21, 22, 27, 29, 38, 50, 59, 60, 81, 82, 95, 96, 97, 98, 99, 100, 101, 103, 105, 107, 108, 109, 110, 111, 113, 115, 116, 117, 118, 119, 120, 121, 123, 125, 127, 128, 129, 130, 131, 132, 133, 134, 135, 145, 150, 151, 152, 159, 162, 165, 166, 167, 168, 169
Aleje Ujazdowskie, 124
Armia Ludowa, 120
Ateneum Theatre, 124
Babiak, 12
Bełżec, 4, 148
Brest-Litovsk, 112
Chełm, 101
Chłodna Street, 111
Ciepłe, 121
Czerniaków, 121
Czerwony Krzyz, 123
Dąbie, 12
Deby Szlacheckie, 12
Falencia, 113
Gęsia Street, 107
Garwolin, 101
Grodziec, 12
Grójecka Street, 122
Grzybowska Street, 110, 121, 156

Index

Gwardia Ludiwa, 120
Izbica Kujawska, 12
Janowska, 116
Jasna Street, 121
Kałuszyn, 113
Kampinos Forest, 96
Kielce, 109
Kilinski, 124
Kleparow, 115
Kłodawa, 12
Koło, 7, 12
Kowale Pańskie, 12
Łódź, 11, 12, 101, 106, 115, 120
Łosice, 101
Lubliniec, 101
Lviv, ix
Malachowicze, 112
Malczewskiego Street, 121
Majdanek, 9, 18, 19, 22, 101, 132
Mińsk Mazowiecki, 113
Mokotów, 121, 162
Mokotowska Street, 124
Moti Pinkiert, 107
Mrozów, 101
Napoleon Square, 121, 124
Narodowe Siły Zbrojne, 120
Nowiny Brdowskie, 12
Nowy Dwór, 113
Ochota, 121, 122, 126, 164
Okopowa Street, 107, 123
Opaczewska Street, 122
Pawiak, 97, 110, 111, 119
Peltewna Street, 115
Pius XI Street, 124
Praga, 121
Rembertów, 113
Sadyba, 121
Sobolew, 101

Sompolno, 12
Średnicowy Bridge, 124
Stanislav, 108
Stawki Street, 111
Stutthof, 8, 22, 23
Świętokrzyska Street, 121
Sztutowo, 22
Szucha Street, 124
Upper Silesia, 22, 96, 101, 164
Vistula River, 120, 124, 128
Wodzisław Śląski, 22
Wola, 121, 125, 160, 164
Zamarstynow, 115
Zamenhof Street, 104
Zielna Street, 124
Żoliborz, 123
Zwierzyniec, 101

Radio Prague, 157
Raoul Wallenberg, 75, 79
Ravensbrück, 8, 31
Red Cross, 44, 58, 97, 124, 150, 154, 155
Rezső Kasztner, 76, 164
Richard Hildebrandt, 102
Richard von Weizsäcker, 67
Richard Walther Darré, 100
Roman Catholic, 27, 169
Romania, xiii, 76, 80, 81, 82, 86, 87, 95, 128, 144, 155, 161
Bucharest, 87
King Michael 1, 80
Rudolf Creutz, 102
Rudolph Hess, 4, 153
Russia, viii, xv, xvi, 47, 48, 62, 63, 65, 82, 97, 103, 108, 115, 134, 135, 136, 139, 151
Königsberg, ix

Moscow, 25, 40, 47, 59, 63, 64, 75, 78, 113, 128, 140, 145, 146, 157
Stalingrad, 74, 140
Russian Liberation Army, 34, 35, 125, 157
Samu Stern, 75
Siegfried Line, 95, 140
Serbia, 71, 73, 78, 79, 80
Bačka Topola, 75
Bácstopolya, 79
Baja, 75
Belgrade, 71, 73
Bor, 78, 80
Budapest, 21, 41, 46, 74, 75, 76, 77, 78, 79, 85, 86, 89, 158, 164
Cservenka, 80
Kistarcsa, 79, 93
Pirot, 71
Vojvodina, 73, 79
Banat, 71, 73
Baranja, 71, 73
Syrmia, 73
Sergěj Ingr, 33
Škoda, 63

Slovakia, 19, 27, 28, 29, 55, 63, 81, 163
Janovy Lehota, 55
Kežmarok, 55
Žiar nad Hronom, 55

Slovenia, 71
Sonderkommandos, 13, 15, 16
St James Palace, 107
Stanisław Mikołajczyk, 121
Sturmbannführer, 5, 15, 111, 168
Szentkirályszabadja, 80

Transferstelle Agency, 107
Tuberculosis, 92
Typhoid, 73, 91, 92
Typhus, 12, 18, 22, 92, 106, 130

Ukraine, 17, 70, 72, 73, 96, 108, 115, 128, 166, 168
Doroshich, 73
Drohobych, 108
Kowel, 108
Równe, 108
Stanisławów, 108
Stryj, 108
Tarnapol, 108
Yasinia, 72
Zhytomyr, 72
Vinnytsia, 72
Babi Yars, 72

Ulrich Greifelt, 102
London, ix. 25, 27, 33, 39, 51, 98, 107, 113, 117, 119, 166
Václav Havel, 67
Václav Kopecký, 39
Václav Nosek, 63
Vilmos Nagybaczoni Nagy, 78
Vladimír Clementis, 41, 45
Vladimir Sviridov, 88
Vojtěch Černý, 61
Volksbund, 83, 84, 90
Volkssturm, 138
Voronezh, 73
Vyacheslav Molotov, viii, 41, 107, 127, 167
Waffen SS, 38, 84
Washington, 65, 113, 128
Wenzel Jaksch, 48
Werner Catel, 2

Index

Werner Lorenz, 102
Wilhelm Keitel, 38, 153
Władysław Gomułka, 129
Yitzhak Zuckerman, 104
Yugoslavia, ix, x, xiii, 17, 43, 70, 71, 73, 78, 82, 86, 91, 113, 144, 154, 163
Kamianets-Podilskyi, 72
Kolomyia, 72
Macedonia, 71
Novi Sad, 73
Temerin, 73
Titel, 73
Montenegro, 71
Žabalj, 73
Zdeněk Fierlinger, 49, 62
Zsidó Tanács, 75
Zyklon B, 4, 157, 158